NEVER AGAIN

NEVER AGAIN

SECURING AMERICA AND RESTORING JUSTICE

~~~

Former U.S. Attorney General

John Ashcroft

CENTER STREET™

NEW YORK   BOSTON   NASHVILLE

Center Street
Hachette Book Group USA
1271 Avenue of the Americas
New York, NY 10020

Visit our Web site at www.centerstreet.com.

Center Street® is a division of Hachette Book Group USA. The Center
Street name and logo are trademarks of Hachette Book Group USA.

Printed in the United States of America

First Edition: October 2006

10 9 8 7 6 5 4 3 2 1

Library of Congress Control Number: 2006928292
ISBN-13: 978-1-59995-680-0
ISBN-10: 1-59995-680-2

ACKNOWLEDGMENTS

This story would have been told by someone else had not the people of Missouri and of America accorded me the profound privilege of public service. I am grateful to them first and to their courageous leader, President George W. Bush, for the incomparable opportunity of protecting lives and liberty in this matchless nation, America.

My service focused on the direction and encouragement of the dedicated, selfless effort of thousands of career and politically appointed members of the Justice community. Daily, they reminded me that the Department of Justice is the only agency of government with a value as its title. "Justice" is a noble value, the worth of which was compounded by the devotion and dedication of their lives to the securing of the rights and freedoms of humanity.

To all the interviewees who contributed valuable insights and recollections to this work, I give my thanks, especially in light of their compelling schedules. Special thanks to:

FBI Director Robert Mueller
Homeland Security Secretary Michael Chertoff
Former Deputy Attorney General Larry Thompson
Kris Kobach
Mindy Tucker
David Israelite
U.S. Attorney Johnny Sutton
Jerry Jacobs

My wife, Janet, deserves more credit than could be accorded for her patient, valued advice and counsel.

ACKNOWLEDGMENTS

To Rolf Zettersten of the Hachette Book Group, my appreciation for his patience and kind coaching.

To David Ayres, without whom the organization necessary to assemble this effort, and without whom many facts necessary to assure accuracy would not have been ascertainable, I owe the greatest of debt. He has made my public service during the past two decades possible for me, and valuable for America.

The daunting job of evoking and extrapolating the thoughts of this book fell to Ken Abraham, whose experience, persistence, and dedication have made this endeavor a positive experience for all of us.

CONTENTS

CONTENTS

NEVER AGAIN

CHAPTER ONE

CRASH IN THE NIGHT

A Nightmare While Awake

I'm a country boy at heart. Few activities are more enjoyable to me than getting out in the country, working on a tractor, or fixing up an old shed on the edge of a green pasture. That's why my wife, Janet, and I hung on to our property near Springfield, Missouri, at the northern base of the Ozark hill country when I was elected to the U.S. Senate in 1994. By 2000, even though we now lived at least half our year in Washington, D.C., I relished every opportunity to spend time at our traditional, two-story, white farmhouse located near a gently rippling river.

Ten miles from town, the serenity of the farm with its bucolic beauty beckoned me away from the stark severity of city life. Something about returning to the farm, a sanctuary amid the hustle and bustle of the workaday world, refreshed me, restored my spirit, and reminded me that life is more than the latest opinion poll or Washington intrigue.

The old farmhouse provided a welcomed respite for me, especially when the weather turned ugly, as it had earlier on this mid-October night. The sturdy construction offered a place of warmth and security, impervious to the pelting rain and the flashing lightning. Eventually, the booming thunderstorm moved off eastward, leaving behind a persistent drizzle and a dense fog that painted a thick gray mist across the hillsides, shrouding the valleys, and casting an eerie pall over the area. I glanced out the window at the soupy sky and shook my head. *I'm glad I'm not traveling in that mess tonight.*

I tossed a stack of papers aside and moved to my favorite chair in the TV room, kicked off my shoes, and reached for the remote control. I wasn't really interested in watching any more news coverage, and it was still too early in the year for a basketball game, but it was nice to have a bit of background noise in the house. Janet was in Washington, D.C., attending to her teaching responsibilities at Howard University, so I had returned alone to our Springfield home following a televised Sunday night debate in Kansas City against Mel Carnahan, the governor of Missouri, my opponent in the upcoming election for U.S. senator.

The jangling of the farmhouse phone jolted me out of my silent reflections. I pulled myself out of the chair and ambled over to the telephone. David Ayres, my former Senate office chief of staff and my current campaign manager, was on the line. David had worked with me for years and was one of my most trusted advisers. It was not unusual for him to call me after office hours, but late night calls were rarely ever good, and this call was no exception. I could tell quickly from the tone of David's voice that this was no ordinary call.

"John, there's a problem."

"What kind of problem?" I asked, still relatively at ease. Problems go with the territory when running for office or serving in office, so I was not surprised or alarmed to learn that another issue had popped up three weeks prior to election day.

"I just received a call about a press report that Governor Carnahan's plane is missing . . . apparently, it has disappeared from the radar."

"What?"

"Word is that Carnahan and his campaign aide Chris Sifford were attempting to fly from St. Louis to New Madrid tonight, and the air traffic controllers lost contact with the plane sometime around seven-thirty or eight o'clock. Carnahan's son, Randy, was flying the plane, and they can't raise him on the radio."

"No . . ." I was stunned as the full realization of David's words began to sink in. "You don't mean . . ."

"We don't know," David anticipated my question. "But the weather here in St. Louis has been awful tonight, and there's fear that the plane may have crashed in the woods south of the city, in Jefferson County. We're checking with local authorities and all the news services right now, but it does not look good. We also need to start thinking about what we're going to do if the reports are accurate."

"Do? There's only one thing to do. Pull down the campaign . . . put everything on hold until we find out what's going on here."

"That's what I thought, too," David concurred. "Try to settle yourself. I'll call you back as soon as I hear anything."

I had no sooner hung up the telephone and turned the television to a local station for news when the phone began ringing, one call after another. "John? Have you heard? Is it true? Is Carnahan okay? Have they found the plane yet? Is Mel dead or alive?"

My mind was racing. *How could this be?* Just a few weeks ago we had accepted an invitation for a debate to be held on Monday, October 16, in southeast Missouri at Cape Girardeau, but the Carnahan camp had declined the invitation, opting instead for a fund-raiser in St. Louis that day, and then a trip to the boot heel of the state later that evening. Now I couldn't help but wonder how the events of the evening might have been different had we still been on the debate platform in southern Missouri.

Mel Carnahan and I had served together in Missouri politics for a couple of decades. Mel had been the state treasurer during my first term as governor of Missouri, and the lieutenant governor during my second term. Missouri's term limits allow for only two consecutive terms of office, so after serving eight years as governor, I stepped aside and planned on retiring from politics.

But when the Missouri seat in the U.S. Senate opened, my friends and family encouraged me to run for office. I won the Senate seat in 1994. Meanwhile, Mel had won the governor's job in 1992. He went on to serve two four-year terms as governor, although he quickly let it be known that he wanted a broader sphere of influence. He publicly announced his intention to run for my U.S. Senate seat the day after the 1998 midterm elections, a full two years before he would complete his second term as governor.

I had no animosity toward Mel; our dealings were properly cordial, but tension filled our relationship from the early days of our working together, when he was the lieutenant governor and I was governor. At that time, Missouri had a law that allowed the lieutenant governor to assume the position of governor whenever the chief executive was absent from the state.

The whole idea was based on an antiquated notion that remained when I took office. Clearly, a modern governor continued in office when outside the state conducting state business. Nevertheless, whenever I traveled outside Missouri's boundaries for an extended period of time, I'd sign a document designating Mel Carnahan as governor until I returned.

On one such occasion, I was traveling in Japan when a reporter back home asked Mel about his pro-abortion stance. Mel unabashedly stated that if legislation modifying the state's abortion laws came across his desk while he was the acting governor, he would sign it. This was totally contrary to, and inconsistent with, my publicly stated beliefs and positions regarding abortion. I was stunned that Mel would suggest such a thing. Historically, lieutenant governors handled the acting governor's responsibilities in a manner consistent with the governor's views. They understood that it was not the intent of the constitution of the state to change the philosophy and law of the state during temporary absences of the governor.

After Mel's statements, I never again relinquished my role as governor. To clarify the legal situation, while in Washington, D.C., on official state business, I signed some documents as governor of Missouri and sent them back to the state capital for formal registration. This evoked a challenge as to whether the Missouri constitution's "absent from the state" clause stripped me of my office as governor when outside the state's boundaries. The Supreme Court of Missouri ruled in a way that allowed the governor of Missouri to remain governor as long as he was able to carry out his duties, even when temporarily performing official functions outside the state.

The state was better served by the clarification, but my relationship with Mel Carnahan was damaged by the decision. It was an unfortunate consequence that I regret, but it was a fact.

Missouri being traditionally a moderate state, its local and state officials elected from the time of the Civil War to Harry Truman had been Democrats. During my lifetime, only one other Republican had been elected governor of Missouri—Christopher "Kit" Bond. Moreover, I had been the only Republican in Missouri history elected to consecutive terms as governor, and amazingly, I had won big. In 1988, I won all 114 Missouri counties and garnered more than 66 percent of the vote in the gubernatorial race, the largest margin for governor ever received in Missouri. In 1994, I was elected to the U.S. Senate by capturing more than 60 percent of the vote. Decades earlier, I had served as the state auditor of Missouri, then eight years as its attorney general, then eight years as governor and six years as a U.S. Senator. Few candidates had held three high-profile state offices, as well as a seat in the U.S. Senate. As the incumbent senator in the 2000 race, it was natural that I was considered the front-runner by many political pundits.

Nevertheless, Mel Carnahan was a formidable candidate. Our battle for the U.S. Senate in 2000 was Missouri politics at its best . . . and at its most intense. At its best, it was an important race with national ramifications, since the seat was regarded as a potential pivot on which the majority of the U.S. Senate might turn. On the state level, it was a clash of the titans, two popular two-term governors vying for a seat in Washington's senatorial club. At its worst, it was a no-holds-barred, political bare-knuckled bout.

The campaign turned tough early on, and it never eased up. Public Broadcasting's *NewsHour with Jim Lehrer* characterized the vitriolic campaign as "downright ugly," noting that the two longtime rivals were:

> clashing on classic hot-button issues such as abortion and the death penalty, in a race that some observers say is becoming downright ugly . . .
>
> Carnahan announced his Senate candidacy just one day after the November 1998 election and criticized Ashcroft ever since . . .
>
> Ashcroft's ads reminded voters that Carnahan accepted money from abortion-rights groups and vetoed a ban on "partial birth" abortion.
>
> The race became increasingly negative this year as Carnahan countered by painting Ashcroft as a member of the extreme right.[1]

It was a grueling battle and I tried as best I could to keep our campaign efforts focused. The opposition continually sought to vilify me as an ultraconservative, racist, insensitive, heartless pol. Some of those themes even found their way into the mid-October debates.

"Carnahan, Ashcroft Use First Debate to Rip Each Other's Records," the *St. Louis Post-Dispatch* headline read following the first debate between Mel and me, held ironically on Friday the 13th, and broadcast live on KMOX radio in St. Louis. The newspaper reported that Carnahan:

> . . . was particularly combative during Friday's one-hour joint session. Ashcroft returned fire in a milder manner, reflecting

his promise at the beginning of the debate to "raise the level of discourse" . . . Ashcroft's strongest criticism arose during their exchanges over abortion. Ashcroft, who opposes abortion, began by observing, "I do understand that good people can disagree." He then called Carnahan "extreme on the issue" because he has vetoed measures to outlaw a mid-to-late-term procedure that critics call "partial birth abortion."[2]

Two evenings later, Mel and I debated again, this time at the Gem Theater in Kansas City. The debate was broadcast live on television throughout the state. National media including reporters from the *New York Times, Washington Post,* and others traveled to Kansas City to see the bloodletting. But it didn't happen. Mel and I engaged in a vigorous but dignified debate. Mel was actually more animated than usual, taking off his suit coat, sitting down occasionally during the debate, and appearing quite comfortable. At the close of the telecast, we shook hands. "Well, John, it looks as though we're going to survive this," Carnahan said.

Bill McClellan, a reporter who covered the campaign, wrote that he was disappointed at the "remarkably civil" debate: "Ashcroft had gone into a nice-guy mode . . . the very image of good cheer and respect.

"That meant the burden was on Carnahan. If there was going to be a fight, he'd have to start it. He didn't seem so inclined. The men disagreed on almost all the issues, but they did so with little rancor . . . a strange stance to take in a campaign noted mostly for its nastiness."[3]

The debate over, I left the Gem Theater that night with no reservations about whether I had won, but I was especially pleased that I had resisted engaging in acrimonious statements about my opponent. Besides, as we entered the final month of the campaign, I felt confident that I was on the way to victory.

Throughout the summer, most pollsters reported that Mel and I were running neck and neck, as every public poll gave me a slight lead.

A month earlier, the Zogby poll taken for the *St. Louis Post-Dispatch* in the first week of September had found me running ahead of Carnahan, 45 percent to 43 percent, with a 4 percent margin of error.[4] Although the race was by no means a runaway, going into the mid-October debate, a new public poll indicated we were ahead by ten points and stretching our lead over the Carnahan camp. My campaign team emphasized that our own polling research revealed a much stronger position and growing. We were breaking away finally after a twenty-three-month-long pitched battle. Our advertising campaign was working well, and we had just locked in a huge advertising buy for the homestretch. We were not on autopilot, but with only three weeks before the election, barring any unforeseen circumstances, we were on a clear track to win. I was exhausted but encouraged.

And now, suddenly, winning or losing an election seemed not to matter. Mel's plane was down and nobody knew whether he was alive or dead.

The farmhouse phone continued to ring. More calls poured in from frantic people, posing questions I could not answer.

Memories flooded my mind as I recalled an incident in which I had been flying a small plane during a turbulent storm. It was one of the most frightening experiences of my life. I could picture all too well what the men aboard the Carnahan plane may have experienced, and it caused chills to run down my spine.

Rrrrriiing! The phone rang again. It was David again.

"John, we're still not absolutely certain, but it looks as though the reports are accurate. The plane has gone down, and by all indications, there are no survivors."

I stood holding the phone in my hand, unable to speak, feeling as though someone had suddenly punched me in the stomach, knocking the wind out of me. Finally, I mustered the wherewithal to respond. "Pull down the campaign, David," I whispered. "No advertisements, no public appearances, nothing. Put out a release to the press letting them know that we are on hold."

David went to work attempting to stop a large campaign machine that was energized with momentum, rolling under its own power. He issued a press release, before midnight on Monday, October 16, reflecting that we were still uncertain about many of the details regarding the Carnahan crash. David's statement read simply:

> We hope and pray that this tragedy has not occurred. Out of respect for Governor Carnahan and his family we've suspended the campaign indefinitely. We're suspending all campaign advertising and canceling Senator Ashcroft's appearances, effective immediately.

The moment I placed the phone back on the receiver, it seemed to ring again . . . and again . . . and again. Instead of answering, dazed, I wandered to the couch. Waves of emotion overwhelmed me, and large tears coursed down my face as I held my head in my hands. "God, help us . . . please help the Carnahan family." I thought of Jean, Mel's wife. Not only had she lost her husband, but her son, Randy, as well. I prayed for our state and for our country. And I prayed for myself, as well. "Please, God, give me wisdom, that I might respond with compassion and be a unifying force in the midst of this heartrending tragedy."

It dawned on me that the phone had been ringing again. "Hello?"

It was Steve Hilton, my press secretary, warning that the press would soon begin chasing me for my reaction to the developing story. I had scarcely begun talking with Steve when a sharp knock at the back door caught my attention. I looked at the clock. *Who in the world would come out here close to midnight?*

"Who is it?" I called from behind the door.

"It's me, John. Jerry."

I recognized the voice of Jerry Jacobs, a television reporter from the NBC affiliate KY3-TV in Springfield. Jerry and I had met a number of years earlier as supporters of the University of Missouri basketball team. We had grown to be friends, and he had been to the farm before a few times.

I unlocked the door and swung it open. "Thanks for coming," I said, almost as if I'd invited him. "Come on in. I'm on the phone. I'll be right with you."

The expression on Jerry's face alerted me that I was a mess. My eyes were red and puffy and my hair was disheveled. Jerry later told a friend that I looked as though someone had punched me in the face. If Jerry had any thoughts of interviewing me that night, they were doused right there at the door.

I concluded my phone conversation and sat down with Jerry. The TV reporter had some solid information regarding the crash. Mel Carnahan's six-passenger Cessna 335 took off from Cahokia, Illinois, right across the Mississippi River from St. Louis. The small twin-engine plane carried three people: forty-four-year-old lawyer Randy Carnahan at the controls, Chris Sifford, a campaign aide, and Governor Mel Carnahan. Apparently, as David had heard earlier, they were traveling from St. Louis to New Madrid, about a 145-mile flight, when they encountered the vicious storm immediately after takeoff. Chris Sifford had even called from his cell phone to tell the rally organizers the Carnahan group was concerned about the lightning and was thinking of turning back.

"Although most everybody advised against it, they took off in the inclement weather with extremely low visibility," Jerry said. "The governor's son has been flying for some time now, and I guess he had expressed some concerns about risking it, going or not, and all that. The early reports indicate that he became disoriented due to the storm, although there is already talk about a possible equipment failure aboard the plane. In weather like this, it's hard to tell."

"Have they found the . . . have they identified . . . ?" I couldn't bring myself to finish the questions.

"No, not yet," Jerry said. "They are still dealing with the wreckage. It's going to take a while."

"It must have been awful," I said. I told Jerry of my terrifying experience in a small plane, and about the frightful feelings I had known in the darkness of the storm. The telephone continued to ring, and I repeated the same questions and answers over and over. Even with Jerry's help, I had little information to offer. Jerry and I talked for a while longer. Sometime around one-thirty in the morning, I stood up, grabbed a cap and a jacket, and said, "I've got to get some air . . . clear my head. Let's take a walk."

The young reporter didn't flinch; he quickly reached for his coat to come along with me. Jerry and I stepped into the drizzle drenched night and started walking down the lane from the farmhouse, back through the woods to our fields near the river's edge. On better days, I oftentimes watched bald eagles fish there. Tonight, the dark, hovering clouds, ominous tree branches, and gurgling sound of the river made for a more surreal scene.

The rain halted, but the storm clouds remained as Jerry and I walked and walked, intermittently questioning: Why? Pondering, soaked, sometimes simply walking in silence.

Near three o'clock in the morning, we trudged onto the back porch of the farmhouse. Sometimes the act of walking in the face of the elements helps us come to grips with reality. Or it simply exhausts us to the point of seeing the futility of resisting reality and the futility of denial. Spattered and soaked, we gave in.

Jerry shook the moisture from his jacket and stayed a little longer to knock the chill off his body before heading back to town in time to be on camera for the six o'clock morning news.

"Thanks again for coming, Jerry," I said as he opened the door to leave. "I appreciate you being here."

"I really didn't think you'd want to be alone," the reporter replied. He was right.

As soon as Jerry departed, I peeled off my damp clothes and climbed into bed. In a few hours, I'd have to get up and go to St. Louis to make a formal announcement about our campaign cessation. I was deeply grieved and suddenly depleted by a draining weariness. This day had been a nightmare, and I had not yet been asleep.

ENDNOTES

1. Public Broadcasting Service, "A Missouri Battle Royal," *NewsHour with Jim Lehrer*, October 13, 2000; www.pbs.org/newshour/election 2000/races/mo_10-13.html.
2. Jo Mannies, "Carnahan, Ashcroft Use First Debate to Rip Each Other's Records," *St. Louis Post-Dispatch*, October 14, 2000, p. 5.
3. Bill McClellan, "When Given Chance to Excite, Governor Chose the High Road," *St. Louis Post-Dispatch*, October 18, 2000, p. B1.
4. Glen Johnson, "MO Governor Dies in Crash; Impact Seen on Senate Balance," *Boston Globe*, October 18, 2000.

CHAPTER TWO

DEFEATED BY A DEAD MAN

The Controversial 2000 Senate Reelection Campaign

⫷⫸⫷⫸

The morning sun over Missouri provided little hint of the vicious thunderstorms that had lashed our area the night before. Nor did the brightness of a crisp new October day do anything to dispel the notion that all was well with the world. Like so many mornings after a rain, the air possessed a freshness, a hopeful promise that renewal would come even out of the previous night's storms.

I paused momentarily in the farmhouse yard, to breathe in fresh air before climbing into my vehicle and heading toward the airport, where I'd catch a plane to Jefferson City and then on to St. Louis. David Ayres planned to meet me there. Members of the media also met me at the airport and immediately peppered me with questions regarding my knowledge and feelings about Mel's death, as well as my plans for our campaign. I quickly curtailed the questions by giving a brief statement.

"Obviously, this is not a time for politics," I said. "This is a time for the state to come together."

Regarding my former opponent, I attempted to offer words of consolation, while acknowledging Mel's long career in public service. I commented to the reporters, "Governor Carnahan served the people of Missouri with dignity and honor over the course of four decades. I will remember him and all of Missouri will remember him for that exemplary public service, and for his dedication to his family."

There was no need to say anything further. I hurried on to our campaign headquarters in St. Louis, where David had assembled the key members of our team. The campaign was over. He had instructed his leaders to "pull your team off the field," even though we knew it could be impossible to get everybody back up to speed when or if we decided to jump-start our campaign. It just seemed like the right thing to do. David placed a statement on our campaign Web site reading, "We, as a state and nation, join together to mourn the loss of these men. During this time of mourning, I have directed that all campaign activities cease. That our Senate campaign could have ended so tragically is shocking."

The mood at our headquarters was somber as we gathered together to decide our next steps. The election was a mere three weeks away. It was an awkward situation. I grieved the loss of all three men in that aircraft, reliving over and over what their last moments might have been like. With as much time as political candidates spend aboard small aircraft nowadays, it could have been any one of us in that crash. I wanted to be considerate of the pain and grief that the families touched by this tragedy must be feeling.

Nevertheless, events soon took on a life of their own.

"Missouri Mourns Its Leader," the headlines read. With the sitting governor's sudden death, the media launched into round-the-clock coverage mode, extolling the fallen public servant's virtues. Newspapers overflowed with articles on the governor. Local television stations ran documentaries describing the outstanding career of the governor whose life had been tragically cut short. Jo Mannies, political correspondent for the *St. Louis Post-Dispatch* wrote a series of effusive articles with statements such as "Governor Carnahan was never too big for his britches."[1]

Nowadays, that sort of "instant history" can be expected when a public figure meets an untimely death. News networks all scramble to put together a fitting compilation of the person's life and influence. I wasn't surprised, nor did I have any qualms about the desire to review Mel's career for the public. The governor and the men who had died trying to get him to the campaign meeting in New Madrid deserved our respect. My family and I felt grieved for the families of the deceased. The public responded compassionately, too, pouring out a flood of emotion and support at the positive coverage of Mel's career.

The day after the tragedy, the *St. Louis Post-Dispatch*, the area's largest newspaper, wrote that Governor Carnahan's name would remain on the ballot, and noted that people could still vote for him. The newspaper reported that many St. Louis residents said they would indeed vote for Mel Carnahan, though he was deceased.

Surprisingly, the next day the paper ran an editorial titled "Finishing Mr. Carnahan's Work," suggesting that the most logical possibilities to replace Governor Carnahan, should he win the election posthumously, were members of the governor's family: his wife, Jean; or his daughter, Robin; or his son Russ, who was already running for a position in the state House of Representatives.

By October 19, 2000, before Governor Carnahan had been laid to rest, front-page articles in the *Post-Dispatch* suggested that "Some Want Jean Carnahan to Carry Democrats' Torch." The new governor, Roger Wilson, may have thought those statements inordinately crass as he declared that it was still too soon for such a discussion.

Early on, I attempted to contact the Carnahan family to offer my condolences. *This isn't about politics*, I thought. *This is about one human being reaching out to another, to say, despite our differences, I hurt for you, and with you. I care about the agony you and your family are experiencing.*

An elaborate, formal state funeral was planned for Friday, October 20, 2000: "A Celebration of the Life of Mel Carnahan." After being invited along with other Senate members to be a part of the ceremony, we received a signal through a murky backdoor channel that the family—or perhaps some of the governor's staff or supporters—might not want me to attend. It was never totally clear to us what was happening. Was some distraught political opponent playing an ugly trick? If the signal was legitimate, and I attended the funeral against the family's wishes, would I be inflicting further pain on them? Would it seem that I was attempting to draw attention to myself? But if I did not pay my respects to the governor properly, would it be considered a political snub? In any event, did I not have a duty as a former Missouri governor, and a seated U.S. Senator, to be present? In such case, the public might receive the impression that I did not respect the memory of Governor Carnahan, nor had I sympathy for his family.

It was a strange conundrum, but in the end I decided to attend the funeral as a part of the official Senate delegation, rather than as a candidate for reelection. Along with the delegation, I flew to Jefferson City on a plane provided by the U.S. government. The congressional delegation was ushered into the Governor's Mansion, where the governor's body laid in state. We slowly made our way to the front of the room, where each of us expressed our condolences to Mrs. Carnahan. When it was my turn, I gently expressed my sympathy to Jean. She didn't seem to respond negatively to me. *Perhaps we had received some misinformation suggesting that the family and friends preferred that I not attend the funeral,* I thought.

This relief was to be but momentary.

The state funeral—the largest in Missouri's history since President Harry Truman's 1972 funeral—started out as a fitting tribute to a fallen leader, but the service, broadcast "live" statewide, took on a subtle political undercurrent. I sat there along with Senator Kit Bond, former senator Jack Danforth, and other members of the congressional delegation, wondering if I was the only person picking up on the speakers' remarks. I was distressed, but my responsibility required me to sit politely and listen stoically.

President Bill Clinton eulogized Mel Carnahan in glowing terms. "I loved the guy," President Clinton said. "I'm grateful that I knew Mel Carnahan; grateful that we worked together."[2]

Former Missouri Senator Thomas Eagleton compared Mel Carnahan to Harry Truman. "Like Harry Truman," Eagleton said, "Mel will be remembered not for what he accomplished, but for what he was: a decent, honorable, forthright, and quietly courageous man whose life and career were driven by the values he learned here in Missouri. Like Harry Truman, Mel didn't have to preach about 'family values.' He lived those values and led by example."[3] Most people in attendance that day knew that my campaign slogan was "Ashcroft: Missouri Values."

Robin Carnahan, Governor Carnahan's daughter, especially stirred the audience with a poignant and heartrending story about her father. According to Robin, on mornings around the Carnahan homestead, Mel would regularly build a fire in the fireplace before the children got up for breakfast. Later, when leaving for work, he'd heap up the fire with the admonition to the children, "Don't let the fire go out." At the close of her eulogy, Robin adamantly declared, "We won't let the fire go out!"[4]

The implication to the audience was obvious.

Robin' story elicited the desired response from the mourners.

Ironically, the essence of her story sounded strikingly similar to one from literature, not simply a tale from the Carnahan family lore. In *The Skin of Our Teeth*, a 1942 play written by Pulitzer Prize–winner Thornton Wilder, the hero repeatedly tells his family, "Don't let the fire go out."[5]

Jean Carnahan, Robin's mother, had told the Thornton Wilder story in a speech less than a year earlier as a means of calling her audience of Democrats to action, closing her remarks with the phrase, "Don't let the fire go out." She also included her speech story in a book published in 2000, *Will You Say a Few Words?* in which she specifically credits Thornton Wilder as the story's creator.[6]

Nevertheless, the crowd paying their respects to Robin's father was deeply moved by the daughter's remarks. Two days later, on October 22, 2000, Jean Carnahan spoke at the funeral of Chris Sifford and evoked the same images, urging the mourners, "Don't let the fire go out."[7]

Watching the Carnahan funeral on television, David Ayres stiffened the moment he heard Robin's words. They were so well delivered, so strategically placed. Looking at several other people in the room, he said, "*That* is their new campaign slogan."

David was absolutely right. Within days, signs bearing the slogan began popping up all over Missouri. Candlelight vigils evoked similar imagery, reminding the "Show Me State" of the new theme. Al Gore fanned the flames when he brought his presidential campaign to Missouri a week or so later. "Still for Mel" posters adorned the outdoor rally, as Gore shouted to his audience, "Keep the fire burning! You know what that means."[8]

Complicating matters was that Mel's death had occurred three days after the legal deadline for making name changes on the election ballots. Consequently, even though he was deceased, Carnahan's name would remain on the ballot for the upcoming election. On October 24, 2000, eight days after the accident, Governor Roger Wilson, Carnahan's lieutenant governor who assumed the office, made it known publicly that he would appoint Jean Carnahan to the Senate seat for a two-year term if voters elected her deceased husband. In other words, a vote for the deceased Governor Carnahan would in fact be a vote for his wife.

Wilson's voice was literally shaking as he made the announcement. The new governor said he felt an obligation to inform voters of his intentions to fill the vacancy should Carnahan win. "If people choose to vote for the ideas or values of what they think the person represented or his surrogate would represent, then that is the best alternative we have," he said.[9]

When Ann Wagner, state GOP chairperson, Kit Bond, and other

Missouri Republicans suggested that there were legal and constitutional matters to be considered (for instance, is a deceased person a citizen of the United States, which is one of the requirements for holding a U.S. Senate seat?). Roy Temple, executive director of the Missouri Democratic Party, accused them of "the most disgusting attempt to mislead and confuse voters that I've ever seen. They want to create doubt in voters' minds, apparently because they don't believe they can win the seat straight up."[10]

The dilemmas with which I wrestled were not so much legal, political, or even constitutional as they were moral and ethical. How should I respond to this confusion and commotion? My primary desire was to do the right thing. For me, the issue of paramount importance was this: *What is the most moral and ethical thing for me to do under these challenging circumstances?*

For eight days following the tragedy, I had ceased all campaigning and joined Missourians in mourning.

Jean Carnahan was not a declared candidate, and in any case, I believed it would have been inappropriate to direct any political comments toward one who had so recently suffered the devastating compound loss of both her son and her husband. Certainly there were both statutory and constitutional questions about whether Jean's husband, now a deceased person, could be a candidate in an election, or whether votes for a deceased person—a person who no longer existed as far as the law was concerned—could be counted at all. No doubt, there were plenty of potential lawsuits and other legal options that could have been pursued, but my campaign advisers and I concluded that it was best simply to let the system work itself out.

After eight days of our respectful suspension of public appearances, we felt it appropriate to begin activities again. I appeared at several community events, and spoke to children at a school about government and how our political system works.

It was an awkward position, not opposing a formally announced candidate, yet trying to avoid being cast as the evil, mean-spirited fellow who was campaigning against Mel's memory. During the campaign, I had tried to delineate my positions regarding taxes, education, abortion, gun control, and other issues of importance to Missourians and to the nation. But now there was no way to mention such things without evoking the truth that Mel Carnahan and I differed radically in how we felt the government should operate. I didn't feel right debating against the positions of my former opponent, even though his wife held most of those same opinions and had strongly intimated in public that she and Mel had in fact been partners in forming his political agenda.

The media continued the accolades for the now deceased Governor Carnahan. *Post-Dispatch* political correspondent Jo Mannies pointed out:

> Womens-rights groups. African-American leaders. Teachers' Organizations. Unions. Not all backed Mel Carnahan early in his political career. But over the course of his two terms as the state's chief executive, they became his staunchest political defenders and lauded him as the best governor in their lifetime.
>
> "We have never had greater political support or respect from another political official," said E.C. Walker, assistant executive director for the Missouri National Education Association.
>
> Carnahan's staunchest supporters from the beginning were Missouri's women's groups—who saw him as their first public champion of reproductive rights and women's health care issues. And he never let them down, even though he took some of his toughest hits from anti-abortion groups and others who called Carnahan a threat to family values. "He was a great champion and extraordinarily grounded,"

said Paula Gianino, chief executive of Planned Parenthood of the St. Louis region. "He never wavered."[11]

I still felt compassion for the Carnahan family, but I was fed up with what the press was doing. I was not alone. Former Missouri senator Jack Danforth remained a true statesman, one of the most highly respected men in Missouri. Both Democrats and Republicans spoke well of him, and listened when he spoke. Like me, Danforth was willing to accord my opponent the commendation of a fallen leader, but when it became obvious that the newspaper was engaging in blatantly political gamesmanship under the guise of venerating the former governor, while castigating me for restarting my campaign, Danforth could no longer sit by idly. He spoke at a rally along with Barbara Bush, wife of former President George H. W. Bush, and told the people of Missouri that things had gone too far.

"Governor Carnahan's death was a loss for the entire state, not just for Democrats," Danforth said. "It's not right to take the great loss of our state out on this good man," Danforth said, referring to me. "He is trashed on the front page of the newspaper for daring to be a candidate to the United States Senate. . . . I just don't think that's right. . . . What I think is wrong is to take the highest feelings that we can have as people and try to use those for partisan political advantage, and that's what I think Governor Wilson is trying to do, and it's wrong."[12] Jack felt so strongly about what was happening, not simply to me but to the entire political process in Missouri, that he appeared in a political commercial with that same message: "It's not right what is happening to John Ashcroft." I appreciated former Senator Danforth going to bat for me, but by October 24 his designated-hitter role and my renewed campaign may have come too late in the game.

During the weekend of October 27–29, Jean Carnahan announced that she was meeting with her family to decide whether she should accept an appointment to the Senate should her late husband win the election. She said that if she accepted the challenge, "It will be because I am ready to do this with my entire heart and soul, just as Mel did every day of his life." In the meantime, Carnahan supporters sent out 750,000 letters to Democrats across the state urging them to vote for Mel Carnahan on November 7. The letters were signed by former Lieutenant Governor Harriet Woods, an early proponent of Jean Carnahan's appointment.

On Tuesday, October 31, one week before election day, Jean Carnahan spoke to the press from the porch of her home and announced that she would accept the appointment to the U.S. Senate if Missourians voted to elect her deceased husband. "I think that I'll be trying to let people be informed that a vote for Mel Carnahan is a vote they can make," she said. "It's a proper way to carry his ideals forward. They still have a choice."[13]

The newspapers loved it. "It's Jean Carnahan vs. John Ashcroft," the *Post-Dispatch* announced; "Carnahan says she would fight for husband's values; she'll serve if Mel Carnahan wins." Meanwhile, our campaign kicked off a twenty-five-city tour of the state, with me speaking several times each day emphasizing my experience in government and my "Missouri values."

On Thursday, November 2, 2000, the Carnahan campaign began airing a sixty-second television commercial in which the deceased governor's wife looked into the camera and said, "Mel Carnahan's name will still be on that ballot, and his vision for Missouri can still prevail if we want it. With the support of my family, I've decided to do what I think Mel would want me to do—what he wants all of us to do—to keep fighting with all the strength we can muster for the values and ideals he lived for." The ad ran through Sunday, costing an estimated $700,000.

Singer Sheryl Crow headlined an event on Friday, November 3, titled "A Tribute to Mel Carnahan and the Democratic Ticket." Robin Carnahan thanked the crowd for "making Dad proud."

On the Sunday before the election, November 5, Jean Carnahan appeared in a prerecorded interview with Cokie Roberts on the ABC News program *This Week with Sam Donaldson and Cokie Roberts.*

On election day 2000, the Ashcroft team gathered at the hotel just off Highway 40 in St. Louis County, near the West County Assemblies of God church Janet and I had regularly attended when we lived in the neighborhood. Campaign supporters for several Republican races convened in the hotel ballroom, nervously conversing as they awaited the first batch of election returns to be broadcast on the large screens in the cavernous room.

Upstairs, we had set up a "war room," from which our staff and campaign workers could monitor the incoming election returns. The war room was a long, narrow area, similar to a partitioned ballroom. Inside, we arranged rows of fold-out tables lined with laptop computers and phones so our staff could track the voting patterns and the returns coming in from every county in Missouri. Televisions dotted the room—each TV tuned to a different channel—keeping our staff abreast of the local and national coverage of the election returns.

Earlier in the day, I visited several polling places in St. Louis, greeting people on their way to vote. If anything could be gathered from the smiles and enthusiastic handshakes I received from the voters, I had good reason to be confident, but I still felt uneasy. Later that afternoon, David and I and some of our friends played basketball for a while to relieve the tension. Early in the evening, I went out for dinner along with a group of supporters at a favorite Italian restaurant owned by my friend Charley Gitto. Then together with our children, Janet and I retreated to an upstairs suite in the hotel to monitor the election returns coming in. Meanwhile, about fifty staff members and campaign volunteers hunkered down in the war room to watch the tally and anticipate election problems, while getting early returns.

In the hotel ballroom, others were watching on the large mounted screens. Several Republican groups, including the Missouri headquarters for the George W. Bush presidential campaign, gathered to receive the results, and hopefully to celebrate our victories.

Shortly after nine o'clock that evening, David came upstairs from the war room. I could tell by the expression on his face that he was not happy. "I don't like the numbers that are coming in," he said. "We're not getting the margins that we had hoped for."

I nodded in understanding. He had directed a comprehensive campaign focusing on the issues about which I felt strongly, and our workers had done a fantastic job of getting our message to the people. But information, voting records, and policies are no match for an emotional tsunami of compassion and sympathy. We watched helplessly as the televised election results showed Mel Carnahan running neck and neck with me. Based on historical results, we knew the kind of winning margins we needed in particular regions across the state, and we simply were not reaching them, especially in the St. Louis area.

Meanwhile, in St. Louis, a voting fiasco was taking place that bid to surpass any supposed confusion over "hanging chads" reported in Palm Beach, Florida. As seven o'clock approached—the time for all polls to be closed in Missouri—the Missouri Democrats convinced a state judge, St. Louis Circuit Court judge Evelyn Baker, to ignore the law concerning the 7:00 p.m. closing time, and to arbitrarily extend the voting hours in St. Louis long after voting ceased in every other part of Missouri.

Beyond that, the Democrats complained that 33,000 registered voters had been removed from voter registration rolls. This, the Democrats contended, made it imperative that the polls in St. Louis (a strongly Democratic city) be kept open an extra three hours *after* polls in every other part of the state had closed. The proposal was outrageous on its face and offensive to any standard of fairness, but the judge agreed!

Actually, 33,000 people had been removed from the rolls because they were not eligible to vote. Apparently the Democratic opposition, the judge, and a large number of potential voters conveniently looked past the fact that in St. Louis, registered voters are removed from the rolls if they did not participate in previous elections, and if they did not respond to reregistration notices sent out by the election board, intended to verify their residence in the city. If a person does not register, he or she is not permitted to vote.

The law notwithstanding, on a "live" election night television interview, several distraught voters complained, "Why do we have to register to vote anyway?"

Worse yet, hundreds of people who were not registered were *permitted* to vote. To this day, no one knows how many other unregistered voters were allowed to cast ballots in Missouri during the 2000 election.

Within minutes of Judge Baker's decision to operate the election on her own timetable, a prerecorded telephone message by Jesse Jackson—obviously prepared ahead of time—hit phone lines all over St. Louis. Jackson's message said that the polls would be open until ten o'clock, and even later at the Board of Election Commissioners, so come on out to vote, emphasizing, of course, that people still had time to vote for Mel Carnahan and Al Gore.[14]

Fortunately, the Board of Election Commissioners appealed the improper extensions of voting time and the rulings to allow unregistered voters. A three-judge panel of the Missouri Court of Appeals summarily reversed Judge Baker's opinion, ordering the polls closed immediately. The responsible judges saw through the sham, and acted as promptly as possible. But in the confusion, many of the St. Louis polling stations stayed open long past closing time, as Democrats rallied voters to "keep the fire burning."

Even after the three-judge panel declared that the polls should be closed at 8:15 p.m., Jackson's message continued to be broadcast, flagrantly ignoring the Missouri Court of Appeals' decision, and voters continued to be permitted to vote—in some areas as late as 10 p.m. As a test to see whether the polls had in fact stayed open longer than legally allowed, one of our campaign workers made a 9:00 p.m. call to a Central St. Louis city polling place after the time the Board of Appeals had closed all voting places. "Can I still come in to vote?" the worker asked.

"Come on down; we'll get you in here," was the response.

At ten o'clock, David returned to the suite, looking even more solemn than during his previous visits. As it became increasingly obvious that the vote count was not going to turn in our direction, the tone in the suite became more sullen. My family members searched David's face and eyes for any sign of a last-minute surge, but he had little good news to report. Janet remained quiet and reserved, more concerned about me than herself. My brother, Bob, who had been a strong bulwark of support in the midst of numerous other tough elections, sat somberly watching the returns. Only my son Jay was particularly animated, energetically holding on to hope against hope that we could miraculously pull out a victory.

For my part, I tried to soothe the family's fears. I had always maintained a deep sense of gratitude for the privilege of being in public service. My family background was not from the rich, upper class; I didn't hail from a family filled with robust political connections— far from it. My father began his preaching ministry as a high school dropout who later struggled to get his education, eventually becoming a college president. We attended an Assemblies of God church during a time when many people misunderstood Pentecostal experiences as signs of instability, heresy, or worse!

I felt privileged to have served two years as state auditor following Kit Bond, and a stint as assistant attorney general under the tutelage of Senator Jack Danforth, eight years as Missouri's attorney general, eight years as governor, and six years representing our state in the U.S. Senate. While serving as governor and as attorney general of Missouri, I had been elected to lead each of the national associations.

As far as I was concerned, nobody owed me anything. It would be the height of ingratitude and greed to think that I should be entitled to more than I had already experienced, or that I should feel cheated or disappointed. It would be sheer arrogance on my part if I refused to accept that I could be voted out of office, that there could be an end to my political career. I had enjoyed a great run in public service. I was content knowing that I had served my country to the best of my abilities, that we had accomplished a great deal of good, and that I had made a positive difference in my state. If Missourians sent me back to the U.S. Senate, I would continue to serve them with passion. If they chose not to return me to Washington, well, I'd just have to find something else to do.

I paced back and forth across the suite as I mulled the possibilities in my mind. Although anxious about the election results, I was not agitated or distressed; strangely, I was at peace.

Downstairs, peace seemed less possible. While the votes were not yet in, the trends were undeniable. Speaking to Republican supporters in the hotel ballroom before the final outcome of the election was known, Missouri senator Kit Bond pulled no punches in revealing the Democrats' election abuses in St. Louis. Kit's sense of justice was so offended by the voting irregularities that he injured his hand pounding the podium while speaking. I winced when I saw Kit's pain as video of the statement replayed on television.

Back upstairs, David and I knew that we would have a choice to make: we could concede the election to the Carnahan camp, or we could contest the result. Regardless, we agreed to wait until morning before making any final decisions. Too much emotion from the past three weeks engulfed us; we needed to be able to look at all the facts; dispassionately review the situation. A bit of sleep—fitful as it might be—and a fresh perspective would be imperative before contemplating our next action.

I received phone calls from several friends and colleagues, whose counsel I listened to carefully. One of my best friends in Washington, Republican Senate leader Trent Lott called, as did Senator Mitch McConnell, a senior strategist in Republican senatorial circles, Senator Larry Craig, and others. Many—but not all—encouraged me to consider contesting the election results, not to give up too easily.

I pondered the serious issues, not the least of which was how a Democrat in the Senate seat would affect the national political picture. If there was any possibility of preventing that from happening, did I not have an obligation to my party to contest the election? More personally, I didn't want to let down the many people who had poured their time, love, sweat, and labor into our campaign, not to mention those who had sacrificially supported us financially. Would I be doing them a disservice if I did not fight the election procedures? Nor did I want to let down the Republican Party that had been counting on me to bring home a victory, in light of the Democrats' intensive targeting of my Senate seat.

Then there was the overshadowing concern of the Republican majority in the U.S. Senate. We had been monitoring the election results coming over the wires and by reports from the field. The stakes heightened when Senators Slade Gorton and Spencer Abraham seemed to be going down to defeat, as well. To lose my seat could well turn control of the U.S. Senate back to Democrats, which would have national ramifications concerning the effectiveness and the success or failure of the new administration. If George W. Bush had indeed been elected president (and there was still a question about that in the minds of many people), would I be letting down the entire country if I did not fight to contest the election in Missouri, especially if my seat would help give George Bush the majority he would need to implement his programs? Clearly, the question of whether to contest the election or not superseded my personal feelings.

These were tough issues, to be sure, yet I couldn't get away from the truth that the people of Missouri were making their wishes known at the ballot box. Ultimately in a democracy, people should decide the elections. The will of the people is to prevail. Can anything be more basic to self-government and freedom? When courts intervene, it should be to achieve the will of the people, rather than displace it, to support, not subvert the will of the people. Was I to attempt to overturn that process?

By ten-thirty or eleven o'clock, we could guess with a fair amount of certainty what the results portended, but because the numbers were so close—Mel garnering 50 percent of the vote to my 48 percent—we decided against conceding or contesting the election that night. Ann Wagner, our state party chairman, who later became chairwoman of the Republican National Committee then U.S. ambassador to Luxembourg, went downstairs and encouraged our supporters to go home for the evening. She told them that we would not be making any announcements until morning.[15] Before retiring for the night, David and I also went downstairs to share the same sentiments with our team in the war room.

Emotions ran high; exhausted staffers leaned forward in their chairs, head in hands as though trying to relieve a headache. Anger flashed over the election abuses. Others were disappointed and sorrowful; some just sobbed. A few wept openly. I felt like the coach of the team that had just lost the Super Bowl. For more than two years, the campaign staff poured their lives into our cause. Now, the settling awareness that there were more votes for the deceased governor than for me in an election environment of questionable integrity festered into a sore feeling that several staffers vocalized. "This just isn't right!" one longtime staffer blurted.

Before lowering the flag and retreating for the night, I asked a small group of advisers and friends to meet with me at eight o'clock the following morning so we could confer regarding our options and determine a plan of action. I returned to the suite, got ready for bed, and slept as hard and fast as I could, knowing full well that within a few hours I could be conceding my seat in the U.S. Senate to a man who was no longer alive.

The questions surrounding the 2000 Missouri Senate race will probably never be adequately answered. Were there serious election irregularities and illegalities? Probably. Did people vote with their sympathy for the Carnahan family? Possibly. Were some votes cast for Mel Carnahan in a compassionate attempt to honor his memory? Most likely. Nevertheless, a vote is a vote. And after more than 2.36 million votes were counted, I received 48,000 fewer of them than my competitor. I became the first and only incumbent U.S. senator to lose an election to a deceased opponent.

The morning after the election, Janet and I and our advisers gathered at eight o'clock in what was left of the war room in the downstairs area of the campaign hotel. The staff had not yet arrived to straighten up the room, so it looked as though a hurricane had swept through it, chairs in disarray, coffee cups and papers strewn everywhere. Computers and phones still lit up from the night before remained in place, although shoved to the side of the room.

The staff had arranged some chairs in a small circle, so I sat down and looked around at the faces of the dedicated individuals in the room. My wife, Janet, my brother, Bob, and my son Jay sat near me. My family has never suggested to me that my identity or value to them depended on my station in life. I knew that they did not consider me any more or less valuable because I held some political office. They valued me as a husband and father, whether or not I won an election. Nor did they regard holding office on Capitol Hill or in the Missouri statehouse as the epitome of success. Quite the contrary, my family had endured numerous personal sacrifices because of my public positions.

Janet, especially, recognized that I was leaning away from contesting the election. An intensely private person by nature, an accomplished lawyer, author, and university professor in her own right, Janet's sense of value did not depend on my being in office. She was more than willing to accept the opportunity for us to have a more private lifestyle. At the same time, she understood the tensions and the political realities we were facing.

Around the circle were David Ayres; my friend and advisor Rich McClure; Republican party leader Ann Wagner and her husband, Ray; Steve Hilton, our deputy campaign manager; and others whose wisdom and expertise I depended on—all of them affirming their willingness to support me in whatever decision I was about to make.

We opened the meeting with prayer, asking God for wisdom. I made a few brief remarks, and we quickly got down to business. The question was, what should we do? Certainly we had grounds to challenge the election in regard to some of the voting irregularities. If we contested the election, a final decision would have to be made by a vote of the U.S. Senate. Given the strength of legal arguments, I might well have been seated, especially since Republicans maintained the majority in the Senate.

One of the key concerns put forth that morning was something that I knew all too well—that a political candidate at his best is a trustee of the people. A trustee has a responsibility to guard the assets of others with a higher degree of care than he does his own. Those who nominated the candidate deserved the best effort possible. From that point of view alone, I wouldn't dare concede the election without a fight.

On the other hand, it would discredit democracy to drag the state through a prolonged court battle sure to plunge the political system into a quagmire.

Beyond that, the campaigns had been the most expensive in the history of Missouri politics, with each campaign spending in excess of $10 million and advocate groups spending millions more. I couldn't see any reason to shovel more money into the fire.

I was familiar with the feelings of failure and rejection a candidate inevitably experiences after losing elections. I had lost my first election in Missouri. My family and I had prayed about whether I should run for office, and we genuinely believed then, as I do yet today, that God was directing my steps. Despite that, I had lost the election. Then I lost my second election. Since then, I've won quite a few elections, and lost some. Through it all, I've learned to trust that God does indeed have a plan and purpose for me. Trust doesn't come into play when you can figure everything out; that's mere reason. Trust operates when you can't understand why circumstances or events happen. That's where it takes faith to believe that God knows what is best for our lives. Anyhow, I've never been too big on challenging God. I refused to shake my fist at God, demanding to know, "If You led me here, why didn't I win?"

He might just tell me, and I'm not sure I could handle that.

Nevertheless, whether I won or lost, there was always a sense of relief when the election campaign was completed. Maybe that's why as we walked out of the war room that morning, I felt as though a heavy load had been lifted off my shoulders.

Our campaign headquarters was in the same building as the Missouri Bush team, so we held a brief news conference outside on the parking lot in St. Louis. Surrounded by my family and about two dozen close supporters, I faced the full arsenal of television cameras and recorders. Because the race was nationally important, the national media had turned out in force.

Nearly everyone who was in the building came out and gathered around, as members of the media crowded in with their battery of microphones to catch my comments. Obviously, they knew nothing about whether I was going to contest the election or concede it—especially in light of the brewing brouhaha propagated by the Al Gore campaign. Gore seemed willing to burn every bridge and do whatever was necessary to insert himself into the Oval Office. For my part, we were dealing with a sacred process that demanded respect, and I had no intention of doing that.

My emotions almost got the best of me as I began to speak that day. I hadn't written a formal speech, but I had a number of things on my mind that I wanted to say. I briefly reviewed my privilege of public service and simply shared from my heart the deep appreciation I felt for that privilege and the many people who had supported me throughout my political career. Finally, I mustered my courage and got to the part everyone had gathered to hear.

"Missouri is a compassionate state, and, I think, in a very special way Missouri voters have demonstrated their compassion." I could feel the emotion welling within me as I continued, "I hope the outcome of this election is a comfort to Mrs. Carnahan."

I paused for a moment to gain my composure before addressing my staff. "In commending the staff, I want to say that I really appreciate the way in which they have helped me to do things that I believe to have been right. And I'm very pleased that in our development of the campaign and in our completion of the campaign, I don't have regrets about the way we handled things. The tragedy obviously raised issues for us, but some things are more important than politics, and I believe doing what's right is the most important thing we can do."

I didn't want to create a stir, but I felt it was important that people hear from me on the issues swirling around the confusing election. Already, the "talking heads" on television were describing the various strategies I might employ in an attempt to maintain my seat in the U.S. Senate. I must have shocked them when I said, "Now, I know that there are some serious constitutional issues that surround the procedures of this election. And I know that there are serious allegations of fraud and corruption as it relates to the conduct of the election in the city of St. Louis." I paused again, as the expressions on many media members' faces contorted. I could almost feel the air being sucked out of the parking lot as they collectively inhaled.

"But I reject any legal challenge to this election in terms of the election for the United States Senate," I said straightforwardly. "I will discourage others from challenging the will of the people in the election of their United States senator. I will not initiate any legal challenge, and I will not participate in any legal challenge."

The media members finally exhaled. A few bolted for their cars to file their reports, but most remained respectfully silent as I wrapped up my statement.

"I believe that the will of the people has been expressed with compassion and that the people's voice should be respected and heard."

I turned to look at Janet and my family. "Now, in that respect, I have an opportunity to respect some individuals who from time to time have deserved more respect than I've given them." I tugged Janet closer to me. "I look forward to spending time with my wife, Janet . . ." I choked up as I tried desperately to conclude my remarks without crying.

Janet leaned over and placed her head on my shoulder. I struggled to maintain my composure as I felt the tears well into my eyes. In a very real way, I felt that I was saying good-bye to all the people who had been part of my political career. It was over; I was finished. It was time for Janet and me to return to the farm, to retire from public life.

"I look forward to spending time with my wife, Janet, who has always been willing to take whatever steps were necessary for us to work in the public interest, even when it dislocated the private interests and concerns of our family."

I turned toward my children and grandchildren who were standing near me. "And of course, I want to spend time with my children. My daughter, Martha, is here with me today, my son-in-law, Jim . . ." I looked to Martha and Jim, as I felt tears trickle down my face.

Just as I was about to lose the battle to hold back the sea of tears, a tiny voice from the front of the crowd piped up: "That's my mommy!" Both the audience of well-wishers and the media members covering the event burst into laughter, mercifully relieving me of the pressure of the moment.

"Yes," I said with a laugh, "that's little Jimmy's mommy. And I look forward to spending a lot more time with Jimmy as well, on the farm just north of Springfield." I quickly concluded my remarks by thanking everyone once again for their kindness to me over the years.

It was over.

Reporters clamored for more information, for insights into my plans, thoughts, and feelings, but there was nothing more to say. I hugged my family members and close friends, shook hands with people, and answered a few questions tossed from the crowd as we moved toward the door and back inside the campaign headquarters.

Later, in public and private I reiterated to my friends, "Regardless of the legal technicalities, we decided that the people of Missouri had spoken, and had expressed themselves in favor of the deceased candidate and his wife. Since the governor had announced ahead of time what the outcome would be if such a result should occur, I took that as an indication of what the people wanted. I am not about to invoke legal technicalities in an attempt to thwart the will of the people."

My exit comments, broadcast by the national media, unexpectedly elicited a huge response. I soon began receiving dozens of calls, e-mails, and messages applauding my "gracious" concession, and more significantly, my willingness to avoid putting the state and the country through any more pain over this issue. There were already loud, contentious voices shouting and arguing with one another over the Bush-Gore results. We didn't need any more divisiveness.

As the crowd of well-wishers slowly dissipated, I looked around at Janet, David, and a few others who stayed close to me. One question lingered in all of our minds. *Now what?*

While I wasn't worried that I'd be standing in unemployment lines, I had no idea what I was going to do after the new U.S. senators were seated in January of 2001. All I knew was that I'd soon be heading back to Washington to clean out my desk and clear out my office in the Hart Senate Building. Besides that, I wanted to assist my thirty-five or more Senate staff members whose lives were soon to be in upheaval because I had lost the election. I wanted to do my best to help them find other jobs on Capitol Hill, if at all possible, so their families would not be disrupted any more than necessary.

Surprisingly, almost everybody I met in Missouri in the days immediately after the election, whether at church, in a restaurant, or someone I encountered at the gas station, offered me words of encouragement. "Boy, that was a tough loss," they'd say. "Well, I sure voted for you," I'd hear over and over again. Of course, if all the people who claimed to have voted for me actually had done so, I'd have probably won by a landslide! But I appreciated their kind, warm sentiments and their desire for me to heal nonetheless.

Back in Washington, the Senate had not yet recessed, so I was caught up in a flurry of activity whether I wanted to be or not. There was much to be done in a short amount of time. As I had done when I had left other offices, I wanted to conduct a "thank-you tour," to express my gratitude and appreciation to the people of Missouri who had accorded me the privilege of serving them. A number of my senatorial friends expressed their appreciation for how I had handled the disputed election with such "grace" and "class."

"Thanks, that's easy for you to say," I'd quip with a laugh.

George W. Bush was reluctantly declared the winner of the 2000 presidential election by most major television networks before election day was over. Within hours after the polls closed, however, one challenge after another surfaced in Florida regarding election processes and the infamous "hanging chads," the partially punched-out portions of the punch cards used for voting in that state and others. Supporters of Vice President Al Gore launched an angry battle to contest the election results. Nine days later, the legal wrangling and debate continued unabated, focused on nebulous issues such as how a partially punched card reflected the voter's intent. Did they or did they not really intend to vote for that candidate if the hole next to the name was only partially punctured? Everything from the dexterity of senior citizens to the intelligence of the voters was called into question during the absurd legal challenges. Meanwhile, America and the presidency dangled in the wind while rafts of lawyers challenged the proceedings at every point.

Along with numerous other Republican leaders and observers, I traveled to Florida twice in mid-November to speak out on behalf of the president-elect. I was honored to do so.

Several news reports contrasted my willingness to step aside rather than create more divisiveness within our state to Al Gore's rapacious tenacity in pursuing the presidency at any cost. In a *National Review* commentary, Deroy Murdock drew an apt comparison while giving me a backhanded compliment. Mildly chastising conservatives as "too nice," Murdock pointed out that "Article I, Section 3, of the Constitution could not be clearer: 'No Person shall be a Senator who . . . shall not, when elected, be an Inhabitant of that State for which he shall be chosen.' On Election Day, Mel Carnahan was not an inhabitant of the state of Missouri. He was dead."

Unlike Gore, Murdock contended, "the gracious and gentlemanly Ashcroft departed rather than demand a special election between himself and a live opponent."[16] Murdock probably gives me more credit than I deserve, but to me the best interests of my home state and the nation were at odds with my personal and political self-interest. That made my decision much easier.

When George W. Bush was finally confirmed by the courts as the forty-third president of the United States, I sent him a handwritten note of congratulations, including, "If I can ever be of service to you, please don't hesitate to call upon me."

Had I known what that service would entail, I might have thought twice.

ENDNOTES

1. Jo Mannies, "Gov. Carnahan Was Never Too Big for His Britches," *St. Louis Post-Dispatch*, October 22, 2000, p. E2.
2. Terry Ganey, Virginia Young, and Bill Bell Jr. "Family, Friends, Dignitaries Pay Tribute to Governor," *St. Louis Post-Dispatch*, October 21, 2000, p. 1.
3. Ibid.
4. Ibid.
5. Thornton Wilder, *The Skin of Our Teeth* (New York: Harper Collins Publishers, 1942).
6. Jean Carnahan, *Will You Say a Few Words?* (Marcelline, Missouri: Walsworth Publishing Company, 2000), p. 145, 151.
7. John Gizzi, "Terra Incognita," *Human Events*, November 3, 2000.
8. Robert Novak, "'Still for Mel' Partisan Plea," *Chicago Sun-Times*, October 30, 2000.
9. Jo Mannies and Eric Stern, "GOP Doubts Wilson Can Name Fill-in Now," *St. Louis Post-Dispatch*, October 25, 2000, p. A1.
10. Ibid.
11. Jo Mannies, "Carnahan's Actions Earned Him the Support of His Core Groups of Backers," *St. Louis Post-Dispatch*, October 22, 2000, p. A1.
12. Terry Ganey, "Danforth Assails Critics of Ashcroft's Campaigning," *St. Louis Post-Dispatch*, October 27, 2000, p. A10.
13. Terry Ganey, "It's Jean Carnahan vs. John Ashcroft," *St. Louis Post-Dispatch*, October 31, 2000, p. A1.
14. Julie Foster, "Something Smells in St. Louis," WorldNetDaily.com, November 11, 2000; www.worldnetdaily.com/news/articles/article.asp?ARTICLE_ID-18006.
15. At this writing, Ann Wagner is the U.S. ambassador to Luxembourg.
16. Deroy Murdock, "The Right's Too Nice," *National Review*, December 15, 2000.

CHAPTER THREE

A MARKED MAN

The Senate Confirmation Battle, Part 1

⧫⧫⧫

When the mobile phone in my car rang, I knew it must be someone important. My office never gave out my cell phone number to the general public, only to people who had reason to get in touch with me quickly. Nevertheless, I was surprised when I picked up the receiver and heard the voice on the other end.

"John, Andy Card. How are ya?"

"Fine, Andy. How are you?"

"Keeping busy these days, John, as I'm sure you know."

"That's what I've heard."

It was the third week in December 2000, and Andy Card had been recently appointed as George W. Bush's chief of staff, not a surprising choice since Andy had served well in both the Reagan and Bush administrations. He had also directed the transition from the Bush team to the Clinton administration, and now he was back again to serve the younger Bush. I knew Andy was not one to waste words in chitchat, so I wasn't surprised when he swiftly turned the conversation to business.

"Can you bring your wife and a clean suit and come to Texas tomorrow? The president wants to talk to you."

"Sure, Andy. What's this all about?"

"That's all I can tell you right now. Let me know your travel arrangements and we'll have somebody at the airport to pick you up in Austin."

The president-elect had been assembling his cabinet, and most of the major positions had been filled. Although I had indicated in my handwritten congratulatory note to the new president that I would be willing to serve in any way, nobody had contacted me regarding any position in the new administration, and the list of jobs for which I might be qualified was dwindling. The one high-profile cabinet post that remained unfilled was a job that I had done for eight years at the state level—attorney general. Several notable names had already been mentioned in that regard, including individuals such as FBI director Louis Freeh, former New York City mayor Rudy Giuliani, Harriet Miers (George W. Bush's attorney), former Missouri senator John Danforth, former Oklahoma governor Frank Keating, and others, all of whom were highly qualified and competent to fulfill the demands of the office. I hadn't given much thought to the matter, especially after the stomach-wrenching defeat I had recently experienced in Missouri. Nevertheless, I remained willing to serve the new president if called upon.

And Andy Card's call seemed to portend a possibility of my serving in some capacity in the new administration. I hung up the telephone and immediately called my office, rearranging my schedule to accommodate an unexpected trip to Texas. The following day, Janet and I flew to Austin to meet with the new president. I still did not know with any certainty what direction the meeting might take. That same evening, I was escorted to a comfortable sitting room at the Texas Governor's Mansion in Austin, where I joined George W. Bush and Andy Card. After some friendly introductory comments and some background-type questions, the president soon turned the conversation toward the position of attorney general. He made clear the lines of authority in the new administration: in the George W. Bush administration, they wanted an attorney general who would advise the president, not someone who would discuss his advice to the president with the press.

My previous exposure to George W. Bush had been rather limited. I had met with him two years earlier, when I had been considering a run for the presidency and prior to the announcement that he was running for that office. We had talked for a couple of hours about our roles as governors, and had enjoyed a mutual respect. I had also worked closely with the new president's father, Bush 41, during his administration. I had been loyal to George H. W. Bush from the beginning, when I was trying to help him during his 1988 presidential campaign, all the way through his presidency. I was also friends with the elder Bush's brother "Bucky" Bush, who lived in Missouri, and one of the president's top advisers, Karl Rove. Karl had worked for me as a campaign adviser in the 1970s back in Missouri. I knew him well, and he had been in the room when we made many important decisions at the state level. Now he was a trusted and valuable member of the Bush team. But despite our many mutual connections, George W. Bush and I were not close friends.

The meeting with the president and Andy went well, and I departed that night with a new job—attorney general of the United States—although I was sworn to secrecy and couldn't really speak freely about it. The Bush inner circle was then, and has always been, highly cautious concerning leaks to the press. The president had personally asked me to be his new attorney general and I had accepted his offer. He would make an announcement to the world first thing in the morning, and then it was merely a matter of confirmation by the Senate.

As I left the president that night, I could hardly believe the amazing roller-coaster ride my emotions had been on the past few weeks. After becoming the first person in American history to lose a U.S. Senate election to a deceased person, now here I was being asked to occupy what some might consider the fourth most powerful position in the country. But in a sense, that has been a theme of my life. When I've taken my lumps and felt as though the strain, pain, loss, or humiliation could not possibly be any worse, something good has always come of it. In spiritual terms, for every Gethsemane, there is an Easter morning. To me, failure is not fatal unless you quit; getting knocked down is not embarrassing unless you allow it to keep you down. In my career, I had won some elections and lost a few; some were horribly disappointing, others were wildly successful beyond my grandest hopes. I've lived by the adage that for every door that slams in your face, there can be an open window somewhere, if you are willing to find it, and if you can maintain your integrity in the process.

There was not a lot of preparation for the news conference held the next morning, after the president announced my nomination. It was a rather straightforward affair, at which I told the press, "The president has asked me to give him the best of my legal advice and assistance, and I'll give it to him and not to the public." I fielded a few questions, but it seemed that most members of the media were somewhat surprised at my selection, and were rather benign in their efforts. This was the calm before the storm. Before long, I was on my way home.

One of my first telephone calls was to my former chief of staff, David Ayres. One of the most highly respected chiefs of staff on Capitol Hill, David had already been entertaining job offers since our defeat in Missouri. I wanted to let him know that we still had some work to do if he wanted to come along for the ride. Thankfully, he did.

With the rancor from the hotly contested general election still fomenting, David and I expected that some of President Bush's nominations might be challenged in the Senate, if for no other reason than simply because the Democrats wanted to throw down a gauntlet to the new administration and to let the voters know they were not rolling over in the face of defeat. We underestimated the level of

Democratic vitriol, however, and their marshaling of liberal groups such as the American Civil Liberties Union, the National Organization for Women, and the People for the American Way. We thought the opposition would center on one or two nominees, and because of my record it was assumed that I might be a lightning rod, but we were not expecting that I would be the target of some of the most vehement opposition in the history of presidential nominations.

We should have seen what was coming when Linda Chavez, President Bush's nominee as labor secretary, was excoriated by the media for allowing an illegal Guatemalan immigrant to live in her home and receive some spending money in exchange for doing housework and nanny duties. Chavez withdrew her name from the running almost overnight. One day she was in the transition team office next door, the next day she was gone. But not before pointing out that her critics were expanding their line of fire. "They're out to get George W. Bush's nominees," she told CNN. "I'm only the first person. I can tell you, John Ashcroft is going to face much worse than I have."[1] She was right. Once Linda was gone, the opposition forces focused their sights on me.

At a news conference in Washington, a coalition of liberal advocacy groups announced a coordinated effort to oppose my nomination as attorney general. Hilary Shelton of the NAACP's Washington bureau, Elaine Jones, director-counsel of the group's Legal Defense Fund and Education Fund, and Kate Michelman, president of the National Abortion and Reproductive Rights Action League (NARAL), were among the first to speak out in opposition to my appointment, but they were certainly not the last or the loudest.

Opponents talked about my nomination as being troublesome for two main reasons. First they were concerned about my deeply held personal beliefs that influenced my conservative record on matters regarding desegregation, abortion, and capital punishment, and they feared what I might do as a public official with such broad responsibilities. Second, they wanted to signal the president that he was going to have enormous opposition to any appointments of conservative judges and attempts to influence the judicial branch of our government.

For my part, I never thought it important that I be confirmed by a unanimous opinion, or even by eighty-five of one hundred senators. My job was to get confirmed—period. I knew that a simple majority was enough, and perhaps all that could be expected after such a tumultuous election season. Even before the public announcement of my nomination, I started, at David Ayres's suggestion, calling my friends and foes in the Senate, asking for their advice and support. It is not appropriate to ask certain members of the Senate to vote for someone who holds positions contrary to theirs, so I asked those individuals, "Can you advise me? Can you give me some help?" Oftentimes, they did.

One of the first calls I placed was to Senator Patrick Leahy. Leahy is one of the nicest, most gregarious fellows you would ever want to meet, but at the same time, he can be extremely cutthroat when it comes to his partisan dealings. "Well, I'll work with you, John," he said whenever I called him to ascertain his feelings about my nomination. I felt that was a good response, coming from Leahy.

After I talked with Patrick Leahy, I made several calls to other key congressional leaders, including Orrin Hatch, Henry Hyde, and John Conyers. "I have something that I need to discuss with you, and I need your commitment that it will remain in confidence," I started. Most senators could hold a secret at least till nine o'clock in the morning, so I knew I was on relatively safe ground. Senators in powerful positions don't like to be caught off guard, so I said, "You may have already heard, but I wanted to tell you personally that the president has asked me to join his cabinet as attorney general, and I'm inclined to do so. I just wanted to give you a heads-up on what was going on."

My basic approach was simple: I attempted to make a personal connection with each person I called, expressing a desire to work together. I always asked for support, and if a senator indicated that he or she might be willing to go on record, I'd ask for a contact person so we could follow up. If the senator was reluctant to support me, I'd ask if I could stop by his or her office for a chance to discuss the nomination. Most senators welcomed such visits. "Oh, I'll be glad to see you," they'd say in the classic senatorial style of offering whatever you can without giving away too much. "I'll be glad to keep my ears open; I'll be happy to let you know what's going on . . ."

"I'm asking you to vote for me," I'd sometimes press.

"Oh, well, now . . . there are a few things I need to know yet, a few questions I want to ask before I make my final decision . . . I'm leaning toward voting for you . . ." some senators hedged.

While it could be assumed that conservative Republicans would support me, the more moderate members of the Senate were wild cards. I wanted to firm up my relationship with Arlen Specter and Lincoln Chafee, two leading moderates in the Senate, both of whom were quite encouraging.

Then I called Joe Lieberman, a man for whom I hold the greatest respect, and a genuinely nice person. Joe was quite cordial when I called to ask him to vote for me. "Well, John, I'd like to," he said, "but there are some things . . ."

I could tell that Joe wasn't merely putting me off, so I blurted out, "Wait a minute. Are you going to run for president sometime in the future?"

My directness took my friend almost by surprise, but Joe recovered quickly. "Well, I can't say that I am not, or won't . . . I might."

"Joe," I said, "if you ever plan to run for president, you can't vote for me."

I could almost see Joe smiling through the telephone. "Well, you may be right about that," he said.

Chris Dodd, a former chairman of the Democratic National Committee, was another person who responded to my nomination with great integrity. Chris told me, "The president deserves his people;

you're a decent human being, and a capable person. I will vote for you." And Chris Dodd kept his word, despite getting a lot of heat and pressure from his colleagues.

I knew that certain members of the Senate would not—and could not—vote for me for various reasons of political expediency. To them I said, "Look, I understand that you can't vote for me to be confirmed, but we've been friends for a long time. How would you approach this process if you were me?" Frequently, I found that I could reduce some members' opposition simply on that basis. If I knew I could never get their support, at least I could defray some of their opposition.

Several high-profile members of the Senate said things along the lines of "I can't help you, but I'll try not to hurt you." I appreciated that.

One of my closest friends in the opposition party was Russ Feingold. He is a brilliant man and a good friend, but we are at opposite spectrums politically. Russ is liberal and I am conservative, yet we'd worked well together on several Senate committees, and we'd developed a deep respect for each other. I always felt that I could trust Russ completely. I never worried about him saying one thing to my face and something else behind my back. I felt certain I could depend on Russ's support, and he did not disappoint me.

The aggressive calling campaign was modestly successful, since my goal was simply to elicit some sort of public commitment from the senators, a statement of support from which they couldn't or wouldn't want to retreat. Eventually, at least six Democrats who said they would vote for me reneged. On the other hand, I had at least that many Democrats who pledged to help me as much as they could, and who kept their word when it came time to vote, despite the mounting pressure from their own leaders by that time. Had we not secured commitments from these Democrats, my nomination might have been sandbagged.

In any political transition when one party leaves office and another comes to town, dozens of appointments must be approved in a relatively short time. Both parties have a sort of standard "playbook" for getting confirmed to a cabinet position, Supreme Court judgeship, or other high-level positions. The basic game plan is to lie low, don't make any waves, don't talk to anybody in the media, don't make any promises or commitments that you might not be able to fulfill.

The preconfirmation preparation is quite elaborate. To help me prepare, I received huge briefing books from the incoming administration's transition team regarding a multitude of issues. Moreover, we built a team of advisers to help with the process, including Bill Barr, a former attorney general; Fred Fielding, a former White House counsel; Mindy Tucker; and Barbara Olson, all of whom offered invaluable assistance. Fred McClure was our direct liaison with the Bush transition team. He had handled the preparation for Clarence Thomas prior to the Supreme Court justice's confirmation hearings. For several days prior to my hearings, the group quizzed me on potential questions and appropriate answers.

When I wasn't cramming for the big test, I continued my phone confirmation campaign between the time the president announced my appointment on December 19 and the Christmas holiday. From the responses I had received, I felt confident of a relatively easy confirmation. After all, most of President Clinton's appointments were confirmed with a mere voice vote; only one had gone to a roll-call vote, much less a prolonged confirmation process. With several strong Democrats leaning in my direction, I hoped the negative voices would be quieted.

But as the new year dawned, opposition from various liberal groups intensified. Scathing articles appeared in major newspapers and magazines. *TIME* magazine ran a cover story that sounded as though it had been written by a Democratic campaign speechwriter. The *Washington Post* published a litany of articles castigating me as the president's choice. Many of the liberal leaning talking-head news programs trotted out guests who took great pleasure in presenting a choreographed litany of reasons why I was the worst nomination George W. Bush could have possibly offered the nation.

By mid-January 2001, the language of the opposition to my nomination as attorney general became more damning. Particularly offensive to me were the articles and statements calling me a racist. Clint Bolick, of the Institute for Justice, tried his best to set the record straight on a PBS interview with Gwen Ifill. When Ifill asked if my opposition to Ronnie White, an African American jurist nominated for the U.S. District Court, was discriminatory, Bolick replied, "There was not discrimination in that selection. John Ashcroft as governor appointed the first African American judge to the Western District Court of Appeals. He voted for the vast majority of minority nominees. This is race-baiting, pure and simple. It is an effort on the part of the left wing and the Democratic Party to inflame the base by injecting race. Ashcroft opposed a lot of nominees because he disagreed with them fundamentally on their view of the law, not because of their race."[2]

I appreciated Clint Bolick and others like him who adamantly defended me against such false accusations. Frequently, just about the time one of the vicious vendettas threatened to discourage me, someone would rally to my defense. Occasionally, the words of encouragement came from quite unexpected sources.

One day I rode the Washington Metro subway system from our home to the Bush transition office, located three blocks from the White House. As I walked down the street, I noticed an old black street musician, dressed in a tattered high school band uniform, playing his trumpet. Even from a distance, I recognized the strains of "Amazing Grace" wafting across Pennsylvania Avenue. Just as I was about to pass by him, the trumpeter stopped playing in mid-note, and I was surprised to hear him call out, "Hang in there, Mr. Ashcroft."

I stopped on the street and replied, "That's mighty nice of you to say that."

"Well, we're for you, man. We really care about you."

I thanked the street musician and started to walk away. As I walked a few steps farther down the street, the trumpeter began playing a lilting old gospel tune to which I knew the words:

Love lifted me; Love lifted me;
When nothing else would do,
Love lifted me!

That was a good reminder as I made my way down the street toward the transition office where I'd spend the rest of the day preparing to be grilled by the Senate Judiciary Committee. The process would be grueling, no doubt; at least two, possibly three days before the Judiciary Committee, then if all went well, a few more days of tension as the full Senate would debate my qualifications to be attorney general. The tune "Love Lifted Me" would come in handy in the days ahead.

The accusations and negative publicity became so virulent that the FBI decided I should have a security detail with me, especially as I entered and exited the hearing room. The FBI was concerned for my safety because threats had been made against my life.

On January 16, 2001, the first morning of the confirmation hearings, Janet and I were scheduled to meet with Senator Orrin Hatch, the ranking member of the Judiciary Committee, prior to going into the hearing room. We got out of our vehicle, accompanied by the FBI agents, David Ayres, Fred McClure, and some staffers and began walking toward the entrance of the Russell Senate Office Building, the august chamber where the hearings were to take place. The scene outside the building was complete bedlam. Protesters bearing large placards and picket signs shouted obscenities and other vile comments, and some shook their fists at me ominously, while others waved, smiled, and offered support. News cameras protruded out of the throng, filming from every angle, with the large boom microphones hanging over the tops of our heads as we pressed into the crowd.

Then I saw them. A large delegation of African American Christians led by Bob Woodson, a man well-known for his conservative approach to helping people lift themselves out of poverty, had bused to Washington from hundreds of miles away, some from Georgia, Alabama, and other locations. Three or four busloads of people had traveled to the Capitol to pray for me during the confirmation hearings and had congregated outside the Russell Building.

As we walked through the mixed crowd of protesters and supporters, the black well-wishers pressed in as though to protect and insulate me from the nasty harangues launched in my direction by the detractors. By the time I reached the steps of the Russell Building, the delegation of African American Christians had virtually surrounded me, wanting to lay hands on me and offering to pray for me.

On high alert, my security detail was not happy. "Stay close to us, sir," one burly fellow said through tight lips. "We'll make a way for you to get you inside safely."

"No, no, it's all right," I said. I appreciated the security detail's desire to protect me, but these people had come to pray for me. I was deeply moved, especially in light of the recent attacks accusing me of being a racist. The fact that this group had gathered at the Russell Building was an implicit refutation of such charges. If I was a racist, why would these people travel hundreds of miles simply to pray for my success, and to ask God to guide, direct, and prosper my efforts? I knew we were on a tight schedule, and I was aware of the security risks, but I could not possibly turn away from this crowd of believers whose only desire was to encourage me and to pray for God's best in my life. I waded into the crowd and allowed the group to place their hands on my head, back, and shoulders as they prayed for me. "Oh, God, please give this man wisdom," a black pastor prayed loudly, with television cameras rolling and reporters scribbling. "Heavenly Father, let Your will be done!" another man prayed. It was the kind of sponta-neous event that rarely makes it onto most newscasts—as far as I know, the media chose to focus their attention on the relatively small crowd of protesters. I doubt that the African American Ashcroft sup-porters were written about in most major newspapers or magazines, but they were a part of the confirmation hearings that I will treasure all the days of my life.

It was truly an emotional moment. I thanked the people as best I could. "Thank you for your prayers," I managed to say without losing my composure. I was deeply troubled that anybody could perceive me as a racist, that someone might think that I would judge a person by the color of his or her skin. I knew beyond a doubt that I had never harbored a racist inclination in my life, but with the incessant pound-ing of the press and liberal interest groups, after a while I had begun to wonder, *What must black people who hear this nonsense think of me? Do they really believe this smear campaign?* I certainly hoped not, but it is hard to know such things. Now, there, right on Capitol Hill, a large delegation of black Americans had gone out of their way to let me know that they understood and believed not just my words, but my heart.

We moved inside the Russell Building and made our way to Sena-tor Hatch's office. He was waiting for me and greeted me warmly. Orrin had been the chairman of the Judiciary Committee until the balance of power shifted because of my loss to Democrat Mel Carna-han and the defection of former Republican senator Jim Jeffords. Consequently, the Democrats held a majority, and Patrick Leahy was the new chairman of the committee.

Always the gentleman, Orrin Hatch made no mention of such matters. Instead, after some brief introductions and some casual small talk, he suggested that we gather in a circle for prayer before going into the Senate hearing chamber.

The entire group of us joined hands in a circle, and Senator

Hatch prayed a heartfelt prayer, asking God to give me peace and to guide my thoughts and statements. Orrin's prayer was not a rote repetition of trite, spiritual-sounding words; quite the contrary, he prayed passionately and confidently, not just for me, but for my wife and children as well. His prayer vocalized the thoughts and concerns in my own heart. When he finished, I felt a sense of peace and calm, and there was no doubt Orrin believed that God had indeed heard our prayer. The irony was not lost on me, that the last thing we did before stepping into a room predominantly filled with individuals who opposed prayer in public institutions—members of groups such as People for the American Way, the American Civil Liberties Union, and others—was to stop and invoke Almighty God's presence in the proceedings. I felt a bit like what I imagined the early Christians must have felt as they stepped through the archways into the Roman Coliseum to face the hungry lions.

But we were ready. Senator Hatch led the way, and Janet and I walked into the Russell Caucus Room, a Beaux-Arts-style architectural design, replete with huge marble Corinthian pilasters and marble walls, with richly detailed, ornate ceilings, enhanced by the red carpet on the floor. It is the same room in which public hearings had been held regarding the sinking of the *Titanic*, the attack on Pearl Harbor, the Watergate affair, the hearings on Supreme Court nominee Robert Bork, and the confirmation hearings of Supreme Court justice Clarence Thomas. It is the room where senators love to hold court when they want to regale themselves with the grand traditions of their offices.

The first thing that strikes a person on entering that high-ceilinged, cavernous environment is the brightness of the room. It was not built for television coverage, so the large battery of television cameras depend on high-wattage lights for quality indoor shots, and the cumulative effect is nearly blinding. Before long, the floodlights heat the room, regardless of the thermostat setting, adding another discomforting element to an already uncomfortable situation.

Janet slipped into a row of seats behind me, joining David and my advisers. I took my seat at the table at the front of the room, facing a U-shaped arrangement of nineteen senators seated at elevated tables in front of me. A lone microphone stood ready to capture every word I uttered. Behind me, the gallery of about two hundred seats was nearly full. A large contingent of people, I later learned, had come simply to pray for me throughout the hearings.

As a U.S. senator myself, and a former state attorney general, I had experienced both sides of the confirmation process. Beyond that, I had served for four years on the Senate Judiciary Committee; I had been one of the guys sitting at the elevated tables and I knew how the responsibility weighed on me when I considered the confirmation of various appointments. On the other hand, I knew how it felt to be the guy under the gun, the man in the spotlight. Although cabinet members serve at the pleasure of the president, rather than for life as do Supreme Court justices, I knew it wasn't a done deal just because President Bush had selected me for confirmation. Quite the contrary.

In the past, as a senator, I had felt strongly on several occasions that certain individuals should not be confirmed. One of these was Frederica Massiah-Jackson, a judge in Philadelphia whose name was brought before the U.S. Senate to be confirmed as a federal judge. Two things she had done were anathema to me.

One, in open court, she had chosen to identify two undercover police agents, demonstrating that she despised such clandestine efforts by law officers. Identifying the two agents was tantamount to marking them as targets for the criminals on whom they had been gathering information.

Second, in a separate incident, again in open court, she berated attorneys by telling them in no uncertain terms, including her use of the "F word," that they didn't know what they were doing. Despite what I considered to be her less than noble character traits, I did not attempt to keep Frederica Massiah-Jackson from getting an "up or down" vote by the Senate. Quite the contrary, I refused to allow the

Senate to vote on her without a roll-call vote and the opportunity to debate the nomination. The entire Senate was apparently willing to allow the nomination to slide through on a voice vote only—everyone except me.

I received pressure from both sides of the aisle to back down, to let the nomination fly through. Even the venerable Strom Thurmond called me one night when I was traveling through Iowa. "Look, John, you have to let this go."

As much as I respected the senator from South Carolina—a man who had been reelected to the Senate eight times—I dug in my heels. "I'm sorry, Strom," I said, "I can't do that. This is not the kind of person I can recommend as a federal judge. If the nomination goes through after a roll-call vote and a discussion, fine; but we need to demand a vote on this person."

Those supporting Jackson wanted to slip the nomination into the Senate record late at night, as is often done on a wide variety of issues, when the Senate floor is practically empty except for the presiding officer and a few members and clerks. Here's how a "consent" vote works: as the presiding officer is closing the Senate for the day, someone reads something such as, "By unanimous consent, the following nominations are approved."

The presiding officer might say, "Is there any objection?"

Objection? Nobody is even there to object!

"Without objection, the nominations are approved."

To me, tacit consent was not appropriate in this particular case. When I called for a roll-call vote, those who supported Frederica Massiah-Jackson pulled down the nomination.

Now it was my turn to be in the hot seat. As I unbuttoned my suit coat and adjusted my notepad in front of me, I glanced at the senators sitting in judgment on me. I knew these men and women, and they knew me. I could have almost predicted how they were going to vote.

I knew several of the Democrats on the committee would not have voted for me if I were the last man in America qualified for the job. On the other hand, there was my friend Russ Feingold. He just might.

Senator Leahy called the session to order and swore me in. As I stood and raised my right hand, a bevy of photographers scrambled for shot position on the floor, crouching down low to stay out of the way of the television cameras and to avoid blocking the view of the senators. The photographers shot up at me from every possible angle as I repeated the oath.

Leahy fired the initial shots in the conflagration. Following the perfunctory niceties, he subtly outlined the Democratic attack program, saying, "The attorney general is the lawyer for all the people, as the chief law enforcement officer in the country. That's why the attorney general not only needs the full confidence of the president, he or she also needs the confidence and trust of the American people. We all look to the attorney general to ensure evenhanded law enforcement and protection of our basic constitutional rights, including the freedom of speech, the right to privacy, a woman's right to choose, freedom from government oppression, and equal protection of all our laws.

"The attorney general plays a critical role in bringing the country together, in bridging racial divisions and inspiring people's confidence in their government."

Clearly, the battle was on. I stared straight ahead at Leahy, as though not really seeing him. Occasionally I looked down at my notepad and jotted some notes about what he was saying. I had no need to write much down. I'd heard it all before from Leahy and his cohorts on the committee, as well as from their surrogates in liberal organizations given privilege by the media. It was their same old song, different day, different verse. It was rather clear where he was going, and Leahy held true to form.

"Senator Ashcroft has often taken aggressively activist positions on a number of issues that deeply divide the American people . . . On many of these issues and on battles over executive branch or judicial nominees, Senator Ashcroft was not just in the minority of the United States Senate, but in a minority among Republicans in the Senate."

Oh, really? I wondered. *That's news to me.* I wanted to interrupt, but that's not the way things are done in these hearings. I knew I'd get my shot. Besides, Leahy was still banging the drum that the liberals hoped to thump throughout the hearings: that John Ashcroft was far out of the mainstream of the American people.

"Now, we have to ask if somebody who has been that unyielding in a policy outlook can unite all Americans," Leahy asked rhetorically. "And that's an important question for the Senate.

"Now, the hearing is not about whether we like Senator John Ashcroft or call him a friend. All of us do.

"All of us like him," Leahy was saying. "All of us know him. It is not about whether we agree or disagree with him on every issue. Many of us have worked productively with him on selected matters and then we've disagreed with him on others.

"Let me be very clear about one thing: this is not about whether Senator Ashcroft is racist, anti-Catholic, anti-Mormon, or anti-anything else."

In his classic way, Leahy was raising these specters, and then he said, "Those of us who have worked with him in the Senate do not make that charge."

Orrin Hatch followed on Leahy's heels, beginning by thanking Janet and my family for their sacrifices while I had served in public office. He outlined my thirty-year career, noting each highlight, including the fact that I had served eight years as attorney general of Missouri, and had also been elected by my peers, the attorneys general of the other forty-nine states, to head the National Association of Attorneys General. Orrin's stated point was, "Of the sixty-seven attorneys general in the history of this country, only a handful come close to having even some of the qualifications that John Ashcroft brings in assuming the position of chief law enforcement officer of this great nation."

Ted Kennedy was next, and he made no effort to disguise his disdain for me as a potential attorney general of the United States. He stated on the record, "During Senator Ashcroft's quarter-century in public service, he has taken strong positions on a range of important issues in the jurisdiction of the Justice Department. Unfortunately and often, he has used the power of his high office to advance his personal views in spite of the law of the land. The vast majority of Americans support vigorous enforcement of our civil rights laws, and those laws and the Constitution demand it.

"Senator Ashcroft, however, spent significant parts of his term as attorney general of Missouri and his term as governor strongly opposing school desegregation and voter registration in St. Louis. The vast majority of Americans believe in access to contraception and a woman's right to choose, and our laws and Constitution demand it. Senator Ashcroft does not. His intense efforts have made him one of the principal architects of the ongoing right-wing strategy to dismantle *Roe v. Wade* and abolish a woman's right to choose. Deep concerns have been raised about his record on gun control . . ."

On and on, Ted went, filling his three minutes with distortions of my record. I had no illusions that Kennedy was going to vote for me, but at least he could have based his decision on facts and truth. I couldn't wait to hear what he'd bring up when he had fifteen minutes to question me.

Strom Thurmond was next, and promptly set about extolling my virtues. Without saying so directly, Strom hinted that he'd seen a lot of these kinds of hearings, and I was honored when he said, "Senator Ashcroft is one of the most qualified people selected for this position in many years." He reminded the committee, "Twenty years ago, I recommended him to be attorney general for President Ronald Reagan, and I would like to place that letter into the record."

It went back and forth like that for a while, each senator making his or her opening remarks for three minutes. This was the preview of coming attractions, the warm-up before the real questions would be directed to me, each committee member having fifteen minutes during the first round of questions.

Nonetheless, the opening volleys in the hearings set the tone for the confrontational nature of what was to come. Once the senators could ask specific questions, I was grilled about my views on everything from racism, abortion, and special rights for homosexuals to desegregation issues and violence in schools.

With the help of my confirmation prep team, I had established some "rules of engagement" for dealing with the deliberately cutting questions from certain members of the Judiciary Committee. My rules were simple: be polite and friendly, but don't take the bait. I knew that many of the questions that would come my way could be "bait," leading to potential traps wrapped in tantalizing opportunities to state my beliefs or to comment on issues or the conduct of other people. For example, a question may be asked, "Aren't you opposed to homosexuals?"

The answer, of course, is no, I am not opposed to homosexuals; I am opposed to legislation granting *special rights* for homosexuals. Certainly I don't condone homosexual lifestyles, but I believe in treating people equally, regardless of their sexual orientation. Nevertheless, the question is asked in a way that if I succumb to the temptation to go on a soapbox, it is sure to be counterproductive. Instead, my rule was simply to avoid the bait.

The flip side of that principle was also true. Deal quickly with the specifics of the question; don't dodge the question, yet understand that the specific question is often making a general charge. As such, answer the general accusation and don't focus on the specifics of the charge. In most cases, I knew that I was not going to persuade the more antagonistic members of the Judiciary Committee to change their minds. Moreover, I was extremely aware that I could hit all the home runs I wanted, but it would make little impact and most likely not change the score. However, one minor error could lead to losing the entire game.

The tension in the room was palpable. For me, the only upside of the confirmation process was that I made a lot of new friends, mostly people outside the hearing room. Americans like to root for the underdog, and when the public saw nineteen senators, and particularly the Democratic side of the committee, ganging up on one person, the results were an unexpected rise in my popularity. This was especially true when the senators opposing my nomination repeatedly attempted to force me into answering questions that were a political version of "When did you stop beating your wife?" It is difficult to prove a negative and deny culpability for something you didn't do in the first place. Worse yet is trying to prove that you *wouldn't* do something in the future!

In any confirmation hearings, the members of the committee and the person in the dock are all conscious of the time limits placed on most confirmation hearings and inquiries nowadays. Some will ask a question and then petition the person in charge for more time, to explore a subject further in another round of questioning or to follow up on something that someone else asked. Working the clock gets to be almost like a sport, waiting to take your best shot at the right moment, running down the clock in some ways to keep the ball out of the opponent's control.

Senator Ted Kennedy was particularly vehement in his inquisition. His face grew red and his voice increased in volume and pitch. At one point, the senator from Massachusetts was nearly yelling and screaming at me on the first day of the confirmation hearings. At one point, when I was trying to explain my reasons for opposing a mandated desegregation in St. Louis, the hearing room nearly turned into a verbal jousting match. When I expanded my explanation, the following exchange took place:

SENATOR ASHCROFT: I'm pleased to respond to your question about my priority for education. During my time as governor, funding for education in the state of Missouri went up about 70 percent. The vast majority of all state resources that were new and available went to education because I believe in education.

In *Missouri v. Jenkins*, the case in Kansas City—

SENATOR KENNEDY: Could we get on—I don't think we've got—

SENATOR HATCH: Let him answer the question.

SENATOR KENNEDY: The question wasn't about Kansas City. I asked about St. Louis.

SENATOR HATCH: It was about education.

SENATOR ASHCROFT: Fine.

SENATOR KENNEDY: But if he wants to talk about Kansas City—

SENATOR ASHCROFT: I would like to talk about Kansas City, but it's not—I'd rather answer your question than talk about Kansas City.

SENATOR KENNEDY: That isn't the question, but if you want to talk about it—

SENATOR ASHCROFT: Well, I'll just give you an idea—

SENATOR SESSIONS: You challenged his interest in education, Senator Kennedy—

SENATOR KENNEDY: Well, that isn't the—

SENATOR SESSIONS: You suggested he didn't care about children.

CHAIRMAN LEAHY: Gentlemen, gentlemen.

SENATOR HATCH: Let him answer the question.

CHAIRMAN LEAHY: First I would note that whatever questions are asked, if the witness feels that he's not given time to answer all the questions, he will be given time, as will senators be given time to do follow-up questions.

SENATOR KENNEDY: Well, I had one other area to cover, but whatever you want to do, John.

SENATOR ASHCROFT: Well, you're the senator.

SENATOR KENNEDY: Well, you're the—

SENATOR ASHCROFT: You know, I look forward to working with this committee upon confirmation. I do. And I don't know when there was last an attorney general that had previously served as a member of this committee. And, frankly, I think we can work together, and I want to, and I don't want any rancor to characterize our relationship. And I'm very pleased to defer.

SENATOR KENNEDY: Let me just go on to the questions of voter registration, your vetoes on voter registration.

That was probably not the kind of noble exchange the framers of our Constitution had in mind when they ordained these kinds of committees and hearings. It was, however, where the media centered its news coverage of the hearings that day.

Ironically, during one of the breaks in the hearings, Ted Kennedy came over and said, "Oh, John, I know you have your family here with you, and if during these breaks you need a place where you can just get away from it all, I have a conference room right down here near my office. You are welcome to use it anytime."

I thanked him and smiled. Personal kindness and public sparring; that's the way the game is played in Washington. A few minutes earlier, he had been trying to pin me to my chair with his blistering rhetoric. Now he was offering me a place of sanctuary where my family and I could be refreshed. Ted and I have always gotten along well, even though we see many issues quite differently. A few years later when we dedicated the Justice Department building and named it in honor of Ted's brother Robert F. Kennedy, we had a special luncheon reception for the Kennedy family at the Justice Department. Although I don't know if Ted would accept the comparison, even our approach to combating terror under my term was modeled on Bobby Kennedy's approach to rooting out organized crime.

I knew that a firestorm would be occur wherever I chose to fight and contest the accusations lodged against me, and that is where the news coverage would focus. So I tried to choose my battles wisely. Like moths drawn to a flame, the opposition is drawn to where they believe they have drawn blood. It makes for good news coverage.

I remained cool and calm most of the day, but I also wanted to make my case, that I could and would honor the law, even those laws— such as a woman's legal ability to pursue an abortion—with which I personally disagreed. In my opening statement, I emphasized that. "The language of justice is not the reality of justice for all Americans. From racial profiling to news of unwarranted strip searches, the list of injustice in America today is still long. Injustice in America against any individual must not stand. This is the special charge of the U.S. Department of Justice. No American should be turned away from a polling place because of the color of her skin or the sound of his name. No American should be denied access to public accommodations or a job as a result of a disability. No American family should be prevented from realizing the dream of homeownership in the neighborhood of their choice just because of skin color. No American should have the door to employment or educational opportunity slammed shut because of gender or race. No American should fear being stopped by police just because of skin color. And no woman should fear being threatened or coerced in seeking constitutionally protected health services. I pledge to you that if I'm confirmed as attorney general, the Justice Department will meet its special charge. Injustice against individuals will not stand—no ifs, ands, or buts, period."

I directly took on two concerns cited by my critics. I looked straight at Ted Kennedy and Patrick Leahy, then said, "Some have suggested that my opposition to the appointment of Judge Ronnie White, an African American Missouri Supreme Court judge, to a lifetime term on the federal bench was based on something other than my own honest assessment of his qualifications for the post . . . Studying his judicial record, considering the implications of his decisions, and hearing the widespread objections to his appointment from a large body of my constituents, I simply came to the overwhelming conclusion that Judge White should not be given lifetime tenure as a U.S. District Court judge. My legal review revealed the troubling pattern of his willingness to modify settled law in criminal cases. Fifty-three of my colleagues reached the same conclusion. Another issue merits specific mention in these opening remarks, and that is the issue that we would identify with the case of *Roe versus Wade*, which established a woman's constitutional right to an abortion . . . If confirmed as attorney general, I will follow the law in this area and in all other areas. The Supreme Court's decisions on this have been multiple. They have been recent, and they have been emphatic."

I've always believed abortion to be repugnant, a horrible evil foisted on our nation by an unwise Supreme Court decision. I had stated numerous times that as a U.S. senator I would do all that I could to see *Roe v. Wade* overturned. But now as attorney general, I would have to follow the existing laws of the land until they were changed.

It seemed almost silly to have to state such an obvious fact, but such was the nature of the day, answering questions designed to be more like knives in the back rather than honest inquiries. At the conclusion of the first day of hearings, Thomas L. Jipping wrote an op-ed piece in WorldNetDaily.com describing the attacks on my character: "These leftists are demonizing a man, not debating his qualifications."[3]

When we walked out of the hearing room that first day, Janet was quick to tell me what a wonderful job I had done. She was a tremendous encouragement to me. "I'm so proud of you," she said. "I'm so glad that is over."

"Thank you, Janet," I said as I gave her a quick hug. "But the game is only at halftime. We have to come back again tomorrow."

ENDNOTES

1. CNN, "Retribution Sank Nomination Chavez Says," *Wolf Blitzer Reports*, January 9, 2001; www.transcripts.cnn.com/2001/ALLPOLITICS/stories/01/09/bush.wrap.
2. Public Broadcasting System, *NewsHour with Jim Lehrer*, January 2001.
3. Thomas L. Jipping, "Outrage Over Ashcroft Hearings," WorldNetDaily.com, January 25, 2001; www.worldnetdaily.com/news/article.asp?ARTICLE_ID_21470.

CHAPTER FOUR

THROWING HEAT

The Senate Confirmation Battle, Part 2

M y parents taught me that you get only one chance to make a good first impression. Unfortunately, I missed that chance with the vast majority of the American public. Prior to the Senate Judiciary Committee confirmation hearings of January 2001, many people across America knew relatively little about me. I had discovered that fact when I considered running for president in the late 1990s and found that I didn't have the levels of support necessary. Many people didn't know me or the values I embraced. Unfortunately, despite my spending more than a quarter of a century in public service, the first impressions of me many people formed stemmed from the news reports covering the 2001 confirmation hearings. Many of those impressions were not positive.

I was introduced to the country in ways that more accurately reflected the views of the liberal groups attacking me—that I was a racist, a bigot, and a plethora of other derogatory terms. Anybody who knew me recognized that those tags were totally untrue and inappropriate, but for two solid days the high-intensity assassination of my character before a national television audience continued unabated.

For the second day of the hearings, January 17, the proceedings moved to the larger, newer hearing room at the Hart Senate Office

Building. The hearing room in the Hart Building is the modern equivalent of the Coliseum, complete with the gladiator pit, where Washington blood sport is displayed. It was built with television coverage in mind, although the cameras are placed so as not to intrude on the proceedings. It is the same room that more recently was used for the Supreme Court confirmation hearings of John Roberts and Samuel Alito. The fact that our hearing was moved from the Russell Building to the Hart was something of a statement in itself, announcing to the press, "This is going to be a big show."

And indeed it was.

As the confirmation process dragged on, the strategy of my opponents came into clearer focus. One person after another referred to my "deeply held personal beliefs," a politically correct euphemism for "Christian." They then raised the questions of whether I could serve "all the people," and would I be willing to enforce laws with which I personally disagreed because of my spiritual beliefs. Or, worse yet, would I attempt to "impose" my spiritually based viewpoints on others through the significant powers of the U.S. Department of Justice?

Liberal interest groups had already done a good job of branding me as "right-wing extremist" and "controversial," thinly veiled words for "conservative Christian," the implication being that for all my other tags—racist, bigot, and more—my Christian faith was the worst of all, the cornerstone upon which all my other beliefs and conduct stood or fell. Of course, in some ways, they were correct in that assertion: I am a Christian and I do my best to conform my attitudes, words, and deeds to the teachings of the Bible. I have a Christian worldview and I don't apologize for that. On the other hand, I've made this a rule in my life: "It's against my religion to impose my religion." More about that later, but in 2001 my Christian faith concerned many liberal leaders more than anything else about me.

Barry Lynn, of the liberal group Americans United for Separation of Church and State, said my nomination "may please television evangelists like Pat Robertson and Jerry Falwell, but it's a disaster for anyone who cares about maintaining constitutional principles." Similarly, Ralph Neas, of the People for the American Way, a group that aggressively led the charge against my confirmation, said that I "might make an excellent choice to head the Christian Coalition . . . but he is not qualified to lead the U.S. Department of Justice."

Funny, not even my most contentious opponents on the Senate panel questioned my "qualifications," but these groups concerned about my faith in God fretted—for the good of the American people, of course—that a man who had a Christian faith could not function in a government founded on principles of, and formed largely by men of, that same faith.

I wasn't surprised. Politics disabuses a person of the notion that you can please everybody. It is an inescapable fact that people will always have different opinions, and some people are going to disagree. Sooner or later, a person constructs his or her own "platform" and stands on it, regardless of what others think, say, or do. It is also true that some people delight in another person's demise. That was certainly obvious to me as I looked around the hearing room at the Hart Building.

But there were also people in the room who were there to support me. My family and coworkers, of course, but also several senators on the Judiciary Committee were eager to see me confirmed. Senator Orrin Hatch, for instance, was a tremendous help and encouragement, a prince among his peers. Kit Bond introduced me and spoke eloquently on my behalf. Susan Collins, Jon Kyl, Jeff Sessions, and members of their staffs worked diligently to help me get confirmed. Senator Kyl framed the battle well:

> I think at the end of the day, one thing is very clear. There have been two interesting assertions made with respect to Senator Ashcroft by opponents. The first is that he has very strong convictions, faith, and belief in God. Indeed, he does.

The second is that he may not enforce the law and the Constitution. Well, the second assertion is at odds with the first. You can be assured that when John Ashcroft places his hand on the Bible and swears to uphold the laws and the Constitution that he will do that on behalf of the people of the United States of America.[1]

I didn't hear directly from the president-elect—the president does not get involved personally in cabinet nominee hearings—but members of the transition team were quite positive in their review of the first day's proceedings. That was reassuring, since I was keenly aware that should I make mistakes in my hearings, the nomination could go down in flames. The last thing I wanted was to be an embarrassment to President-elect Bush at the beginning of his administration, setting a negative tone. In the chess game of cabinet nominations, one of the first rules is this: protect the king.

On the second day of hearings, I walked in and shook hands with each member of the committee. It was always interesting to watch their responses to me. Several of the Democrats had already made their intentions known—Senator Joe Biden had indicated that he would not vote to confirm me, as had Kennedy, Dick Durbin, Charles Schumer, and others. Dianne Feinstein, always a model of gentleness, gave the impression that she wanted to consider fairly the issues raised in the hearings, but I had little doubt which way she would vote.

Near the end of the hearing, Senator Feinstein went on record, stating: "The background record of this nominee is not mainstream on the key issues. I know he is strong and tough on law-and-order issues. However, his views on certain issues—civil rights and desegregation, a women's right to choose, and guns—make him an enormously divisive and polarizing figure."[2] It was futile to attempt to persuade most of the Democrats on the Judiciary Committee to change their minds; they'd already staked their claim, and now their job was to please those to whom they had pledged a negative vote.

The opening day of the hearings had been an emotionally charged event. Pennsylvania senior senator Arlen Specter put it in perspective when he noted in his initial remarks that the battle lines had been clearly drawn. The Democrats resolved to launch an all-out assault against me, and the Republicans vowed to defend me. I knew, of course, that my vilification wasn't completely about my qualifications or even about what I believed. This was, as CNN reporter Jonathan Karl put it, "the first great ideological showdown of the Bush presidency. This is the spring training before further battles on other nominations, on issues, possibly Supreme Court nominations."[3]

The day had seen its bizarre moments as well. Early on, the hearings were disrupted by four demonstrators who had jumped up in the hearing room right after I had completed my opening statement. "Ashcroft kills!" they shouted. "Dead addicts can't recover." Apparently, they were protesting my opposition to government-funded free needle exchange programs for intravenous drug users. The demonstrators were hauled away by the Capitol police and the hearings continued without delay. But the incident added to the tension in the room.

Senator Jeff Sessions, a Republican from Alabama, was a strong voice in my support throughout the hearings. Jeff had once been nominated to be a federal judge, but two Judiciary Committee members with whom he now sat were instrumental in blocking his confirmation. Although I had never seen that incident color his decisions, he certainly was not reluctant to buck those "old bulls." Sessions is not among the larger senators in stature, but none has a more gallant heart. He is neither loud nor confrontational, but neither does he back down. He is stronger than ten acres of garlic when it came to supporting his friends, especially me.

I maintained a sense of composure throughout the hearings,

regardless of everything that was thrown at me. In baseball, when a pitcher is throwing hard fastballs, he's often referred to as "throwing a lot of heat." In the confirmation hearings, every time I stepped into the batter's box, the opposition was hurling vicious curves, beanballs, and a few downright wild pitches. When it was my turn, occasionally I had to return some heat, throwing what I like to call "chin music," brushing a hitter back from home plate a bit. Nevertheless, I did not go looking for fights; I knew that if I allowed the opposition to rattle me, if they could in any way say, "Look, he is not able to separate his personal, deeply held spiritual beliefs from the actions of the attorney general," I would be striking out when I was at bat, or allowing my enemies to hit a home run when they had the opportunity.

Instead, I emphasized, "I know the difference between enacting and enforcing the law." I had spent the past six years as a U.S. senator helping to make laws. But for eighteen years prior to that, I had been in the business of enforcing the law, as both attorney general and governor of Missouri. I am so strongly committed to keeping the law that I knew I could deal objectively and enforce laws that were not my personal preference, even those that were at odds with my Christian beliefs. Christians are commanded in the Bible to obey the governing authorities. That is not always easy, but it is the right way for me to operate, especially as a Christian. When the committee members pressed me as to whether I would uphold the law in regard to abortion—a practice that I personally consider as taking a human life—I responded that I would uphold the law. "I believe *Roe v. Wade* as an original matter was wrongly decided," I reiterated. "I am personally opposed to abortion, but the role of the attorney general is to enforce the law as it is, not as I would have it."

On the second day of hearings, Senators Ted Kennedy and Joseph Biden once again went for my jugular on the issue of Ronnie White, the black judge whose appointment to a federal bench I had opposed on the basis that I felt he was too lenient on convicted criminals. Ted was virulent, and several members of the committee jumped on his bandwagon.

I tried to keep my mind on the confirmation, rather than trying to prove a point or to retaliate against my opposition. Consequently, I simply absorbed many blows from some people I didn't feel obligated to contest. Through it all, I felt strongly that I was on the right track toward confirmation. I was determined not to allow the news coverage or the comments of the committee members to get to me. Ultimately, we are all accountable for our own behavior, not that of others. I tried my best to keep mine above reproach.

At the end of the second day of hearings, I said to Janet, "Let's take a little trip down to the Outer Banks of North Carolina, just to get away from all this for a few days." Although I still had to be available for recall as a witness, I did not have to attend the third day of hearings. There had been a lot of saber-rattling, with certain members implying that they wanted to call me back for testimony. But it didn't happen. That was just as well, since the next day's hearings were to feature Ronnie White, whom the opposition expected to blast me with open shots in his testimony.

Beyond that, the committee submitted more than four hundred pages' worth of questions that had to be answered in writing before they would take a final vote. It was a massive amount of work to be completed in an extremely short period of time, answering questions that, for the most part, had already been answered thoroughly in the verbal inquisition.

It was a difficult and, at times, exasperating experience to sit before the Senate Judiciary Committee for confirmation, but I believe I came away from the hearings a stronger person, more confident than ever about what I believed and what I stood for. It is not an easy thing to have every public word you've ever spoken for over twenty-five years subjected to scrutiny, or every deed examined to discern your motives. But it was a marvelous feeling to walk away from that sort of rigorous exam knowing that my words and actions passed muster before a highly critical group—whether or not they appreciated what I had said or done, or agreed with me—and that I could do so without a trace of rancor or animosity toward any of them. Indeed, I gained a new appreciation for several members of the committee. The inquisition revealed more about trust than I ever dreamed possible.

Following the two days I spent in hearings, the committee took several more days of testimony. When the vote was taken, it was ten to nine in favor of confirming, with the committee members voting straight down party lines, except for Russ Feingold, who voted for me. When the confirmation went to the full Senate for approval, I was confirmed 58 to 42 on February 1, 2001, and was sworn in the same evening by a man with whom I had shared office space in 1975. Together we had served in Jack Danforth's Missouri Attorney General's Office. He'd done all right for himself and America since then. I was highly honored to have the oath of office administered to me by Supreme Court justice Clarence Thomas.

I looked forward to throwing myself into my new job. I'd heard that there was much work to be done at the Justice Department, that there were numerous areas, particularly at the FBI, that were in disarray, and that I was sure to have some surprises once I got inside. I just couldn't imagine how surprised I would be, and how much housecleaning needed to be done.

ENDNOTES

1. Senator Jon Kyl's opening statement; Senate Judiciary Hearings on the Confirmation of John Ashcroft, January 16, 2001, p. 23; U.S. Government Printing Office, Washington, D.C., 2001.
2. Senator Dianne Feinstein; www.senate.gov/~feinstein/releases01/ashcroft%20opposition.html.
3. Jonathan Karl, "Ashcroft hearing first ideological battle of Bush presidency, *All Politics*, CNN, January 16, 2001; http://transcripts.cnn.com/2001/ALLPOLITICS/stories/01/16/karl.debrief/index.html.

CHAPTER FIVE

TROUBLE AT THE FBI

The Hanssen Spy Scandal

━━━⟊⟊⟊ ⟊⟊⟊━━━

I awakened early and played a couple of gospel songs on the piano, much as I do most every morning. But this was a special morning; this was my first day at my new job. At the time, Janet and I lived "on the hill," beyond the Capitol, so I decided to walk from our 130-year-old house down Constitution Avenue along the Washington Mall. I never cease to marvel at the majesty of the view, with the U.S. Capitol's glistening dome in the sunshine behind me and the Washington Monument and the Lincoln Memorial in front of me. I had an extra lilt in my step as I walked toward the Justice Department building located on Constitution between 9th and 10th streets. I liked the idea of the Justice Department being located on *Constitution* Avenue—it seemed fitting. As I walked to work, I looked up and noticed an unmarked car tailing me. I now had constant, round-the-clock security. Behind the security vehicle, another vehicle slowly followed at a distance, television cameras rolling. The news media wanted to catch my first day on the job, too.

I stopped briefly outside the entrance to the U.S. Department of Justice and simply stared at the massive building over which I was now to serve as presiding officer. Beyond that, I now was considered the top law officer in America. Had anything changed? I still put on my suit the same way I had yesterday. I was still the same fellow I was a few weeks ago when I had been immersed in a tough election campaign. Yet everything had changed. I walked up the steps, through the main doors, and into the historic art deco "Main Justice" building.

I shook hands with the security guards and walked every hall of floors one through four, on my way to the fabled fifth floor. I walked the length and breadth of the huge building, stopping in each office, greeting each person I met, shaking hands and thanking them for working in Justice, slowly making my way to the attorney general's office on the fifth floor. I couldn't possibly shake hands with all 120,000 employees, but I wanted to convey the attitude that I would if I could. I wanted to signal to the Justice Department employees a new era of teamwork, openness, and accessibility.

I wasn't certain what kind of reception to expect from the seasoned employees at Justice, especially the career people. Would they be hostile toward me, or excited about working with me? In many agencies, the career people view the president's cabinet members with grudging respect if not out-and-out disdain, since the leaders change with each new administration, and in some cases, several times during an administration. Consequently, the cabinet members never know as much about the bureaucracy as the career guys. At least that's the way some of the career guys tell it.

I couldn't blame them. After all, I was just coming out of a volatile confirmation process, with some high-profile U.S. senators suggesting that I was a racist and a bigot, claiming that I was opposed to equality of the sexes, and alleging I would probably not execute the attorney general's job in a fair manner. These were evils the people in the Justice Department loved to fight. Now here I came, painted as a troglodyte. No wonder some regarded me skeptically.

One of the activities on my schedule was to attend a reception held in my honor at the department. A small crowd gathered outside my conference room to celebrate my swearing in and to welcome me as the eightieth attorney general of the United States. Near the end of the reception, as lingering guests made small talk over cookies and sipped the sweet, government-issue red fruit punch from clear glass cups, FBI director Louis Freeh pulled me aside. "I need to have a word with you in private," he whispered.

I looked back at Louis with surprise, but not concern. After all, we were at a party. "Sure, Louis; let's step over here." I motioned toward an open area in the room.

"Maybe we should talk over there." Louis nodded toward the attorney general's office, a secure location known as a SCIF (Secure Compartmented Information Facility), a specially constructed room built to prevent spies or other unauthorized people from eavesdropping on secret government conversations. Louis's request was not in itself all that unusual. In Washington government circles, it is illegal to discuss certain classified matters outside of a secure location specially engineered to be impermeable to outside "eyes and ears." Ordinary glass resonates, and with the right equipment, conversations can be captured with relative ease. Individuals or representatives of foreign countries with high-tech surveillance capabilities roam freely in Washington, hoping to pick up information that can be used or sold. The U.S. government does all it can to prevent the compromise of such information, but it can happen.

Once inside the secure area, Director Freeh spoke bluntly. "We have a serious problem within the FBI."

I nodded, expecting to hear about some morale problem that had seeped out into the Bureau.

"Apparently, we have a mole in the Bureau . . ."

"A mole."

"Yes, a spy," Louis said quietly. "Someone inside the FBI who has been selling top secret, classified information."

I felt as though all the air had instantaneously been sucked out of the room. I swallowed hard, my mind racing. "Selling information to whom, what kind of information, for how long . . . how long has this been going on?" The questions were forming faster than I could speak them.

"Top secret materials, highly classified. To the Soviets," Louis replied. "The KGB, back when the Soviet Union was still together. Now the Russians. We think it has been going on for a number of years, but we don't know yet."

"And?"

"We've known for a while that there has been leakage, but we thought it was coming from the CIA. Now we know better. We're on to him, but we don't quite have the goods to make an arrest. We're close, but not there yet."

I understood what Director Freeh meant. To make sure a charge like this would stand up in court, prosecutors needed airtight proof about what the traitor had done—ideally to catch him in the act. But that entailed an enormous risk.

"Can we let him hang himself, or do we need to nab him now to stop the hemorrhaging of information being lost?" I asked.

"It doesn't seem that the mole has been active lately, but we have indications that he might be active soon," Louis replied. "We've moved him around inside the Bureau so he doesn't have the access that he once had, but we don't want to move him completely out for fear that he will flee the country."

I looked at Louis's face as we talked. His eyes never left mine. He seemed like a straight shooter, if a bit intense. I didn't really know Louis Freeh all that well before I became attorney general. We had met briefly when I was a U.S. senator and a member of the Commerce Committee. The FBI director had come to the Hill to discuss the need for strong encryption laws regarding computer software made in the United States and being shipped all over the world. Louis thought the legal amounts of encryption should be limited, and the FBI should have the "keys" to all the encryption codes. I wasn't so sure about that; I wanted American companies to have as much freedom to compete in world markets as possible. Besides, for the FBI to have that sort of access to private businesses and possibly even private individuals seemed a bit heavy-handed to me. At the time, Louis and I hadn't seen eye to eye on how the encryption matter should be handled.

Notwithstanding our differences, I respected him a great deal. Raised in a devoutly Catholic home, Louis had a sense of right and wrong based on absolute values, not the latest polls. He had earned a reputation as a man of integrity, someone who was not afraid to stand up for what he believed to be right. I appreciated that about him. A square-jawed, gritty New Jersey native, who always looked as though he needed a shave, Louis brought a bit of that edge with him to the FBI. He'd made his mark by doing undercover surveillance work in New York, getting in close with Mafia mobster Mike Clemente, a leader in the Genovese family, who at the time was the undisputed crime boss of the Manhattan waterfront. Louis worked the case for four years, and in March 1979 Clemente was indicted on charges of racketeering, tax evasion, extortion, and other crimes. Freeh passionately pursued other organized crime members all the way to Sicily, and with the help of the Italians brought many mobsters to justice.

In 1991, Freeh was nominated by President George H. W. Bush to be a federal judge in New York. Then in 1993, Bill Clinton—already knee deep in scandal due to improper handling of FBI files—sought out someone to replace embattled FBI director William Sessions. Freeh seemed like the perfect guy, straight as an arrow, earnest, and nonpartisan. Clinton tapped Louis to be his new FBI director, a choice that both men would live to regret, no doubt, although for far different reasons.

The following year, Louis Freeh was flying high. His bureau had just nailed the most flagrant spies in CIA history, Aldrich Ames and his wife, Rosario. Ames, a career CIA officer, had been spying for the KGB since 1985, selling America's secrets at a time when the United States and the Soviet Union were both nuclear behemoths with the capability of obliterating a large percentage of the world's population.

Beyond that, Ames betrayed numerous double agents—agents that the United States had recruited within the Soviet Union's ranks—and the Soviets promptly recalled and executed at least ten of them. Altogether, Ames received more than $2.3 million for selling out our country before he was caught by the FBI. He was sentenced to life in prison, in exchange for cooperating with the government to reveal the extent of his espionage. His wife was sentenced to five years in prison as part of that deal.

Following the Ames case, Louis Freeh and his FBI agents were feeling their oats, notwithstanding the disastrous operations at places such as Ruby Ridge and Waco as well as the fiascos that resulted from the cases of Wen Ho Lee, an engineer with access to sensitive information at the Los Alamos National Laboratory who was accused of stealing nuclear secrets for the Chinese, and Richard Jewell, falsely accused of exploding a nail bomb in Atlanta's Centennial Park during the 1996 Olympics. One major success had been the arrest of Timothy McVeigh, and the FBI was riding high once again, until it was discovered that someone within the Bureau was making Ames's treason seem like small potatoes. The traitor's name, Louis Freeh informed me, was Robert Hanssen.

Even people who liked Bob Hanssen acknowledged that he seemed a bit odd. Aloof and sullen, he prided himself on being the quintessential old-fashioned FBI man, wearing dark suits to work, maintaining a serious, rigid presence, speaking in hushed, mysterious tones in the hallways, with a forced half-smile that looked more like a smirk. Some of his coworkers secretly referred to him as "the mortician"; others called him "Dr. Death" behind his back. He was a quirky, twenty-five-year veteran whose job as a counterintelligence agent was to help track enemy agents and protect American security.

On the surface, this son of a Chicago policeman was a most unlikely spy. A dental school dropout turned accountant turned police officer, Hanssen was staunchly anticommunist. A loner with few friends outside of the neighborhood in which he and his wife, Bonnie, raised six children, they lived quietly in a modest four-bedroom, split-level home in the Washington, D.C., suburb of Vienna, Virginia. His children attended Catholic school with FBI director Louis Freeh's children, and the Hanssens attended the same church as Freeh and Supreme Court justice Antonin Scalia. By all outward appearances and reports from his neighbors, he was supposedly a good man—one who went to church frequently, sent his kids to Catholic school, and was devoted to his wife. In reality, the so-called devoutly religious husband had a penchant for visiting Washington's nude bars, and had initiated a bizarre affair with one of the strippers he met there.

A devious conniver who hid the dark side of his personality under a religious cloak, Hanssen, along with his wife, Bonnie, was part of the Catholic group Opus Dei, a religious organization known for its almost cultlike piety and strict adherence to the teachings of the Catholic Church. But while Hanssen claimed to follow Jesus, his tactics were more like those of Judas—a traitor of the worst kind.

He meticulously devised a system by which he could send packages containing top secret information to the communists, and receive payment for his services, all without ever meeting or even seeing the Soviets face-to-face. Over time, he compromised some of our nation's most valuable secrets, betraying other agents and causing at least two agents to be executed by the KGB, and another exiled to Siberia. Worse yet, his actions were not isolated incidents. Robert Hanssen traded on America's security for more than twenty years, during fifteen of which he actively pursued opportunities to sell out our country, handing over top secret information first to the Soviet Union at a time when that country was determined to surpass the power of the United States, then to the Russian Federation after the collapse of the U.S.S.R. In return, Hanssen collected more than $600,000 in cash from the Soviets, as well as expensive cut diamonds and two Rolex watches. Ostensibly, the Soviets also deposited another $800,000 in his name in a Moscow bank, for a time when Hanssen would exit his own country and seek exile in the U.S.S.R.

But Hanssen didn't compromise his country merely for money. He did it because he felt that the FBI didn't appreciate his talents, disrespected him, and passed over him for promotions; he did it to prove that he was smarter than the best men and women in the Bureau. Besides being horrendously damaging to the security of the nation, Hanssen's deeds were insulting to the FBI agents with whom he worked. He sold out his country right under the noses of the men and women who were supposed to be the best in the world at keeping tabs on such things.

Single-handedly, he devised and operated his traitorous operation from within the offices of the FBI headquarters in Washington. He had computer access to some of the most closely guarded secrets in the U.S. government, and he willingly gave them away to our enemies. Yet, amazingly, his activities went undetected by the Bureau for more than fifteen years.

Behind the façade of normalcy, Hanssen was a seething caldron of anger, arrogance, and hostility. He thought he was smarter than the system, smarter than any of his FBI coworkers, and for an astounding period of time, he was. Nobody suspected him of espionage until a few months before my appointment as the new attorney general in 2001.

As Louis Freeh filled me in on the basic information regarding Hanssen's treason, my stomach churned. I didn't want to believe that any American citizen—especially an FBI agent—would purposely place our nation at such risk. And for what? Money? Sex? Political ideology? Ego gratification? What could possibly be worth it? I was disgusted.

"I'm not going to tell you how to do your job," I said to Louis as we concluded our conversation in the SCIF, "but keep me informed.

Get me a report that will allow me to make a decision about whether we should take him immediately or if we can forebear a bit. I want to know what is going on every step of the way."

Louis and I returned to the reception as though everything was normal. I thanked the late arrivers and hangers-on for coming, and tried to greet with a smile my new staff members, some of whom I was meeting for the first time. But somehow, the fruit punch had turned horribly sour. This whole sordid Hanssen affair agitated me. Yet I couldn't go out and shout, "Hey, everybody! Guess what? Our nation's security has been compromised and our country's top secrets have been handed over to our enemies by one of our own people." No, the lonely sense of isolation that accompanied the confidential information I had received weighed heavily on me. I couldn't discuss this matter. I didn't yet know who on my staff had clearance for sensitive matters at Justice, or if I could even hash this out with David Ayres, my chief of staff. I decided to keep the information to myself, operating on a strict "need to know" basis.

The thought continued to nag me: *How can an organization like the FBI—the nation's top crime-fighting agency—be susceptible to this pilfering of top secret materials for nearly twenty years and nobody noticed?*

I was convinced that the incident revealed more about the FBI than it did about Robert Hanssen. *What structural problems exist within the Department of Justice if this could happen to us?* I wondered. *What changes need to be made so this sort of thing never happens again?* I didn't want to simply "get Hanssen," although I wanted nothing more than that at the moment. But I also wanted to fix the system that allowed Hanssen to exist within our ranks.

During the next seventeen days, while Louis Freeh's agents shadowed Hanssen's every move, I dug in and studied the information we were learning about him. The more I read, the more nauseated I became. Robert Hanssen had joined the FBI in January 1976, and had served continuously through February 2001. For most of his FBI career, he had worked in the FBI's Intelligence Division, later renamed the National Security Division. He had direct access to classified information relating to the foreign intelligence and counterintelligence activities of the FBI and other U.S. intelligence community agencies, including the Central Intelligence Agency (CIA), the National Security Agency (NSA), and the Defense Intelligence Agency (DIA).

Upon entering the FBI, Hanssen had signed an oath of office in which he swore, "I will support and defend the Constitution of the United States against all enemies, foreign and domestic; that I will bear true faith and allegiance to the same; that I take this obligation freely, without any mental reservation or purpose of evasion; and that I will well and faithfully discharge the duties of the office on which I am about to enter. So help me God." That same day, he signed the FBI Pledge for Law Enforcement Officers, in which he pledged, in part, "I accept the obligation in connection with my assignments to . . . consider the information coming into my knowledge by virtue of my position as a sacred trust, to be used solely for official purposes. . . . In the performance of my duties and assignments, I shall not engage in unlawful and unethical practices." For a man so devout, Bob Hanssen disregarded his oaths rather flagrantly.

Exacerbating matters further, Hanssen had top secret clearance from the beginning of his FBI career. In U.S. intelligence circles, classified information can fall into a series of categories, each with increased sensitivity and risk, accompanied by a commensurate increase in the need for clearance before an individual can handle such materials. The unauthorized disclosure of such information could be expected to result in damage to the national security of the United States. Where that damage would be "serious," the information is classified as SECRET. Where such damage would be "exceptionally grave," the information is usually classified as TOP SECRET. Access to classified information at any level may be further restricted and placed in SENSITIVE COMPARTMENTED INFORMATION (SCI) categories. Robert Hanssen held top secret clearances continuously from the time he joined the FBI in 1976, and periodically over the years he had access to a variety of SCI programs as well. The man had unobstructed view of many of our innermost secrets when it came to intelligence information, and he had betrayed that trust at every level.

During the entire time Hanssen had been with the Bureau, he had never taken a lie detector test. Although periodic polygraph tests were administered to employees of the CIA, Louis Freeh resisted having FBI agents and employees tested. Ostensibly, the prestigious reputation, the camaraderie and fraternal bonds of the FBI would shield the Bureau from any miscreant behavior. For the majority of agents, that was sufficient. But nobody had picked up on the deviant signs Robert Hanssen flashed for years. Not until it was too late.

Almost daily, Freeh called me at the Justice Department to brief me on some new aspect of the case. It was obvious that the FBI had Hanssen clearly within its sights. They had bugged his car and purchased the house across the street from his home in Vienna, Virginia, from which agents kept a continuous watch on the suspect's activities. Anytime Hanssen pulled out of his neighborhood, an FBI surveillance team was close behind. We felt sure he was going to make contact with his Russian handlers soon; we just didn't know when or where.

My biggest concern was the balancing act in which we were engaging. Every day was a risk. Louis and I discussed the possibilities, the flight risk the mole represented, and if he did take off, would we ever find out what he had given away to people willing to pay for inside information on U.S. security and weaponry? It was a gamble either way. If we continued to allow him to operate, he might pass along information that could compromise our government, our nuclear facilities, or something worse. If we stuck with him too closely, he might not do the drop; we might alert him that we were onto him, and he'd be gone, taking with him the knowledge of who and what he had compromised, and we'd never know for sure.

Sunday morning, February 18, 2001, found Bob Hanssen attending church, like any other weekend. Our guys had watched him load the family in an aging beige Volkswagen van and drive eight miles to attend the 10:30 a.m. Mass at St. Catherine of Siena Catholic Church in Great Falls, Virginia. Numerous churches dotted the neighborhoods between the Hanssen home and St. Catherine's, but Bob liked St. C's because the church was one of the few in the area that still conducted the traditional Mass in Latin. Only the two youngest children accompanied Bob and Bonnie that morning.

Following the service, the Hanssens returned to their home in Vienna, where Bob spent part of the afternoon throwing a Frisbee to the family dog before taking a visiting friend back to Dulles International Airport. They took the Hanssens' 1997 gray Ford Taurus rather than the van. By all appearances, it was just another ordinary afternoon in the Washington suburbs.

Hanssen dropped off the friend at Dulles and waved good-bye. But instead of going directly home, he detoured into Foxstone Park, not far from his neighborhood, and pulled the Taurus to a stop within walking distance of a nearby wooden footbridge spanning Wolftrap Creek. He pulled out a small package wrapped in a black plastic garbage bag. Inside the package were seven documents marked SECRET, and a computer diskette on which Hanssen had included a letter in code. He stopped long enough to place a piece of white adhesive tape on a crosswalk pole—a sign to the Russians that he had dropped the package—and then he proceeded to the footbridge, where he stuffed the package into a concealed spot between a beam and the dirt below.

Hanssen then headed back to his car, walking briskly but not in haste, careful not to attract attention. Just as he was about to get into his car, a white SUV roared around the corner and two young men wearing jackets bearing a yellow FBI logo jumped out. Two SWAT team members wielding submachine guns followed close by. In an instant, it seemed the entire area sprouted agents—from cars, from the brush, everywhere, blocking Hanssen's potential exit routes whether on foot or in his vehicle.

"Freeze!" an agent shouted, as he aimed his gun at Hanssen's heart in case he reached for a weapon. "Mr. Hanssen, you are under arrest," the agent called. He rattled off a Miranda warning as other agents patted Hanssen down, pulled his wrists behind his back, and handcuffed the turncoat agent.

Hanssen didn't seem surprised. As the agents locked the cuffs on his wrists, he simply glared at his former coworkers and said, "What took you guys so long?"

It was a good question.

A lot of people thought Hanssen's arrest was a sign that there was a new sheriff in town, that I was managing the case from the Justice Department. Not so. In truth, the FBI had been tracking Hanssen for several months before I took office. I made no changes to the FBI's procedures in handling the case, but I certainly wanted to learn from them. Why had it taken us so long to catch this guy? And how could we prevent similar sellouts in the future?

As the Justice Department put the case together, preparing the indictments against Hanssen, I was appalled at the extent to which he had compromised our nation. During his fifteen years of betrayal, he had provided our enemies with more than 6,000 pages of highly sensitive documents, and at least twenty-seven computer disks loaded with secret and top secret programs. Besides handing over intelligence information about the inner workings of the CIA and FBI, including the FBI's 1992 counterintelligence budget and information about how U.S. intelligence operations identified enemy agents, recruited double agents, and planned surveillance of Soviet sites and individuals, Hanssen compromised the safety of every American citizen by giving the Soviets the Continuity of Government Plan, a super-secret program to ensure the survival of the president of the United States and other government leaders in the event of a nuclear attack. This was a key element in a policy that was known during the cold war as MAD, "mutually assured destruction," a major deterrent to the United States and the Soviet Union's using nuclear weapons, since a retaliatory strike would surely ensue and would be as deadly as the first strike. But by providing the enemy with our plans for keeping the government alive and the country functioning in the face of such a horrific attack, Hanssen had given them an advantage in the nuclear chess game.

Hanssen also sold top secret documents from the National Security Council, which advises the president on intelligence and national security matters. He described the location, methods, and technology involved in FBI eavesdropping and surveillance of a Soviet spy station. He warned the KGB about a successful new American intelligence operation against a Soviet target.

He divulged the identities of at least nine Soviet officials recruited to spy for the United States. In one of his first letters to the Soviets, Hanssen proved his credibility by alerting the KGB that three of its high-ranking officers were serving as double agents for the FBI. Two of them, Valery Martynov and Sergei Motorin, were ordered to return to Moscow and were put to death. The third, Boris Yuzhin, was sentenced to a long period in a Soviet prison work camp.

Hanssen also informed the enemy of an ongoing FBI espionage investigation of Felix Bloch, a U.S. State Department officer who was believed to be spying for the Soviets. Hanssen's information allowed the KGB to warn Bloch about the investigation; consequently, the FBI was never able to find key evidence proving that Bloch passed secret documents to the enemy.

In one of the most outrageous and costly disclosures, Robert Hanssen informed the Soviets about the existence of a secret tunnel constructed beneath the new Soviet embassy in Washington, D.C. The tunnel was built at enormous cost to American taxpayers so FBI and NSA agents could eavesdrop on the Soviets' conversations and communications. The Soviets had acquired property on one of the highest hills outside of Georgetown, greatly facilitating their "listening ability," and the tunnel was the U.S. attempt at evening the odds. But Hanssen told the Soviets about the existence of the tunnel, rendering it completely useless. Worse yet, because the Americans didn't know that the tunnel had been compromised and continued to scarf up any tidbit of information they could glean, the Russians were able to feed the U.S. sleuths misleading information through the tunnel. Eventually, the FBI had little choice but to fill in the tunnel at a cost in the millions of dollars.

The Justice Department brought twenty-one counts of espionage and conspiracy to commit espionage against Robert Hanssen. Initially, I wanted to press for the death sentence in this case, as did Secretary of Defense Donald Rumsfeld. But eventually I opted to pursue life in prison instead of the death penalty in exchange for his cooperation, so that the government could get information from him regarding the extent and seriousness of his crimes. On July 6, 2001, Hanssen pleaded guilty to fifteen counts of espionage and conspiracy in the plea bargain.

Hanssen was smart enough to know that in some ways he was in the driver's seat. He knew what information he had given enemies of America, and we did not. He wanted his wife to be able to continue living in their modest home, and that was his strongest motivation for dealing with us, more than concern for himself or fear of being executed. He used his leverage to win concessions from the Justice Department, making a way for his wife to sustain herself during his imprisonment. One of the reasons why the government was willing to negotiate with him was the disturbing truth that we didn't know what we didn't know. We needed Hanssen to help us identify what we had lost. We wanted to know his contacts, and how he had managed to deceive so many for so long.

Oddly, Hanssen had not amassed a fortune from selling out his country. The family's $290,000 home was still heavily mortgaged the day he was caught. He had opened a Swiss bank account, but there was little in it. The KGB had supposedly been depositing his pay-checks in an account inside the Soviet Union in a Moscow-based bank. In a game of duping the dupe, Hanssen would never receive more than $800,000 supposedly laid up in his name. He had betrayed his country, at a cost of hundreds of millions of dollars and several human lives, for a relatively paltry sum. In the end, he had nothing to show for it.

Several dozen FBI agents and Washington field office workers sat in the first two rows of the U.S. District Court in Alexandria, Virginia, on July 6, 2001, when Robert Hanssen shuffled into the courtroom wearing a green prison jumpsuit with PRISONER stamped on his back. Hanssen did not appear ashamed or repentant in the face of his former colleagues. Quite the contrary, before he sat down to be sentenced to life in prison without parole, he turned toward the FBI representatives and smirked his quasi-smile at them as he had for years. It was impossible to tell whether he was implying, "You finally got me," or "I got you."

CHAPTER SIX

A NEW CULTURE

Don't Ever Stop

❦

As if the Hanssen affair wasn't enough of a welcome to the big leagues, I found another rude awakening awaiting me in my own department. My management style was very different from that of my predecessor, Janet Reno. At the time I became the attorney general, the Department of Justice was an enormous organization that included the FBI, the Drug Enforcement Agency (DEA), the Bureau of Prisons, the U.S. Marshals, and the Immigration and Naturalization Service, and employed more than 120,000 people worldwide. My chief of staff, David Ayres, and I decided early on that we were not going to manage by "in-box," focusing on the crisis of the day. Besides its requirement for inordinate amounts of time spent trying to stomp out sparks, the problem with in-box management—especially in a large organization like the Justice Department—was that by the time a problem landed on my desk, it was already a five-alarm fire.

Instead, we set priorities and pursued them. We established workable plans to reduce crime, to fight racial discrimination, to deal quickly and firmly with corporate fraud, to go after the big drug-running organizations, and to deal with other areas under the department's purview. This marked a change in the way things were done in the Justice Department, and we smacked up against resistance from individuals and groups more accustomed to crisis management.

A second attitude we encountered in the early days on the job at

Justice was a "We don't do it that way" attitude. It wasn't so much a know-it-all mind-set as it was an attitude steeped in tradition: "We are the Justice Department and this is how we have always done things." This sort of attitude permeated the entire organization.

When my confirmation as the new attorney general was announced, friends and well-wishers inundated me with cards of congratulations, flowers, fruit baskets, and potted plants welcoming us to the Justice Department. On Friday afternoon, as everyone prepared to leave for the weekend at the end of my first full week in office, I asked one of the secretaries, "Could you please get someone from the support staff to water these flowers so they will stay fresh through the weekend?"

"I'll make the call," the secretary said.

A short while later, the support staff sent back word: "We don't water flowers."

I didn't know whether to laugh, to be shocked, or to be furious— or a bit of all three. I couldn't believe that attitude. I said, "Well, if they won't water them, I will."

From the mundane, simple tasks like watering flowers to much more significant matters, that attitude was pervasive. "We've never done it that way, General Ashcroft," I heard people say over and over again. "Let me explain to you how things have been done here at Justice for the last three decades."

I always tried to listen patiently and politely. Then I'd say something along the lines of, "I hope it won't be offensive to the department to improve. Improvement always involves change."

"How we've always done it" is the process of fighting the last war, which is the bane of losing generals. To experience success and victory, we must fight the next war rather than the last. If you are still fighting the last war rather than getting ready for the next, you will always be at a disadvantage, whether it is watering flowers or dealing with national security. I decided this early on at Justice: if the traditional way was the most effective way of doing something, then we'd maintain it. But if it was not functioning at optimum levels, we would be doing the country a disservice by continuing to do things "like we've always done them."

I realized quickly that I could not afford to maintain the status quo as I tried to instill dynamic operating principles into the culture at the Justice Department. I told people, "Don't tell me what can't be done. Help me find the way to do it."

Of course there was never anyone who willfully, openly disobeyed my commands—at least not that I knew of. Nobody exhibited direct insubordination, but many entrenched department members revealed their passive-aggressive behavior, and when they did, I let them know that we did not appreciate such attitudes. It wasn't that people were antagonistic; it was more that they were accustomed to doing their work in a certain way, and change always causes some people to be uncomfortable. I observed that the quality of work of many Justice Department employees was directly related to their enthusiasm and willingness to embrace our common objectives. Over time, we were able to redirect the department and reap substantially improved performance at every level. But it was tough going at first.

Part of the resistance, of course, stemmed from the fact that the U.S. Justice Department is significantly populated by lawyers, men and women who are accustomed to contesting everything. The safest, easiest answer for most lawyers is "No."

That was unacceptable to me. I wanted them to find ways we could accomplish our goals, rather than spend most of their days identifying hazards and roadblocks to progress. I was kind to our coworkers, but I wanted them to know that we were reshaping the department in a coordinated effort to better secure the lives and liberties of Americans.

I attempted to model the new openness in the department by the way I conducted my own meetings. My office was a large, square room with plain seats spread around its periphery to accommodate ten to fifteen people comfortably. I had a simple desk facing out from the window nook, with a swivel chair, so for meetings I simply spun around in my chair and the meeting was on. No desk between the others and me. An open forum, if you will. I preferred meetings based on inquiries. I'd ask questions, probing to see if staff had pursued the correct lines of inquiry, attempting to ascertain whether they had gone to the necessary depths in their investigations. It was not my practice to second-guess their conclusions.

Someone once asked me if George W. Bush was a "micro-manager." I said, "No, President Bush is not a 'micromanager'; he is a 'micro-auditor.' He asks questions that require you to have dug deeply into the facts before you answer." That's the technique I employed at the Justice Department as well.

The first gathering of the president's full cabinet took place in early February at the White House Cabinet Room. It was an awe-inspiring moment to sit down in that room, around the table with the president's advisers. The seats are not assigned at random; rather, each person is seated in the same place for every meeting. Seated at the center, of course, is the president. Next to him on his right is the secretary of state; on his left is the secretary of defense. Across the table from the president sits the vice president, Dick Cheney. On his right is the secretary of the treasury, and on his left, the attorney general.

As the cabinet meeting came to order, President Bush looked over to me and asked, "John, would you lead us in prayer this morning?"

It was a habit President Bush established and maintained throughout the time I served as attorney general. Every cabinet meeting opened with prayer, and he spread around the honor of praying to various members of the cabinet. I've served on all sorts of church group boards that do not invite the wisdom of the Almighty at their meetings, and I have been to all sorts of gatherings with high-profile ministers who are quite vocal about getting prayer back in our schools yet don't open their meetings with prayer. But the forty-third President of the United States consistently called upon a member to start his cabinet meetings by acknowledging God's supremacy and seeking His help and direction.

The Bush cabinet meetings were not general discussions in which members offered suggestions on wide-ranging topics. Most meetings revolved around crisp reports from specific cabinet members. Apart from that, there was little exchange between them.

Nevertheless, the Hanssen spy case brought the magnitude of my responsibilities into focus in a hurry. At times during those first few months, I felt somewhat like Chevy Chase in the movie *The Three Amigos*. Chase and his two friends, played by Martin Short and Steve Martin, are acting the parts of three lawmen in a movie when they meet a real group of outlaws. After a tough confrontation with "El Guapo," the leader of the bad guys, Chase's character returns to his two friends and exclaims, "They're using real bullets! They're gonna kill us!"

Like most Americans, even those in the U.S. Congress, I wondered at times if some of the James Bond 007 images resembled anything near to real life for our intelligence agencies. I didn't have to wonder for long. I discovered all too soon that our enemies were "shooting real bullets."

Similarly, on the domestic front, it didn't take long for us to encounter our first potential powder keg. It happened, ironically, in a church.

Shortly after I took office, a highly volatile situation threatened to explode following a sixteen-year dispute between the Indianapolis Baptist Temple and the Internal Revenue Service. The church, comprised of more than a thousand members, stopped withholding federal income tax, Social Security, and Medicare taxes from the paychecks of its employees back in 1984 on the grounds that church employees were serving the congregation and received "love gifts" for their services rather than wages. The employees paid their own taxes on the money they received from the church, but the church itself continued to accrue back taxes, penalties, and interest amounting to more than $6 million. The case went all the way to the Supreme Court, where the justices rendered a decision against the church. That didn't deter the church leaders one bit. Finally U.S. District Judge Sarah Evans Barker issued an order that the church and the pastor's parsonage be surrendered to the IRS as partial payment on the debt.

Rather than let the IRS take their property, some pastors and a number of congregants holed up inside the building and refused to come out. The standoff between the church and the U.S. Marshals dragged on for more than three months. The Reverend Greg J. Dixon, who had pastored the church for forty-one years before turning the reins over to his son, the Reverend Greg A. Dixon, defiantly resisted the IRS and declared that he would never walk out of the church under his own power, that the U.S. Marshals would have to come in and take him. He made it well-known to everyone around him that "I will not leave this church. They'll have to carry me out of here." No one knew if the senior Dixon was armed or if he intended to harm himself or others.

The confrontation contained the seeds of another "no-win" situation similar to the one Janet Reno's Justice Department encountered when the cult leader David Koresh and his followers, the Branch Davidians, were suspected of hoarding weapons and ammunition and abusing children in a religious compound in Waco, Texas. We knew it could attract the attention of militia groups, fringe groups opposed to the IRS, and other self-styled vigilantes who often challenged the authority and legitimacy of the U.S. government.

At this time in U.S. history, the country's intelligence concerns centered on threats of terrorism overseas. Only two large-scale terrorist attacks had occurred on American soil: the 1993 bombing of the World Trade Center and the 1995 attack of Timothy McVeigh on the Federal Building in Oklahoma City. McVeigh had been part of a larger militia movement in the United States that seemed a more present threat than international terrorism at the time.

At the Justice Department, our strategy was patience, not provocation. Bleed out the energy; keep it low-profile. Violent conflicts through the 1990s—Waco, Ruby Ridge, the Oklahoma City bombing—loomed large in our minds. We knew a simple act could set off a conflagration, like a spark on gasoline. So we waited. Day after day, we maintained a posture of restraint, hoping the standoff could be resolved peaceably. By early May, our patience was rewarded. We did not want the conflict to escalate into a larger confrontation, so I developed a plan to forcibly remove the people from the church at a time of least resistance.

Bob Mueller, the acting deputy attorney general, traveled to Indianapolis to view the circumstances firsthand and to confer with our people. A highly decorated Vietnam veteran and a former U.S. Attorney in San Francisco, Bob carefully surveyed the plan on-site to ensure that we could indeed get the people out of the church with a minimum of opposition. The night before we planned to make a move on the church, we received word from the White House: they wanted to send a representative to negotiate with the church leaders.

I thought that was a bad idea and told the White House so. So far, our efforts had remained low-key, and we had been successful in defusing the situation. The mainstream media had barely noticed the brouhaha. The last thing the White House needed to do was to give the fringe elements free publicity by bringing real attention to the situation. Exacerbating the matter further, convicted Oklahoma City bomber Timothy McVeigh was awaiting his execution scheduled for May 16, 2001. We did not wish to provide an excuse for McVeigh sympathizers and other militia-type radicals to become inflamed over another supposed "government oppressing the little guy" type of story.

Besides, it seemed that the people inside the church had lost some of their enthusiasm, and interest from the outside was diminishing. As many as 250 congregants had been sequestered in the church early on in the confrontation. Four hundred people from various groups, some from as far away as Texas, had gathered at times for the vigil inside the church. But the longer we waited, the more their numbers dwindled. We maintained our low profile, watching all the while for the number of protesters to get to a point where we could risk moving in. We counted heads daily; it appeared the group was down to about six core members; our patience was paying off. If Temple leaders had any hopes that the conservative Bush administration would not take their building, it was dissipating rapidly.

Making these points as strongly as I could, I was finally able to convince the White House that sending in a negotiator to deal with the people cocooned in the church would only invite outside attention and could provoke anarchist types or militia sympathizers. Late that night, the White House dropped their objections to our recommendation, and our plan proceeded. "If you want to do this, the burden of responsibility is on you," they said.

I gave the order to go ahead at dawn the next morning. Fully armed U.S. marshals stormed the church, executing the plan perfectly. Not a shot was fired, nor a single person hurt. Marshals rounded up the last six people and ushered them out of the church. When the marshals attempted to apprehend the elderly Reverend Greg J. Dixon, he insisted that he would not go out standing up. "This is a matter of principle to me," he said. "I promised God, my people, and everybody else that I would not walk out of this church under my own power."

David Ayres and Bob Mueller were monitoring the situation from the command center on an upper floor of the Justice Department and passed on this information to me.

The U.S. marshals negotiated for Reverend Dixon's peaceful cooperation in coming out of the church. They strapped him onto a hospital stretcher and rolled him out of the disputed building. The man saved face with his congregation, and we successfully extricated him and his followers from the building without incident. Barely a peep made the local news, much less the national news, and that was fine with me. Our objective had been to keep the Indianapolis Baptist Temple conflict from mushrooming into another Waco or Ruby Ridge. Thankfully, it had not.

I don't mean to imply that it was easy for me to sit and watch the first incident in U.S. history in which a church was seized by the IRS for tax reasons—I was deeply concerned over the standoff. Yet on the other hand, Christians obey the law and "render to Caesar that which belongs to Caesar." In other words, pay your taxes! The Indianapolis Baptist Temple defied that scriptural injunction as well as the law of the land. And I was sworn to uphold that law. For all the fuss during my confirmation hearings by the ACLU and other liberal groups fretting whether or not I would uphold the law in cases that touched on matters of faith, hardly a word was reported when the Christian attorney general enforced the law in the church tax evasion case.

The Indianapolis Baptist Temple conflict reminded me again of the conundrum Christians and other people of faith face when it comes to protests against the government, and particularly the use of violence. I'm convinced that Christians, of all people, should be people of peace, modeling respect for the authorities under which they live, even when they don't agree with those authorities. Civil disobedience is sometimes necessary, but violence is almost always out of line to further religious views. For instance, the bombing of abortion clinics by Christians is wrong, and such actions have been counterproductive in bringing about positive change in the laws regarding abortion. Similarly, the militia movement in America has been laced with Christian undertones and biblical references, but the actions of these groups often contradict the One who didn't raise a hand in the face of hatred, opposition, and even crucifixion. True Christianity is a nonviolent religion. Certainly, at times resistance is necessary; had the colonists of 1776 not used force to resist the British, our nation would not exist in the form it does today. But armed resistance must always be taken as last resort. The Bible teaches that Christians should live in peace with all people insofar as possible.

I'm convinced that faith is a matter of inspiration, not a matter of imposition. It is something a person models rather than mandates. Faith does not impose itself on other people. Imposition usually sacrifices somebody else; it seeks to injure or extort others. This is what the terrorist does in an attempt to impose his religion on the world.

In contrast, Jesus said, "If I be lifted up, I will draw all people to myself." In matters of faith, more is achieved through sacrifice than through violence.

We had no sooner put the lid on the Indianapolis Baptist Temple case when another flap hit the press. Ironically, the *Washington Post* ran an article about my faith playing a visible role at the Justice Department. The *Post* was especially interested in the "daily devotional" time I shared with a group of friends who gathered in my office at the Justice building prior to the start of each workday. Usually attended by ten or fewer, the devotional time was open to anyone—Justice and others, men and women, Christian or not. It was never mandatory, nor was attendance a fast track for those wanting to get ahead in the department. Indeed, some of my closest friends and highest-ranking staff did not attend the morning devotionals. In no way did that impair their relationship with me. But the newspaper found a few disgruntled lawyers at the department who were "discomfited by the daily prayer sessions—particularly because they are conducted by the nation's chief law enforcement officer, entrusted with enforcing a Constitution that calls for the separation of church and state."[1]

One attorney at the Justice Department, who was unwilling to be named, was upset about our group devotional time and told the paper, "The purpose of the Department of Justice is to do the business of the government, not to establish a religion. It strikes me and a lot of others as offensive, disrespectful, and unconstitutional. It at least blurs the line, and it probably crosses it."[2]

To the *Post*'s credit, the writer also interviewed my deputy chief of staff, David Israelite. David emphasized the voluntary nature of my morning get-togethers, stating, "He has never in any way insinuated that I should be going to these meetings, and I never felt I've been hindered by not attending." As for the matter of imposing my views on David and his coworkers, David answered straightforwardly, "He's a religious man, and he's been attacked by folks because of that. I've known John Ashcroft for 15 years, and there is no more tolerant person that I've been around in my life."[3]

Actually, the pre-work office devotionals were not something new for me. Starting my workday with a time of Bible study and prayer was a personal habit that stretched all the way back to the 1970s, when I was serving as attorney general of Missouri. When I opened the pre-workday time to members of my staff, I was pleasantly surprised that others wanted to join me in the practice. I held similar meetings in my office as governor, and while I was a U.S. senator. Numerous other officials begin their day by welcoming the wisdom of the Almighty. It is widely reported that President Bush begins each workday with a time of personal Bible reading; it is said that Senator Joe Lieberman does something similar by reading the Talmud regularly, and Bible studies on Capitol Hill are not nearly as rare as one might think. The House and Senate each begin daily proceedings with prayer. Many members of Congress participate regularly in Bible studies that meet in the Capitol and Capitol offices.

When I became U.S. attorney general, I carried on my long-standing practice of opening the morning devotional to anyone who wanted to attend, although in truth more people attended from outside the department than within. That was okay with me. Our morning devotional time was fast-paced, affectionately known as RAMP—Read, Argue, Memorize, and Pray. We used a book made up entirely of scripture, a combination of Old Testament and New Testament passages, reading a portion each morning. Then we'd discuss what we thought the passage meant to us, which is where we often disagreed and argued. Each morning, we'd strive to memorize a verse or a passage of scripture, and then we'd pray together. On occasion I would lead the session, but more often other participants led. For my convenience, others came to my office, relieving me of the need to join them somewhere else.

Shortly after the morning devotional sessions hit the news, I was riding in a car with President Bush. The president looked over at me and cocked his head slightly to the side. "John, I hear some folks join you before work at the Justice Department to pray and ask for God's direction. Is that right?"

Oh, boy, I thought. *Maybe the president is upset or embarrassed by the devotionals. Maybe I have caused a problem for him.*

"Yes, sir; that's right," I replied.

The president looked me in the eyes and a hint of a smile formed on his lips as he nodded his head and said, "Well, don't ever stop."

ENDNOTES

1. Dan Eggen, "Ashcroft's Faith Plays Visible Role at Justice," *Washington Post*, May 14, 2001, p. A-1.
2. Ibid.
3. Ibid.

CHAPTER SEVEN

THE BOTCHED PROSECUTION OF TIMOTHY McVEIGH

An Innocent System

———✦———

Praying for wisdom about how to conduct my duties as attorney general seemed especially crucial when it came to handling the case of convicted Oklahoma City bomber Timothy McVeigh. On April 19, 1995, the cold-blooded murderer had carried out the most deadly act of terrorism on American soil in the twentieth century, setting off a truck bomb in front of the Alfred P. Murrah Federal Building and killing 168 of his fellow American citizens. At least three women who died in the explosion were known to be pregnant at the time. Two years later, on June 2, 1997, McVeigh was found guilty of murder and conspiracy. Eleven days later, he was sentenced to death. Then the appeals process took over. Finally, McVeigh tired of the seemingly interminable appeals on his behalf. On December 11, 2000, he asked U.S. District Judge Richard Matsch to end his appeals and set an execution date. McVeigh had the legal right to request that his execution take place within 120 days, even if his lawyers objected, which of course they did. The judge granted McVeigh's request, but gave him until January 11, 2001, to consider changing his mind. When McVeigh did not contest the action, the execution date was set for May 16, 2001, death by lethal injection.

I inherited the McVeigh case, and had the dubious distinction of overseeing the process for the first federal execution since March 15,

1963, when the U.S. government executed Victor Feguer, convicted of kidnapping and murdering a doctor, ostensibly for drugs. Feguer had appealed to President John F. Kennedy for clemency, but Kennedy was so appalled at the brutal slaying that he refused, and Feguer was hanged from a gallows. Feguer had murdered one person; McVeigh had murdered 168 innocent people.

Not only did the Justice Department have to plan the logistics and security measures for McVeigh's execution, we also had to consider how to accommodate family members of victims who wanted to watch the sentence being fulfilled. McVeigh sat on death row at the federal penitentiary in Terre Haute, Indiana, where the execution chamber seated about thirty people. But the large number of victims in this case complicated how we decided who was permitted to view McVeigh's demise.

Timothy James McVeigh, a young Gulf War veteran, began plotting to blow up the Alfred P. Murrah Federal Building in Oklahoma City back in 1994. For nearly a year, he worked on the details of his plot, using a massive five-thousand-pound truck bomb made from a base of ammonium nitrate—farm fertilizer.

Recruiting friends Terry Nichols and Terry's brother James to help him, on April 19, 1995—the second anniversary of the Branch Davidian incident in Waco, Texas—McVeigh pulled a Ryder truck in front of the Murrah Building in downtown Oklahoma City. At 9:02 a.m., an enormous blast ripped through the building, shredding brick, flooring, and human bodies—168 of them, including several pregnant women and nineteen children. More than eight hundred people were injured in the bombing. The powerful blast shattered the Murrah Building and damaged more than three hundred buildings in the surrounding area. The horrific explosion was felt as far as thirty miles away.

Making matters even worse, the Murrah Building housed a daycare center, and much of the debris from the blown-out portion of the building was littered with children's clothes, papers, crayons, and body parts. The carnage was sickening.

Meanwhile, Timothy McVeigh hightailed it out of town on Interstate 35, heading north in his 1977 Mercury Marquis getaway car, purchased just five days earlier in Junction City, Kansas. Maybe that's why the vehicle did not have a license plate. Within ninety minutes of the bombing, he was stopped by an Oklahoma highway patrolman on suspicion of speeding and driving without a license plate. The state trooper noticed that McVeigh had a handgun stuffed in the waist of his jeans. Although possessing a firearm was not uncommon in Oklahoma, the officer became suspicious at the way McVeigh was carrying the weapon, and upon investigation, he arrested him on a firearms charge. Two days later, shortly before McVeigh was to be released, he was identified as a suspect and charged with the Federal Building bombing. His friend Terry Nichols was later caught in Kansas.

Both McVeigh and Nichols were linked to antigovernment "militia" groups, self-styled warriors with their own political and military agendas for the United States. Indeed, in some inexplicable way, McVeigh conceived his terrorist attack as retribution for the government's overreacting at Ruby Ridge and at Waco. In McVeigh's world, the murders at Oklahoma City were necessary, even justified as "collateral damage," as he made his garish anti–U.S. government statement. For a while, rumors of a wider conspiracy ran rampant, fueled in part by McVeigh's court-appointed defense lawyer, Stephen Jones. McVeigh himself consistently denied any outside help.

The trial was moved to Denver, Colorado, by Judge Richard Matsch because in his opinion the accused Oklahoma City bomber could not "obtain a fair and impartial trail any place" in Oklahoma.[1]

On June 2, 1997, McVeigh was convicted of eleven counts of murder and conspiracy. The sentencing phase of the trial proved to be particularly gruesome, as friends and family members told their heartbreaking stories. Some people had gone to thirty funerals in twenty days. Strong police officers struggled to maintain their composure as they described finding dead children, some of whom were mere babes, in the remains of the second-floor day-care center in the Federal Building. Firemen told of their valiant but often futile rescue efforts and the recurring nightmares they had experienced since that horrific day. Physicians replayed heartrending decisions to cut off limbs to free people trapped in the rubble of the collapsed portion of the building, while Timothy McVeigh escaped with his earplugs to prevent his hearing from being damaged by the blast.

The jury deliberated for two days, and then on June 13, 1997, delivered their sentence: death. McVeigh sat devoid of expression as the sentence was read. In 1998, Matsch sentenced Nichols to life in prison, the jury allowing leniency possibly because he was at home the day of the bombing.

By the time McVeigh and Nichols were sentenced, the U.S. government had spent $82.5 million to investigate and prosecute their cases. More than $15 million of taxpayers' money went to defend Timothy McVeigh alone. That's not counting the appeals that followed, or the cost of keeping him in Florence, Colorado's "Supermax" federal prison, the same prison in which Unabomber Ted Kaczynski was incarcerated, as was Ramzi Yousef, the man who devised the 1993 attack on the World Trade Center. A year later, McVeigh was transferred to the federal penitentiary at Terre Haute to await execution.

I made several trips to Oklahoma City to meet with the victims' families and survivors during the spring of 2001. It was obvious they were still dealing with a seething caldron of mixed emotions, ranging from anger to overwhelming grief, to a desire to see justice done, and in some, simple revenge. Regardless of their emotional state, the feelings were extremely raw, and as I met with the survivors I often felt as though I were scraping a knife over open wounds that had not yet had time to heal. As best I could, I tried to express my sympathy and understanding for their loss, while letting them know that we were committed to seeing justice done under our system of law.

Most of the survivors expressed appreciation and respect for my coming. A few addressed their anger toward the Justice Department; it was as though they didn't know who they should be mad at, so occasionally I became the best target. Surprisingly, many of the survivors—hundreds of them, actually—insisted that they wanted to view the McVeigh execution personally, so I promised to be as accommodating as possible.

By April 2001, we had developed a plan to allow survivors and family members of the bombing victims to view the execution if they wished. We recognized the need for closure that the victims' families and friends desired, yet at the same time we did not want inflammatory video of the execution showing up on the evening news, or, worse yet, pirated copies of the McVeigh execution making the rounds on the Internet, or profiteers reproducing videotapes of the proceedings and selling them on street corners within hours of the execution. We settled on a high-tech compromise. Ten people would be chosen to witness the lethal injection capital punishment procedure at the federal penitentiary in Terre Haute. At the same time, those with a close family connection to the deceased victims could view the execution on a secure, encoded, closed-circuit television feed in Oklahoma City. The execution would be broadcast only one time in an isolated, tightly controlled facility, a Justice Department airplane hangar used by "Con Air," the prison system air transport run by the U.S. Marshal Service.

In the interim period leading up to the execution, we meticulously limited McVeigh's accessibility to the media, allowing only one or two half-hour interviews. McVeigh himself had sent a letter to Rita Cosby of Fox News, detailing his rationale for the bombings. Other than those isolated incidents, we kept McVeigh buttoned down tightly. Previously, Bureau of Prisons policies had given the media open access, even to death row inmates, assuming the inmate wanted to communicate. We did not allow such open access to McVeigh. We were concerned about the potential for him to become a symbol and his execution to evoke additional acts of terrorism. McVeigh and his ilk often used perceived injustices on the part of the government as an excuse to wreak havoc. We didn't want him attempting to rally support from other militia-type groups, or making rash statements that could incite further violence.

Beyond that, it would be a horrible insult to the victims and their families if the man who bombed the Federal Building was able to speak freely, promoting the twisted reasoning regarding his cause. None of the families of the 168 victims wanted to be lectured by the man who had robbed them of loved ones.

We also wished to avoid giving McVeigh any opportunity for self-serving interviews in which the convicted mass murderer could use the media to aggrandize himself to the public. Such access to the media might well encourage other killers to pursue their own sick form of "celebrity."

Additionally, we sought to dispel any notions of "hero worship" that could reward a person such as McVeigh who is willing to kill innocents and die for his beliefs, regardless of how cruel and inhumane those beliefs might be. McVeigh wanted to die, but should someone do a book or a movie about his life, they could attempt to portray him as a martyr who gave his life for the Koresh group at Waco, or Randy Weaver and the people at Ruby Ridge. We did not intend to give them additional ammunition.

As McVeigh's May 16 execution date drew nearer, we were extremely cognizant that everything we did in this case was setting a precedent for cases to follow. How we did things would no doubt become the pattern for years to come. Moreover, the way in which we handled the execution could possibly precipitate future acts of violence, just as McVeigh himself had chosen to murder and maim on the anniversary of the Waco incident. An improperly handled execution could discredit capital punishment as a societal tool against heinous crimes.

Consequently, although we could not prevent the execution from being a media event, we worked tenaciously to make sure that the McVeigh execution was devoid of "entertainment value." We were well aware that with all the television cameras and media trucks on hand, it would be an ideal place for any anti-American group to stage events seeking free publicity. The Terre Haute Bureau of Prisons facility boasts tight security, so we weren't too worried about breaches by militia groups; nor did our intelligence indicate any were planned, but we did our best to minimize any possible threats from outside the penitentiary.

By the first week of May, preparations were in place for the execution of Timothy McVeigh. Everything was ready.

Then another explosion took place, this one within the FBI itself. Just six days before the scheduled May 16 execution, the FBI revealed that more than three thousand pages of documents had not been handed over to McVeigh's defense team. Although it was believed these documents raised no questions about McVeigh's guilt—he had fully confessed, even boasted about his responsibility for the murders— the ominous possibility existed that somehow the case could turn on a technicality. Beyond that, since this was the first federal capital punishment case in thirty-eight years, the failure of the FBI to be forthcoming with all the promised materials to the defense threatened to damage the justice system itself.

I was beside myself when I heard the news. I could hardly believe my ears. *This can't be happening,* I thought. *Not after federal prosecutors spent two years and millions of dollars making this case; not after the people of Oklahoma City were primed and ready for some long-awaited resolution of justice.* Nevertheless, I determined that we were going to respond correctly. *We're going to do this right.*

I immediately announced a thirty-day postponement of McVeigh's execution date to give his attorneys time to review the documents. To me, any other course of action raised the risk of giving extremist groups a pretext for further violence. I spoke forcefully about the Justice Department's responsibility in this mess. "It is not enough that we have a guilty defendant. We must have an innocent system as well."

In making the announcement, I noted, "I know many Americans will question why the execution of someone who is clearly guilty of such a heinous crime should be delayed. I understand that victims and victims' family members await justice. But if any questions or doubts remain about this case, it would cast a permanent cloud over justice, diminishing its value and questioning its integrity. For those victims and for our nation, I want a justice system that has the full faith and confidence of the American people."

How could the FBI botch one of the highest-profile cases in history? Much of it stemmed from the Justice Department's prosecutors being overly generous to the McVeigh defense team in the first place, when they agreed to a court order promising to provide materials that are not normally required to be given to criminal defendants. This set a new standard and confusion ensued. The "Brady rule" requires that for a person to have a fair trial, the defense must receive any possible exculpatory evidence possessed by the prosecutor. In the McVeigh case, the Justice Department prosecutors went beyond what was necessary. By doing so, we granted McVeigh's lawyers access to every document in the FBI's possession that related to the case, even if the documents had no value in casting any doubts on the defendant's guilt. The FBI had already provided documents necessary to the defense and willingly had given the McVeigh lawyers everything they needed. As far as Justice was concerned, it was an open-and-shut case; the evidence linking McVeigh to the bombing was beyond doubt and irrefutable. Then somebody discovered the file boxes filled with documents. Acting Deputy Attorney General Bob Mueller was notified by the FBI, and Bob brought the matter to me.

On May 11, the same day I postponed the execution, until June 11, I directed the FBI to issue a worldwide alert, ordering every FBI office to identify and produce any and all documents required under the broad discovery agreement in the McVeigh case. Even though eleven previous searches had been done, I wanted the FBI to make a final, thorough search to find any other potentially relevant documents in this case.

These missing documents were scattered all over the country, throughout the fifty-six field offices of the FBI. They had to be collected from each one of these offices, as well as the fifty-five international offices the Bureau maintains, all of which were involved in the investigation of the Oklahoma City bombing, especially in attempting to ascertain whether a broader conspiracy existed. At least 2,592 agents had been actively involved in the investigation in some manner. Consequently, nearly every FBI field office had material relating to McVeigh in some way. The vast majority of these documents were duplicates, or factually similar to other material that had already been turned over to the defense. But they existed, and they had not been given to the defense.

We needed remediation rather than recrimination: there was no use squawking about who was at fault; we just needed to get this problem fixed quickly. I told the FBI directly and clearly that we wanted every piece of evidence that might be remotely relevant to the case. Moreover, we demanded that every field office certify in writing that it had swept its offices, that it had gone through its files and had delivered anything it had found to the court. As a result, even more than the three thousand documents eventually turned up.

"Don't worry," we were assured by people in the field. "There's nothing new in those files." Of course we understood that these were the same voices that had assured us that they had previously provided all the documents.

In the FBI's defense, it is almost impossible to imagine the huge amount of work involved in a case like McVeigh's and the massive amount of paper that accompanies it. FBI director Louis Freeh estimated that the case "generated some 3.5 tons of evidence, nearly a billion separate pieces of information."[2] The FBI conducted more than 28,000 interviews; the Bureau examined press clippings, truck rental records, and airline records, and all of these elements produced mounds of paper that had to be considered relevant or not by somebody in each field office. Although we didn't believe there was any new information or anything of value to either the prosecution or the defense,

I was unwilling to allow the execution to go forward if there was even a shred of doubt and until the justice system had operated properly.

The worldwide search produced 898 additional pages of documents. All of those materials were reviewed by McVeigh's attorneys, and none of the additional documents raised any doubt about the proven and admitted guilt of Timothy McVeigh. Most of the documents had little to no evidentiary value, and much of the information had already been disclosed to the defense through other materials they had received previously. I stated our findings publicly in my report: "No document creates any doubt of McVeigh's guilt, let alone establishes his innocence—which is the legal standard an appeal must overcome." At the end of thirty days, both the U.S. District Court of Colorado (before whom the case was tried) and McVeigh's defense team agreed that the documents provided no new evidence. A new date was set for McVeigh's execution, June 11, 2001.

Louis Freeh and I had serious discussions about the McVeigh files. Both Louis and I were extremely disappointed at the FBI's failure, but we were similarly more concerned about how the delay would affect the friends and family members of the victims. Some people speculated that Freeh's departure as director of the FBI in June 2001 was a result of the missing document debacle. That was untrue. Louis had mentioned to me back in April that he planned to resign from the Bureau. By May, I was already considering Bob Mueller as his replacement.

As embarrassing as the entire affair was, it redounded to the FBI's benefit. If nothing else, our unwillingness to take a man's life unless we were as certain as possible that we had explored every bit of evidence produced a confidence in the public that we were not arbitrarily condemning people to death. The system worked.

Moreover, it was a statement about our integrity. I had already asked Judge William Webster—a man with the rare résumé that included leading both the FBI and the CIA—to head a commission investigating the FBI's performance in the Robert Hanssen espionage case. In addition to that ongoing review, I asked Justice Department inspector general Glenn Fine to examine fully the FBI's belated delivery of the documents and other evidence relating to the McVeigh case.

To the FBI's credit, when the problem was discovered, it was not covered up. Even after the materials had been found, it was a dilemma that we knew about internally, but of which nobody else in the justice system was aware. It might have been suggested that an internal review of the newly found documents be undertaken and it be determined that there was nothing new among them. But we didn't. We brought the matter to full exposure, regardless of the costs or time involved.

It was another lesson to me that the FBI needed reform, a lesson that would be pressed home even more emphatically within a few months' time.

As the new execution date drew near, the question came up as to whether I was going to be in Terre Haute with McVeigh or with the victims' families and friends in Oklahoma City. I decided that on this occasion, the top law enforcement officer in the land should be with the victims rather than the perpetrator of the crime. It was a somber group that assembled at the "Con Air" hangar in Oklahoma City on June 11, 2001. I visited with the victims' families briefly and empathized with their pain and grief.

I stayed until all the people were in the staging area, and then I left before the execution took place. It was not that I was afraid to watch, or that I was unwilling to view the ultimate punishment our judicial system imposed on its worst criminals. I decided not to watch the scene on the screen because I saw no value in my watching. Although I wanted victims' families to have the opportunity to view the execution if they wished, frankly, the sight of a person dying sickens me. I can't stand to watch violence in a movie or a television program. Beyond that, I didn't want to give the impression that the attorney general of the United States took any macabre satisfaction in seeing a person put to death.

On the other hand, I had no qualms about McVeigh receiving the death penalty. If ever a man deserved to pay the ultimate price for the crimes he committed and the pain and grief he caused to so many people, it was Timothy McVeigh. To me, capital punishment is a form of societal self-defense. It should not be employed indiscriminately, but in cases of the most heinous crimes, the death penalty may be the only appropriate punishment. Some people believe it is right to take a life to save the life of someone else, but they would not vote to take the life of a convicted criminal, no matter how horrible the crime. Others believe that killing another person for any reason is simply wrong. I respect those opinions, but I disagree with them. I'm convinced that government has a duty to promote community defense. The death penalty, when applied in appropriate cases, can be a strong deterrent to crime. It is certainly a deterrent to the convicted criminal sentenced to death, and it is also a deterrent to other potential capital offenders.

When I was serving as the attorney general of Missouri, three other state attorneys general and I visited President Ronald Reagan at the White House. Reagan was his usual affable self, when for some reason the subject turned to capital punishment. He told us that he had wrestled with the issue as governor of California, because it is such a difficult matter to end willfully another person's life. Reagan launched into a story about an elderly couple from California who sent him a gift and a note shortly after the first capital punishment was undertaken in California. Paraphrasing the contents of the note, Reagan said it read largely like this:

Dear Governor Reagan,

I'm seventy years old. My wife and I run a small liquor store, and we want you to have this gift because you saved our lives. Two thugs came into our store, and they had me on the floor. They had taken the money out of the cash register and one man had a knife at my throat, ready to kill me. I yelled at him, "You'll get the death penalty for doing this!"

And the thug dropped the knife and ran out of the store. Thanks for saving my life.

Reagan believed the death penalty was a deterrent to murder in that case, and I agree. I'm convinced that in the long run capital punishment saves lives.

Another reason why I favor capital punishment is that it helps promote a sense of justice and closure for family members of a victim. I saw that firsthand in the survivors of the Oklahoma City bombing.

The Justice Department established specific protocol for the countdown to McVeigh's execution. Each step was carefully choreographed, including his transfer in a van from the condemned-prisoner unit to a nine-by-fourteen-foot holding cell in the execution facility. McVeigh had a final medical exam and was given an opportunity to meet with a minister. He was allowed to make a last phone call.

Because McVeigh had not exhausted all of his appeals, up to a predetermined point in the sequence he could have said, "I want to appeal." But I emphatically instructed the department heads, "We are under a court order to execute Timothy McVeigh. Unless we receive a court order to do otherwise, proceed as planned."

The night before his execution, Timothy McVeigh had his last meal, two pints of mint chocolate chip ice cream. Shortly before seven o'clock the next morning, dressed in a plain shirt, khaki pants, and slip-on shoes, McVeigh was led to the execution chamber. Several prison guards strapped him to a padded gurney. An intravenous line was inserted in him, and then the guards opened the curtains covering the glass panels separating the chamber from the viewing area. Twenty-four invited witnesses, including two bombing survivors and eight family members, sat silently on the other side of the glass. Four witnesses were there on McVeigh's behalf. Six hundred miles away, in Oklahoma City, 272 survivors and victims' relatives watched in a hushed airplane hangar as encrypted closed circuit-television brought

McVeigh's face into view. Outside the prison, more than fourteen hundred members of the media waited for any word from inside.

Warden Harley Lappin asked McVeigh if he wished to make a final statement. He did not, although he did leave a handwritten copy of the concluding lines from the William Ernest Henley poem "Invictus": "I am the master of my fate;/I am the captain of my soul."

Showing no emotion, as he had done through much of the trial, McVeigh kept his head down as the warden read an official statement and said, "We are ready."

The lethal injection included a three-step process, the first containing sodium pentothal, which renders a person unconscious. Pancuronium bromide then relaxes the muscles, and potassium chloride stops the heart and lungs. As the lethal injection entered his veins, McVeigh raised his head and glared at the witnesses behind the glass. Then it was over. Timothy McVeigh, the man who had caused such horrendous pain to so many people, looked as though he had simply died in his sleep.

Following the execution, a numbness seemed to set in among the witnesses. Some were happy that McVeigh had paid with his life for the crime he had committed, though all were aware that even the death penalty was not sufficient to make up for the devastation he had caused. Many were disappointed that he offered no apology, nor did he seem in any sense remorseful.

The Oklahoma bombing and the nearly botched prosecution of McVeigh became a dubious milestone in American history. Never again would we think that all the terrorists were "out there," in some foreign land. Now we had learned the hard way that we were vulnerable; worse yet, we discovered that the terrorists could be dwelling among us. It was a lesson we'd be reminded of again all too soon.

ENDNOTES

1. "McVeigh sentenced to die for Oklahoma City bombing," CNN.com., June 13, 1997; www.cnn.com/US/9706/13/mcveigh.sentencing/
2. Louis Freeh, *My FBI* (New York: St. Martin's Press, 2005), p. 212.

CHAPTER EIGHT

TERROR STRIKES

September 11, 2001

❧❧❧

Few days are etched in the American psyche any more indelibly than September 11, 2001. The crystal blue sky appeared unalloyed and virtually cloudless as I whipped through the air aboard a small Citation jet, on my way from Washington to Milwaukee to read with a group of schoolchildren. As part of the White House's initiatives on literacy, several cabinet members were deployed to emphasize the value of reading for young people. The president himself was already in Sarasota, Florida, reading to a group of second graders at the Emma E. Booker Elementary School.

A handful of young staff members from the Justice Department—"kids," as I referred to them, even though they were all in their midtwenties and thirties, and a few older than that—were along with me on my trip. They were Susan Dryden Whitson, now First Lady Laura Bush's press secretary; David Israelite, my deputy chief of staff; Ralph Boyd, the assistant attorney general for civil rights; and some FBI security agents. Susan, David, Ralph, and I were seated conference style, with a table between us. Susan had brought baked goods for us to enjoy, and we were all jovial, happy—leaving Washington for the day.

As I often do when I fly, I was excitedly pointing out various landmarks on the ground as we flew over them. It was such a clear day—a severe clear, as I later described it—that we could see for miles and miles. While I was having a fabulous time, my running commentary was annoying my staff members, especially those trying to catch a few winks of sleep, or those wanting to get some work done during the flight. "Wow, there's Lake Erie, look at that! Yep, that's Cleveland right there along the lake's edge." My staff members nodded at the appropriate moments, as though to say, "Just humor him."

As we passed Grand Rapids, I was pointing out the Grand River flowing right through the center of town, splitting the city. "And guys can go out there on their lunch hours and catch better salmon than you'll find in most restaurants. That's what I call good working conditions," I quipped.

Uh-huh, my staff nodded.

We were about to break over the eastern shore of Lake Michigan when one of the pilots shouted, "Sir, you are to call back to the Justice Department Command Center in Washington immediately."

The Command Center? Why would I need to call there? That can't be good news.

I made the call. As I listened to the report, it was as though I'd been kicked in the stomach: two commercial airliners had struck the two tallest buildings in New York, the World Trade Center towers. I scribbled notes as I talked.

"Wait a minute. Slow down. Say that again," I said, scribbling faster. The other passengers fell silent, sensing something serious was going on.

I felt the color drain from my face as I turned toward the cockpit area. This couldn't be happening . . . but it was.

"Turn this plane around," I said to the pilot. "We're flying back to Washington."

"We can't!" the pilot snapped. "I'm sorry, sir. We don't have enough fuel to make it back to Washington. We'll need to land in Milwaukee and refuel."

"All right, get us down for fuel and back in the air as fast as you can."

I turned and looked back at the young staffers aboard the plane; all of them staring at me like children searching the face of a parent, waiting for me to give them some hint as to what was going on. "The world has changed forever," I said. "The country will never be the same."

I gripped the seat as I tried to describe to them what I'd just learned from the Command Center. The staff members wrestled with their emotions as I grappled with mine. By the time we approached the runway a few minutes later, a silence filled the plane as a protective numbness had already inoculated our hearts and minds. We understood that we didn't have the luxury of crying out in pain; there was work to be done. America was under attack.

When the Citation touched down at the airport near Milwaukee, we were met by black-uniformed SWAT team members brandishing weapons as they surrounded the plane on the tarmac. The pilot directed the refueling chores while the rest of us went inside the otherwise evacuated terminal to find a television. That's when we first saw the horrific scenes that will haunt every American citizen who witnessed them. A short time later, we learned that a third plane had hit the Pentagon in Washington. A fourth plane was off course in Pennsylvania, possibly en route to the Capitol. Reports and rumors were already swirling about other potential targets.

I was on the phone to the Command Center much of the time we were on the ground. Some people were discouraging us from getting back on the plane until we knew whether there was going to be another attack. I didn't want to wait that long.

As soon as the pilot had completed refueling, I gave the order to take off.

"I'm sorry, sir," the pilot said. "We can't take off. I just received orders that we are not supposed to be flying."

"No, we're going. Let's get back in the air," I told our crew, and we all climbed on board as quickly as possible. We headed back toward Washington, and had barely gotten in the air when the pilot called to me again.

"They're instructing me to land outside of Detroit," the pilot said.

"No, keep going," I told him.

Somewhere near Richmond, Virginia, the pilot turned to me again. "They're saying to bring this plane down, sir."

"Keep going!" I directed.

We flew in relative silence for nearly an hour, as I reviewed my notes from the call and began jotting a list of things that needed to be done as soon as we hit the ground. That's when the pilot called out, "Sir, there's a shoot-down order. If we get any closer to Washington, they might blow us out of the sky."

I called the Command Center. Before long, we were informed that an escort plane was on the way. We went into a wide holding pattern while waiting for the escort, and were over West Virginia when an F-16 fighter aircraft streaked toward us. The jet roared by and turned around. The next instant, we looked out the window, and the pilot could be seen in his cockpit; he was flying that close to us. At the time, we thought the jet was protecting us, and no doubt it was, but I now realize that if our pilot had made even a minor turn toward the U.S. Capitol building or the White House as we entered Washington airspace, somebody else might be telling this story.

From about sixty miles away, we could already see the smoke billowing from the Pentagon. We stared out the windows of the Citation in silent horror at the unimaginable sight. Not much later, we heard that our dear friend Barbara Olson had been on one of the planes. Learning that she died on one of the hijacked planes personalized the nightmare to us and intensified our grief immeasurably. Barbara's husband, Ted Olson, was the U.S. solicitor general and a trusted friend who worked diligently with us in the Justice Department. Barbara had been part of the team that had prepared me for confirmation as attorney general. Just three days earlier, Ted and Barbara had hosted a small dinner party that Janet and I attended at their home. Today, Barbara had been a passenger aboard the very plane that had hit the Pentagon—raising the smoke we were observing from the air.

Finally, we were cleared to land, and the pilot brought the plane down and taxied to the already crowded tarmac near Signature Aviation, the private executive aircraft terminal. We were one of the last planes to land at Reagan National Airport that day.

It seemed an army of agents, some with machine guns at the ready, awaited us when we exited the plane. The agents quickly covered me with a bulletproof trench coat, and passed out several bulletproof vests to other people getting off the plane. Apparently they were concerned about possible snipers.

Rumors about a bomb at the State Department building had been reported, and although they were later debunked, at the time it felt like the entire city was under attack. We were hustled into a hangar area to get out of open view as quickly as possible. Inside the hangar, several vans waited. A heavily reinforced SUV was waiting for David Israelite and me as we waved a strange good-bye to our coworkers, who quickly dispersed to their vehicles. As we pulled out of the hangar, none of us could take our eyes off the ominous dark cloud of smoke that seemed to hover in the sky over the Pentagon. The sight made me sick to my stomach.

I called the White House situation room to find out where they wanted me to go to set up operations. I was connected to National Security Advisor Condoleezza Rice, who suggested that I head for the classified site until we knew if any more attacks were forthcoming.

The vehicle whisked us away from the airport, heading away from downtown, toward a prearranged classified site that was part of our government's contingency plan to keep top-level officials alive and as safe as possible in the event of an attack. Just outside the airport, however, our vehicle slowed to a stop. Every road was clogged with traffic. The entire city, it seemed, had disgorged into the streets, either in a vehicle or on foot. Sirens blared from every direction, but few people paid any attention. The congestion was so thick that people walking down the shoulders of the roads were sometimes moving faster than we were in motorized vehicles.

I was able to contact Larry Thompson and David Ayres, who had already left the city and were at the classified location. "It is utter mayhem here," Larry said. "You might be better off heading over to SIOC. The FBI didn't relocate to this site."

I called Condoleezza Rice and told her that we were trapped in the traffic but headed toward the site. "Okay," she said, "make your way back to SIOC."

"Let's turn this thing around," I said to our driver. "Get us back to the FBI building." I directed that senior Department of Justice officials like Larry also meet me there.

Through the median we went, pointed back toward downtown Washington. It was much easier moving toward the Capitol. Before long we were unloading inside the cavernous FBI building. We raced upstairs to SIOC, the Strategic Information Operations Center, a 30,000-square-foot, high-tech, windowless command center inside the FBI building.

Row after row of computer screens in SIOC were all filled with data, and eight large video display screens were being monitored constantly as I walked into the room. For such a tumultuous time in the history of our country, emotions in the room were surprisingly controlled, as highly trained professionals continued to do their jobs, ever conscious that another fuel-laden plane might be headed toward the city, or some other type of disaster might soon befall us.

The room was teeming with people, abuzz with activity, voices and papers everywhere, with dozens of people coming in and out with bits and pieces of new information moment by moment. Bob Mueller, the new FBI director, who had been on the job for less than a week, met us. Fact by fact, he briefed me on what we knew so far. Except for the FBI building, we were shutting down as many nonvital operations as possible, dispersing people to find safety. Most of the White House staff was already gone. Meanwhile, the president was in the air, presumably on his way to an air base somewhere out in the western part of the country, but he had made it clear to Vice President Cheney that he wanted to get back to Washington as quickly as possible.

We braced for more attacks and scrambled to find ways to defend the country from being hit by a second wave. The clear overriding priority was to make sure all the commercial airliners were down, that the skies over America were empty and no more attacks would be forthcoming by air. Of grave concern were the large number of planes that were somewhere over the oceans, both the Atlantic and the Pacific, heading toward the United States. Many of them were past the point of no return; we couldn't turn them back, so our plan was to get them down at the earliest landing location while keeping them as far away as possible from potential targets. Canada took the brunt of the planes coming in for unexpected landings; the airports were crammed full of disoriented passengers coming to the United States from Germany, Spain, Italy, and a few Middle Eastern countries. But airports as far away as Greenland also received planes en route from Europe that were rerouted from their planned landings at New York, Washington, and other major American cities.

Complicating matters further, some planes' transponders were "squawking" garbled or incorrect codes, a few unintentionally sending out distress signals. In a highly charged atmosphere in which we all anticipated more attacks, that got our attention in a hurry. In several cases, we radioed pilots asking if they were in trouble. "No, we're not in trouble," came the response.

But how could we be sure? Already four airliners had been used as weapons; how were we to know whether or not a terrorist was holding a knife or a gun to the captain's throat as we answered a mayday call? Was this a second wave of attacks? Only time would tell. It was nerveracking. We still had domestic flights that were unaccounted for as well. We'd already learned that United Flight 93, the airliner that had crashed in Shanksville, Pennsylvania, was probably intended to crash into the White House or U.S. Capitol. How many other planes were still out there with madmen at or near the controls?

One of the most difficult tasks at SIOC that day fell to Assistant Attorney General Michael Chertoff, who is now secretary of homeland security. He had to call our friend Ted Olson and ask him to talk about what Barbara had told him during their final moments. Every detail mattered. What had she seen? Were there other people involved? What sections of the plane were the hijackers seated in? Did she notice their appearance? Any ideas about what seats the hijackers had occupied? Once we had seat numbers, we could get passengers' names, and begin to do a link analysis. "Ted, I feel terrible doing this," Michael said, "but I need to ask you some questions."

"I understand," Ted replied.

"I'm going to send a couple agents over, and as you know, everything that you can remember about your conversations with Barbara will be very important for us . . ." Michael's emotions nearly got the best of him and his words momentarily faltered ". . . to learn everything Barbara told you, so we can track down the people who did this."

The consummate professional, Ted understood, and as wrenching as it was, he allowed the FBI to drag him back through every painful detail in hopes of helping to prevent further attacks.

Michael later recalled, "Based on what the cell phone callers said about where the hijackers were located, where they had gotten up from, the FBI ascertained the seats where the hijackers had been sitting. That's how we got the first set of names." The FBI immediately sought to obtain the flight manifests for the crashed airliners used in the attacks. Oddly enough, the hijackers on all four planes had used their real names and had purchased seats in similar locations. Patterns became clearly and easily discernible, especially when we were looking for Middle Eastern passengers seated near the cockpit door. As the FBI pursued the theory, someone uncovered a troubling fact— other planes that had already landed had carried passengers who fit the patterns. The passengers had dispersed upon landing, and it was impossible to guess how many other planes may have been designated as potential weapons that day. It was being reported that on another plane, a container of box cutters was found under a seat after the passengers had deplaned. "How many more of them are there?" Michael Chertoff wondered aloud.

As rescue teams and investigators began the gruesome task of sifting through the rubble of the World Trade Center and the Pentagon, and others combed the obliterated pieces of Flight 93, Bob Mueller put together the largest criminal investigation in the history of the world, and he did it almost overnight. No other investigation— not even the first attack on the World Trade Center—was remotely like this. Besides the four crime scenes—at the Twin Towers, the Pentagon, and in Pennsylvania—information soon came in linking the airports from which the flights had originated, adding even more areas of investigation. The sheer enormity of the situation threatened to overwhelm us. But Bob handled each step of the investigation with calm, methodical exactness. He conducted three conference calls per day with all fifty-six field offices of the FBI, pulling in a constant flow of information. Mueller assigned Tom Pickard, the veteran deputy director of the FBI, to be in charge of that part of the investigation.

As we got more names of the terrorists on board the planes, we requested subpoenas and found a rental car in a parking lot that had some "pocket litter" containing telephone numbers and some receipts. The FBI figured out rather quickly that the terrorists had used phony driver's licenses and they found and arrested the man who had assisted many of them in procuring the fraudulent licenses.

Shortly after that, the FBI discovered the hotel room in which Mohamed Atta, the ringleader of the hijackers, and some of his cohorts had stayed in the days prior to 9/11. Investigators found some phone numbers in a waste basket, and that led to other places where investigative interviews were conducted. It was a long, arduous process.

Almost immediately, the Justice Department began focusing on prevention: how can we prevent such an attack from ever happening again? Bob Mueller, David Ayres, Larry Thompson, and other senior Justice Department officials and I met regularly in a bunker-type conference room in the SIOC complex. FBI agents shuttled in and out regularly to brief us on what was going on in the investigation. But we spent most of our time trying to ascertain ways to stop the next terrorist strikes. Our firm expectation was not *if* terrorists would strike again, but when, where, and how.

We quickly devised short- and long-term strategies to thwart additional attacks. In the short term, we recognized that the Bureau, and the U.S. government as a whole, had totally inadequate understanding regarding the terrorist presence in the United States. We were largely blind to what might be out there.

Over the long term, we needed to build a new infrastructure in the Justice Department, including the FBI, that could track and hunt down the terrorist presence in the United States. We needed to reequip our agents and officers with tools, technologies, and legal powers. And we needed to instill a new culture of prevention that supported the overriding mission for a nation that awoke to a stealthy war raging within its borders. For us to survive in this war, as we restructured fundamentally our counterterrorism operations, we had to buy time—time to change laws, systems, and cultures that had been in place for decades.

Consequently, we did all we could to buy that time. We sought to disrupt the terrorist network and put as much "noise" in the system as possible. We later referred to this effort as a "spit on the sidewalk" policy—if a terrorism suspect committed any legal infraction at all, regardless how minor, we would apprehend and charge him. We thus detained and charged numerous people who were suspected of involvement in terrorist activities. We made full use of violations of the immigration laws as a means to freeze people about whom we held suspicions. Even when we couldn't detain them on an extended basis, the short detention did two things: it put the word out on the street that the United States was taking steps to close in on the terrorists, and it caused many would-be terrorists to hunker down for a while.

We knew that Al Qaeda thrived on predictability and routine in selecting and casing their targets. Al Qaeda meticulously planned every detail of their attacks, scouting and surveilling every stage and element. They feared failure and did not take operational risks. They would rather lie low, waiting patiently for the right moment to attack. Al Qaeda's strategy gave us the opportunity we needed to buy time. By changing our own security strategies and tactics, becoming less predictable, we could disrupt their operating environment.

We knew these cat-and-mouse games wouldn't protect us indefinitely, but every bit of time we could buy was worth the effort. We believed Al Qaeda would hold off until they saw what exactly was going to happen next if they were planning any follow on attacks. Every day that passed without another terrorist strike on our homeland or around the world gave the American people a chance to rebound emotionally, physically, financially, and spiritually.

These actions were not controversial at the time, but they were later criticized severely. Some said we were racially profiling. The fact is we detained and arrested terrorist suspects whenever a predicate violation of the law could be proven.

Contrary to media reports and later complaints from civil liberties groups, we did not round up persons of Middle Eastern origins, nor did we detain a huge number of Muslims. Even with our aggressive efforts, we detained close to 750 people, all based on violations, and most of them were held for short durations.

Although it would have been contrary to the national interest to say so at the time, we can now acknowledge that the U.S. government and its elaborate net of security and intelligence-gathering agencies had far too little real awareness of what the terrorist presence within the United States actually was in the days after 9/11. Nor did we have accurate knowledge of how severely vulnerable to terrorists inside our country we really were. We had pitifully little information about who was in the country, plotting what sort of attacks on which cities. We are most fortunate that we did not get hit with another attack during those early days following 9/11. We might have been, had we not acted aggressively.

We kept Reagan National Airport in D.C. closed all the way through the weekend, against the raging discontent of many on Capitol Hill and in the business community. We felt as though we had insufficient airport security, so we redirected federal agents from law enforcement agencies such as the DEA, the U.S. Marshals Service and INS to help plug that gap until we could get new people trained. We weren't as worried about the explosive power of private aircraft, since their fuel load was much less than that of large commercial airliners. Nevertheless, we realized that a small plane could also be extremely lethal if it were carrying a load of "evil biology" such as anthrax or other bioterrorism agents, or if it should be loaded with explosives or crashed into a nuclear energy plant. Consequently, it was necessary to beef up security in our entire air system before allowing the public back on board.

The more we reviewed potential attack scenarios, the more we realized how vulnerable our society is to outside attack. Our schools, churches, apartment complexes, tunnels, bridges, malls, sporting arenas, and more all represented practically indefensible targets for anyone truly plotting evil. Our best hope of interdicting future attacks was to find the terrorists before they found us.

Prior to 9/11, the New York office of the FBI was the center of our antiterrorism investigative capacity. Additionally, when any major criminal investigation took place, it normally was conducted out of the "office of origin," the area in which the crime had been committed. But in the days after 9/11 I wanted to consolidate these strengths and make our terrorist expertise available in Washington. I decided that we needed to centralize the 9/11 investigation, so that information flowed into one location and a coordinated effort flowed out from that one location. I wanted our Justice team to see everything we had on suspected terrorists.

"Bring me the files on all the people we might consider terrorist suspects," I said to our agents in the SIOC complex at FBI headquarters in Washington.

"We don't have them," they replied.

"What do you mean, you don't have them?" I asked a bit impatiently. "We've just been attacked and you're telling me we don't have a list of suspected terrorists to pursue?"

As part of our effort to disrupt the potential terrorist network, I wanted to send agents out to question every person who was under investigation for terrorist connections, unless an intelligence determination was affirmatively made not to contact the suspect because it would tip off the target of the investigation. The FBI had done something similar around the turn of the millennium in an effort to disrupt potential attackers.

Having a couple of FBI agents show up at your door has a sobering effect if you are an aspiring terrorist. First of all, the suspect knows that he is within the awareness of law enforcement. Second, if the terrorist suspect lies to the agent interrogating him, he commits an offense for which he can be arrested and detained under federal criminal law. Lying to the FBI can carry a five-year prison sentence. Word quickly gets around that federal agents are swarming, and the impression is given—correctly—that "If you were thinking of carrying out any sort of malfeasance, you better think twice, because we are onto you."

This tactic contributes to destabilizing those terrorists who operate from the mind-set of "We have to succeed in our attack. A failed attack brings no reward; a failed attack gives no opportunity to earn the rewards of paradise." Attacks with a high possibility of failure, leading to no reward, are not the "normal" way terrorists want to die.

To accomplish this goal, I needed information from intelligence. "How many suspects do you currently have under surveillance?" I asked our agents in counterterrorism at the FBI.

Hundreds of people, they said. But the numbers kept changing with everybody we'd ask. "Does nobody know for sure what we are doing around here?" *I wanted to know.*

I grew agitated. I couldn't even get a precise number of people that we had under terrorism investigations. "Well, that just depends on how broadly you are defining al Qaeda," I was told. "Do you mean all terrorists in the country, or those with ties to extremist, radical Islamic groups that have supported terrorism around the world?"

Finally, I said, "Look, just send me your files. Send over all the

127

files on terrorist suspects to the Criminal Division at the Justice Department in Washington."

"We can't," I was told.

"What do you mean, you can't? Why not?"

"The files are spread out all across the country in the Bureau field offices."

"Get that material from the field, and we will consolidate everything in Washington. Surely you have the information on computer. Just send over the computer records."

"Well, no, sir, they're kept on paper."

"Don't you have duplicate copies here in the Washington headquarters of what you have out in the field offices?"

"No, sir, we don't."

I was irate. "That's not good enough," I said. "This is a national threat. It is clear that these people move nationally and internationally, so we need to consolidate so we can direct an effort to resist terrorism on a national level."

I was even more astonished when I discovered that the FBI had more than forty different computer operating systems and software packages, most of which could not communicate with one another. No matter—the vital information we so desperately needed wasn't on their computers anyhow. The computer records were incomplete because of the FBI's preference for paper records. It was so ridiculous that on the afternoon and evening of September 11, FBI agents had to send images of the suspected terrorists by way of Express Mail service because they did not have the necessary computer capabilities that most ten-year-olds have on their home computers to scan and send photo images.[1]

Beyond that, the FBI expressed serious concerns about passing intelligence information across the invisible "wall," the legal barrier preventing the intelligence agencies from sharing information with the Justice Department prosecutors.

I couldn't believe it. They were worried about the "wall" while our country was at war! "You're telling me that you don't even know the number of people we are tracking," I said hotly, "and you can't provide for me the information that is in our own files?" I was furious.

In several days, the president of the United States would tell the world, "We will direct every resource at our command . . . to the disruption and to the defeat of the global terror network." That sounded real good, and I have no doubt that the president wholeheartedly meant every word. Unfortunately, we didn't yet know who the terrorists were, or where we could find them.

Senior Justice Department officials and I spent the balance of 9/11 in SIOC, with the FBI receiving reports and making on-the-spot decisions about what needed to be done. Throughout the day, we'd hear from members of Congress wanting more information. We tried our best to provide it, but we were still in the heat of battle, in the initial stages of a war unlike any that had ever been fought previously. No matter; Congress wanted answers. Finally, on Tuesday night, September 11, 2001, somewhere between 10:30 and 11:00 p.m., I went up to the police station north of the Hart Senate Office Building to give a briefing to members of Congress who had adamantly demanded an update. I didn't have much that I could say publicly—and telling Congress anything was tantamount to writing an article for the *New York Times*—but I did my best to accommodate their concerns. The place was jammed with members of Congress, all shouting questions, some complaining about apparent inconsistencies, many expressing dissatisfaction that we didn't know everything, and all wanting answers that I didn't know or couldn't say. I stayed there till well after midnight in an intense discussion with the members. I had to say "I don't know" over and over again. One statement I made that night and throughout the first few days after the attacks was, "We will find the people responsible for this." I was convinced at the time that there had to be a large network of supporters and coconspirators on the ground. I told people close to me, "It is inconceivable that they could pull this off without significant ground support."

As it turned out, the terrorists did have significant ground support; but it was found overseas.

My wife, Janet, had been across the street from the Justice Department at the National Archives Building when the attacks on our nation occurred. After going to the Justice Department, she had been brought to the airport to meet me, and then had gone along with me to SIOC. At SIOC, however, she was not cleared for security, so she had to remain outside the sealed-off area for several hours before someone recognized her and offered to take her home. I didn't see her again until after midnight. By the time we actually closed our eyes and attempted to sleep, it was the wee hours of September 12. It had been one of the longest days of my life.

I was back at SIOC well before seven o'clock the next morning, and would remain there except for meetings with the president, National Security Council, cabinet, and press briefings until the day was long since spent; that daily routine lasted for weeks.

Early Wednesday morning, September 12, I joined the president at the White House along with other "principals," top-level officials cleared to handle our nation's most sensitive intelligence matters. We were assessing damages, reviewing our situation and plans when President Bush abruptly stopped, turned, and looked toward me. "Don't ever let this happen again," the president said.

Whether he intended the remark for anyone else in the room at the time, I don't know. But I took it personally. *Never again. Don't let this happen again.* Those words became my guidepost for the next four years. From that moment forward, I devoted myself to an intense, sometimes secret war with a mission many people thought was impossible: stopping terrorists from attacking again on American soil.

ENDNOTE

1. According to former FBI Director Louis Freeh: Louis J. Freeh, *My FBI* (New York: St. Martin's Press, 2005), p. 289.

CHAPTER NINE

NEW PRIORITIES

From Prosecution to Prevention

━━◆◆◆◆◆━━

W hen President Bush called together the National Security Council in the White House cabinet room the morning of September 12, 2001, the tension in the room was palpable. The impact of the previous day's attacks enveloped us like the smoke that still rose from the attack sites. The president spoke briefly but adamantly about bringing the terrorists to justice.

Then CIA director George Tenet made a strong case that the attackers were members of a terrorist group known as al Qaeda, headed by Osama bin Laden.

In light of what the world knows today, it is difficult to imagine al Qaeda and bin Laden being unknown entities, but at the time of the terrorist attacks on our nation most people in America knew little about him. Although the CIA and FBI leaders were aware of al Qaeda's threat, as late as the mid-1990s many agents and state and local law enforcement officers on the front lines had no idea of the danger bin Laden represented.

Born in Saudi Arabia, Osama bin Laden grew up in an enormously wealthy construction family that had made much of its money erecting buildings commissioned by the Saudi royal family— including the renovations of mosques in Mecca and Medina. When the Saudi government allowed American military forces and civilian personnel to operate out of Saudi Arabia during Desert Storm, the coalition response to Iraq's 1990 invasion of Kuwait, Osama bin Laden expressed his outrage. His criticism of King Fahd and his family became so virulent that the Saudis expelled him from his homeland in 1991 because of his antigovernment activities.

Bin Laden moved to Sudan, where he worked with Islamic extremists, fomenting genocide in Sudan and terrorist attacks around the world. His list of evil deeds lengthened every year, as he influenced and took "credit" for various terrorist activities. Since 1996 he had operated out of Afghanistan, conducting or sponsoring terrorist training camps with the tacit approval of the Afghan government and Mullah Omar, the leader of the Taliban, a religious movement that had a habit of converting people at gunpoint—or else. Through his organization, al Qaeda, Arabic for "the Base," bin Laden had declared open war on the United States. In the past, terrorism had most often stemmed from nationalistic groups; now a new dimension was in play: an individual—Osama bin Laden, or "Usama" bin Laden, as most early government sources referred to him—without the direct involvement of a nation behind him, had the money, power, people, and resources to wreak havoc on an international scale. Perhaps even more significantly, he had established a track record of doing so.

Indeed, on Wednesday, September 12, 2001, George Tenet reported that at least three known al Qaeda operatives had been aboard American Airlines Flight 77, the plane that had blasted into the Pentagon, killing 189 people. Tenet expressed his belief that all four planes involved in the previous day's deadly attacks had been hijacked by members of al Qaeda. Although we had no definitive proof as yet, few members of the Security Council doubted the correctness of Tenet's assertions.

Naturally, with al Qaeda and bin Laden on our minds, the president wanted to hear from Bob Mueller, the new director of the FBI. "Give me a brief," he said, turning to Bob. "Where are we on what's happening?"

Bob Mueller, too, believed we were dealing with al Qaeda. From the language the hijackers had used in speaking to the passengers and the announcements that came over the air traffic controllers' radios, especially from United Flight 93 above Pennsylvania, from which the controllers heard clearly the hijackers calling on Allah, "It was quite clear that these were Islamic terrorists," Bob recalled years later. "Although we couldn't put the attacks at bin Laden's feet immediately, one initially thought, yes, this is al Qaeda in some aspect."

At that first NSC meeting following the attacks, Bob described the initial stages of the FBI's investigation and the Bureau's attempts to identify the hijackers. The FBI already had solid identifications for almost all of the hijackers, Mueller reported. They had used their real names on their plane tickets, and the airline manifests revealed where they had been seated. Other members of the Security Council joined in, and we talked about how we planned to track down and pursue those responsible for, or otherwise involved in, the attacks. As the conversation proceeded, Mueller appeared deeply concerned, the consternation visible on his face. I remember him cautioning, "Wait a second. If we do some of these things, it may impair our ability to prosecute."

I interrupted Bob. "This is different." I paused and took a breath before continuing. "We simply can't let this happen again. Prosecution cannot be our priority. If we lose the ability to prosecute, that's fine; but we have to prevent the next attack. Prevention has to be our top priority."

I could see the president nodding slightly, so I continued. "The chief mission of U.S. law enforcement is to stop another attack and apprehend any accomplices and terrorists before they hit us again. If we can't bring them to trial, so be it."

Nobody grasped the message any quicker than Bob Mueller. Bob was more than eager to prioritize prevention, and from that moment, he led the charge.

At the time, I wasn't really sure what we would do with the terrorists when we caught them, especially if we couldn't bring them to trial in our country, but I knew that from 9/11 on, the rules of engagement had changed. That required a major shift on our part. The Justice Department could no longer merely focus on the pursuit and prosecution of criminals; our job was to prevent the attacks from happening, especially the sort of attacks that had leveled our buildings and killed nearly three thousand of our people.

As simple as it may seem, this new emphasis was a major shifting of priorities for the FBI. For years, the Bureau's attention had been centered on destroying organized crime, busting drug rings, pursuing the perpetrators of white-collar crimes such as corporate fraud or the theft of trade secrets, apprehending fugitives and incarcerating criminals, finding bank robbers, solving complicated crimes, and dealing with civil rights offenders. The FBI was the best agency in the world for assembling clues proving that "the butler did it in the pantry with a knife." But after 9/11, while we continued our pursuit of justice in all of the other criminal areas, the priority list had changed—prevention, the protection of our country from terrorism, was now the number one issue on everybody's mind.

FBI director Bob Mueller recalls, "No longer could we look at terrorism as a matter of law enforcement. We made a conscious shift from spending so much time at the crime scene and trying to bring people to justice—the nineteen terrorists were already dead—to thinking, gathering facts, and understanding everything we could in terms of preventing the next terrorist attack."

When Mueller took the oath of office as the director of the Federal Bureau of Investigation on September 4, 2001, no doubt he knew he faced enormous challenges in leading the Bureau's 27,000 employees. One week later, on September 11, those challenges had unbelievably magnified. Yet, as a former Marine officer who had served two tours in Vietnam and received the Bronze Star, two Commendation

Medals, the Purple Heart, and the Vietnamese Cross of Gallantry, Bob well understood the concepts of adapting and overcoming. He went to work simultaneously adapting the Bureau to the new mission of preventing future terrorist activities while overcoming numerous bureaucratic hurdles to restructuring our antiterrorism operations. And he did it all while launching the largest criminal investigation in the history of mankind.

Bob met the challenge head on, first of all by activating the twenty-four-hour-a-day Command Center at the FBI's Strategic Information Operations Center to track terrorists around the world. He deployed 7,000 special agents to the investigation, who tracked over a quarter of a million investigative leads and received close to a half million tips and phone calls.

Bob established new leadership positions to oversee counterintelligence and counterterrorism. He realigned the rest of the FBI's workforce, too, recruiting nine hundred new agents, many of whom possessed special skills in areas like computer technology, languages, engineering, and science. Most important, Bob shifted the FBI structure, culture, and mission to one of preventing terrorism.

On November 8, 2001, I publicly announced that we had made the shift from prosecution to prevention and were reorienting the Justice Department to prevent future acts of terrorism. I emphasized, "When terrorism threatens our future, we cannot afford to live in the past. We must focus on our core mission and responsibilities, understanding that the department will not be all things to all people. We cannot do everything we once did, because lives now depend on us doing a few things very well."

Crafting a blueprint for change and reshaping the FBI's priorities to focus on antiterrorism was no small matter, and I wanted the men and women of the Justice Department to understand that this was a long-term commitment that would affect all of us. "The attacks of September 11 have redefined the mission of the Department of

Justice," I assured them. "Defending our nation and defending the citizens of America against terrorist attacks is now our first and overriding priority."

In the years since 9/11, I've often been asked, "What was it like during those early days following the attack?"

One word says it all: intense.

Whether at SIOC, or the Justice Department, or at the White House, our efforts were intensely focused on preventing future attacks and bringing the attackers to justice. All other issues paled in comparison.

Most workday mornings after 9/11, I met with President Bush, along with National Security Advisor Condoleezza Rice, Chief of Staff Andrew Card, George Tenet, Bob Mueller, and other members of the National Security Council. When it was considered safe for the vice president and the president to be in the same room, Vice President Dick Cheney joined us as well.

Nearly every morning, the president wanted to know what precautions we were taking in regard to possible terrorist threats against a wide variety of potential targets—everything from the Capitol building to schools, malls, bridges, tunnels, any large gatherings of people at sporting events or other public buildings—assessing the odds about likely targets. The unspoken irony, of course, was that we were sitting in one of al Qaeda's primary targets, the White House. Yet President Bush never seemed to worry about his own safety. He was obsessed with keeping the American people as safe as possible without interfering in their daily lives any more than necessary.

In our morning meetings, we dealt almost exclusively with security matters, rarely broaching other topics or discussing nonterrorism issues. We engaged in almost no "small talk"; we certainly didn't come into the meeting and start discussing who won the big game last night. Nor did we discuss peripheral issues. We stuck to terrorism.

Each person in the meeting had more on his or her plate than they had time to handle, so the morning meeting was something that had to be done efficiently and effectively. At almost every meeting, the president called on various people for impromptu reports. He asked specific, pointed questions, often revealing that he had given significant thought to the matters on which he requested further information.

Imagine the war on terror as a large tapestry, comprised of a series of strands, each strand representing a report of some aspect of the overall picture, with new strands being added daily. The president seemed acquainted with all of them, frequently referring back and picking up a strand from two days or two months ago, naming a location or a specific terrorist and asking, "What's happening to that guy?" or "What's happening on that case?"

On any given morning, we never knew who would be queried about which part of the tapestry, so each of us came to the meetings as prepared as possible. Usually it was the FBI or the CIA doing the bulk of the reporting, while the remainder of the council listened carefully and analyzed the information. It was common for some individuals not to say a word throughout an entire meeting. These were not meetings in which everyone needed to be heard; this was unlike the normal "rule of Washington," that the meeting is not over until everyone has had their say.

The president's approach prompted a high level of care and thoroughness on the part of the cabinet and staff. When the president asked for information, he expected the Security Council members to give accurate answers and assessments. If he asked a question for which we did not know the answer, the normal way of dealing with it was to respond, "May I get that answer and get back to you?"

If one of us indicated that we were going to get back to the president with something, he expected us to be prepared at the next meeting. Early on, I got in the habit of reviewing my statements carefully with Bob Mueller as we traveled back to SIOC after the morning meetings. "Is there anything that I said I would do? Did we make any commitments to the president today that you or I must fulfill?"

With the president, you either fulfilled those commitments or you came back with the reason why you could not. You might not be able to have every answer by the next day, but when he expressed an interest in some area under the Justice Department's purview, we wanted to signal that we were responding to his concerns.

This was a management technique of President George W. Bush. It was the president's way of making sure that everything possible was being done to protect the country. Much of what we discussed in the early morning meetings would never see the light of a television camera, but it was information the president deemed necessary to make the many monumental decisions confronting him every day.

Sometimes we had to give the president bad news. For instance, the inspector general of the Justice Department discovered that six months after 9/11, a private Immigration and Naturalization Service contractor sent approvals to two men granting them permission to change their immigration status from "visitors" to "students." The two had enrolled at Huffman Aviation, a flight school in Venice, Florida. The two men then left the country twice after filing their applications, which meant that they had abandoned their request for a change of status, but the INS had not noticed. The two men were Mohamed Atta and Marwan al-Shehhi, two of the hijackers who killed themselves on 9/11.

Although the clearance letters arriving months after Atta and Alshehhi were dead proved inconsequential, they reflected a serious problem in managing the presence of aliens in America. The debacle was an embarrassment for the INS, and thus for the Justice Department as well.

Disappointment filled the president's face as we informed him of the situation, which was sure to make national news, and would no doubt be painted as a glaring example of our ineptitude. He was justifiably upset, but the president was not willing to dwell on mistakes or assess blame. He focused on making things right, keeping our nation safer and more secure.

The president was earnest about these matters. He maintained that same high level of intensity and focus throughout my tenure as attorney general. He got right to the point and remained direct; he refused to put up with any excuses on the part of the cabinet or staff members. He would not tolerate people not working together or sharing information that could be helpful to another department. Occasionally, he'd "take someone to the woodshed" if he felt that the person (or the entire group) was not giving 110 percent. Nevertheless, he was typically upbeat and optimistic, even as he picked his way through dangerous terrain, littered with land mines.

Of course, we did not discuss every facet of the fight against terrorism in those early morning meetings. We had plenty of other meetings during those whirlwind days, regarding what we should do about particular threats. Sometimes meetings started on one topic and then transitioned into a different subject matter, or into a type of gathering in which the Security Council discussed potential targets or other areas outside my expertise. When the discussion moved in those directions, I respectfully excused myself. I didn't need to know about those matters, and I didn't want to know. By remaining in the room, I would have allowed myself to be one more person than necessary who was privy to highly classified or sensitive information. Rather than do that, I'd ask to be excused.

"Where are you going, John?" somebody might ask.

"I'm getting out of here," I joked. "Tomorrow morning this stuff is going to be all over the *New York Times*, and if I'm not here, no one can accuse me of leaking it!"

Those morning meetings reflected an insight on the part of the George W. Bush that he rarely gets credit for having. The morning conferences were not simply "team meetings." They met a real need in the government's culture, assembling the various strands of the national defense and intelligence tapestry into one discernible picture. The president forced this meshing together on an individual basis even before Congress got around to passing legislation that facilitated the intelligence agencies doing something similar on an institutional basis. By the president bringing all of us to the White House every morning to discuss national security matters, he created an integration of the intelligence communities. I felt strongly that if we were going to effectively prevent another attack on our nation, we needed to do something similar among the military, the CIA, and the FBI.

On a dreary Friday, September 14, 2001, I joined President and Mrs. Bush and the other cabinet members and their spouses at the National Cathedral north of the White House for the special national day of mourning for the lives lost in the attack against our nation. Former presidents Bill Clinton, George H. W. Bush, and Jimmy Carter attended, as did most members of Congress. Speakers during the service included a rabbi, a Catholic cardinal, a Muslim cleric, and one of the most respected men in the nation, the Reverend Billy Graham. The president spoke briefly, too, and what he said was memorable. In what was to become a classic statement about the terrorists who killed so indiscriminately, President George W. Bush declared, "This conflict was begun on the timing and terms of others. It will end in a way, and at an hour, of our choosing."

At the close of the service, the entire congregation stood and sang "The Battle Hymn of the Republic." I felt a lump in my throat and was nearly overwhelmed with emotion as we sang the chorus penned by Julia Ward Howe during the Civil War, its lyrics laced with biblical allusions:

Glory! Glory, Hallelujah!
Glory! Glory, Hallelujah!
Glory! Glory, Hallelujah!
His truth is marching on.

As we exited the National Cathedral following the service, I couldn't help noticing that the rain had stopped, the skies were clear and blue, and a bright, warm sunshine bathed the church and the nation's capital.

The president hustled off to Air Force One, to spend the remainder of the day in New York visiting the rescue workers at Ground Zero and later some of the victims' family members. As he walked through the still-smoldering rubble of what had been the World Trade Center that afternoon, the rescue workers began shouting, "U-S-A! U-S-A! U-S-A!" Somebody gave the president a bullhorn, and he and a fireman climbed on top of a buried fire truck, where he tried speaking in the cavernous wreckage. Even with the help of the bullhorn, however, his voice seemed to barely be heard.

"We can't hear you!" one of the grime-covered rescue workers called out to President Bush.

The president shouted back, "I can hear you. The rest of the world hears you. And the people who knocked these buildings down will hear all of us soon!"

Against that enormously wrenching, emotion-charged backdrop, the president left for Camp David, Maryland, where he had "invited" his cabinet members and other top advisers and their spouses for a more concentrated version of our daily meetings on terrorism. By the time I arrived at Camp David for the Saturday, September 15, 2001, meeting, I had a plan in hand for a legislative package that would enhance the powers of law enforcement to fight terrorism.

The group assembled in Laurel Lodge at Camp David early that morning. Almost everyone had arrived the night before and felt at least somewhat rested. Good thing, because the all-day meeting was sure to be . . . intense. As usual, we began with prayer.

Then it was time for the reports and updates. The president started with Colin Powell and worked around the table. I was close to last, following Bob Mueller, who gave the FBI report. When my turn came, I turned the discussion in a slightly different direction.

"It is important to disrupt the terrorists right now, and in the immediate future," I emphasized, "but we need to remember these are

patient people. They waited eight years between their aggressive attacks on our homeland. We need a long-term strategy for dealing
with terrorism abroad, and a continuous, long-term program to go
after terrorists in our own country, because that's the kind of strategy
that they have in place."

"What do you suggest?" someone around the table queried.

"I'm so glad you asked," I responded. I pulled out my notes on the
proposed piece of legislation that members of the Justice Department
and I had been working on all week. It was the framework upon
which America would eventually hang the title USA PATRIOT Act.

CHAPTER TEN

TEARING DOWN THE WALL

Confronting the "Secret Spy Court"

⚜

I've always loved a good acronym. Our pre-work devotional time at the Justice Department, you may recall, was known as RAMP—Read, Argue, Memorize, and Pray. And although I've never done a study on such mundane matters, I'd guess that serving in civilian government affords the opportunity to use more initials than any profession other than the military. But while working on legislation to help fight terror, the Justice Department came up with an acronym that is truly outstanding; the initials not only spell a word; the word describes the true nature of the battle.

The USA PATRIOT Act—*Uniting and Strengthening America by Providing Appropriate Tools Required to Intercept and Obstruct Terrorism*—had been needed in the United States for a number of years, especially since the onset of high-tech crime and the rise of rogue groups of international terrorists. Unfortunately, it took 9/11 to bring the USA PATRIOT Act into law. To understand the intent of the act, it's helpful to recall the context in which it was born.

From the moment our nation came under attack, we were confronted with three simultaneous crises, the resolution of which would form three major components of the Justice Department's—and our entire country's—war on terrorism. First and foremost, we had to identify and disrupt any additional terrorist attacks. We didn't know when, where, or how the next attack would come, we knew only that al Qaeda wanted to hit us again. Years later, Michael Chertoff, currently the secretary of homeland security, acknowledged, "We didn't know if or when another wave was coming, but we felt sure that something else could hit us at any moment."[1]

We knew from past experience that al Qaeda favored multiple, simultaneous strikes. They also had a pattern of returning to targets they had missed previously. In a sense, that is what they had done at the World Trade Center. After inflicting a horrific blow in 1993, the terrorists came back to that same target on 9/11 to finish the devious plot they had started. We couldn't help but wonder what else they had targeted in Washington on 9/11. The Capitol? The White House? The CIA complex? The FBI? We knew that al Qaeda was loath to relent; they wouldn't give up. We had to dismantle them before they attacked us again.

The second crisis we confronted was in our own intelligence and law enforcement system. In the decades prior to 9/11, the U.S. Congress and Department of Justice officials had designed a system that actually made it more difficult for our nation to protect itself against terrorism. Indeed, it was a tragedy waiting to happen, a system destined to fail.

As recently as 1995, the Justice Department had arduously augmented the separation of law enforcement and intelligence agents, strengthening and reinforcing the "wall" between the two groups charged with the responsibility for keeping our nation secure. For example, prosecutors—who had the power to take potential terrorists off the streets—were generally restricted in their ability to communicate with or receive information from intelligence officials who were keeping terrorists under surveillance. It wasn't simply that the CIA could not share information with the FBI or the military; the FBI intelligence division could not even freely share information with the criminal arm of the Bureau. Ostensibly this dividing wall was put in place in an effort to make sure that the various agencies didn't taint evidence that could later be used in court to prosecute effectively cases involving foreign intelligence gathering. But Justice officials kept raising the invisible wall higher and higher. More about that later, but for now, let me say that by 2001, and especially after September 11, we knew we had to do something to change this situation—and we needed to do it fast.

The third crisis to be confronted in the immediate aftermath of 9/11 was one that had become increasingly more apparent every day since I had taken office as the attorney general. Namely, we had serious problems at the Federal Bureau of Investigation in regard to the inadequate technology, especially out in the field, and the morale of many agents and staff inside the Bureau.

It seemed to me that an inordinate number of people at the FBI were biding their time, merely coming to work every day and going through the motions. Shortly after I began as attorney general, I became aware of a number of people with "retirement clocks" on their desks, literally counting down the years, days, and hours till their retirement from the Bureau. The "when can I leave?" attitudes that accompanied those clocks could paralyze any company's success, but when they existed in the nation's top criminal investigative personnel, they could be deadly.

Complacency bred indifference. Numerous weapons assigned to the FBI and other Justice Department agencies were missing. So were an unknown number of computers. It was bad enough that the FBI was years behind when it came to the latest advances in computer technology, but making matters worse, shortly after I took office we discovered that too much of what we did have was being pilfered or lost. Laptop computers, especially, became easy targets. By March 2001, just a few weeks after taking office, I asked the Justice Department inspector general to launch an investigation concerning the rash of missing weapons and missing laptop computers, some of which might possibly contain classified information. The IG's initial report shocked me.

> Five Justice Department agencies, including the FBI, reported hundreds of lost or stolen weapons and computers.

The FBI, Immigration and Naturalization Service, Federal Bureau of Prisons, Drug Enforcement Administration and U.S. Marshals Service reported that 775 weapons and 400 laptop computers were missing. The FBI and INS reported the largest number of lost or stolen weapons: 212 and 539, respectively.[2]

According to the report, the FBI had lost the bulk of missing laptops: 317. Worse yet, the Bureau said that it did not know the classification level of at least 218 of the missing laptops. One missing laptop computer containing classified information could wreak havoc if it were in the hands of criminals or terrorists. We had more than two hundred out there *somewhere*, with information that might be horrendously damaging.

The Hanssen and McVeigh affairs had exposed these weaknesses and taken a toll, as had a spate of other lesser-known debacles, all of which led me to believe that the greatest law enforcement agency in the world had plenty of housekeeping of its own to do. We would never be able to deal with criminal and espionage threats abroad or in our own country if we didn't make some dramatic changes, and make them soon. Speaking of countdown clocks, the countdown clock for the next terrorist strike was already ticking, even though we did not know it.

Within two days of our picking up Bob Hanssen on February 18, 2001, I had ordered an investigative review of the FBI to be conducted by Judge William Webster, a man who had served as director of both the FBI and the CIA. The Webster Commission, as his investigation came to be known, examined every part of the FBI's operation, asking similar questions to those I had asked when I first learned about Hanssen's espionage: How could this happen? How could an FBI agent have gotten away with selling out our nation for more than twenty years? The Webster Commission studied the FBI for nearly a year; they went beyond asking the questions to discovering the answers. And when they brought in their report, the picture was not pretty. I'll say more about that in the pages ahead.

In the days after the September 11 attacks, we didn't have the luxury of working on prevention of future terrorist attacks, then tearing down the wall, and at our leisure or convenience redesigning the FBI. We needed to do all three simultaneously. All three issues demanded immediate and constant attention.

One of the first matters we had to address following 9/11 was the aforementioned "wall" between intelligence and law enforcement agencies. We had to find some way the two groups could legally and freely share the information they were gathering about terrorists and suspected terrorists. Indeed, it surprised most Americans to know that prior to 9/11 our nation's intelligence agents, military intelligence officers, and criminal law enforcement officers were not permitted to help one another by freely sharing information about their investigations. Average citizens were astounded to discover the invisible barrier existing between them. And agents and prosecutors knew that ignoring or crossing over the wall was a surefire way to damage your career in law enforcement or intelligence gathering.

In truth, I hadn't paid much attention to the wall's existence when I took office as attorney general. It was described to me simply as part of the law. Moreover, the courts had issued opinions that seemed to condone the wall, so I accepted that fact. In May 2001, Larry Thompson, the deputy attorney general, issued a directive with my support acknowledging that while the department guidelines that had created the wall in the first place were still in effect, he encouraged the FBI not to give undue credence to the wall itself by overestimating the barrier between criminal investigations and intelligence investigations.

Why was the wall erected in the first place? Originally it was developed as part of a reform movement in the post-Watergate years. Prior to the 1970s, operating on his constitutionally granted executive authority to defend the country, the president of the United States authorized the FBI and the Central Intelligence Agency and other intelligence-gathering agencies to use tools such as wiretaps and other forms of electronics to engage in surveillances when issues of national security were at stake.

Unfortunately, that surveillance was not always handled properly, nor was it limited to foreign intelligence gathering. It is now widely understood that FBI surveillance teams encroached upon the civil liberties of American citizens. Particularly egregious was the case of the civil rights leader Dr. Martin Luther King Jr., whom the FBI closely surveilled. The FBI engaged in extensive use of wiretaps and additional surveillance methods, some instances of which may have been highly questionable. These efforts were later reported as reflecting Director J. Edgar Hoover's personal wish to discredit King. Such surveillances revealed, more than anything, a flagrant misuse of power.

When news of cases such as Dr. King's and others became public, Congress created a special committee led by Idaho senator Frank Church to investigate and offer a plan for rectifying matters relating to surveillance and its possible abuse. Out of that committee came suggestions that eventually melded into the Foreign Intelligence Surveillance Act (FISA), which became law in 1978. Part of that same act also provided for the FISA Court, a special court to deal with the sensitive issues surrounding surveillances. The act provided guidelines regarding authorized surveillance deemed necessary for foreign intelligence gathering, while it also provided safeguards to protect law-abiding Americans from unauthorized surveillance by their government.

The FISA system worked well. When an agency determined that a foreign power or an agent of a foreign power might have evil intentions toward our country, a senior level representative of that agency went to the FISA Court to ask permission and show probable cause to place the suspect under surveillance. If the request was reasonable, permission was granted and an order issued.

Because of the highly sensitive nature of the requests coming before it, and the classified status of its rulings, the FISA Court and its activities remained extremely secretive. Meeting in a secure, soundproof room in an obscure location in Washington, D.C., seven judges gather as needed to decide the fate of certain national security federal wiretap and search-warrant requests. Until recent years, most Americans were unaware of the court's existence. In truth, most lawyers and many judges did not know about it either. Its decisions, however, profoundly shaped how our nation's intelligence agencies operated.

Over the years, attempting to place boundaries around the ability of our government to perform foreign intelligence, the FISA Court together with Congress and Justice Department officials added layer after layer of regulations to the initial standards. This was done as an effort to protect against incursions into U.S. citizens' civil liberties, by keeping separate the intelligence-gathering groups from the criminal prosecution groups. What if law enforcement officers used information gathered by intelligence agencies to harass or discredit American citizens? The abusive surveillance of Martin Luther King Jr. loomed large in the memories of civil liberties advocates.

Besides, nobody wanted to see a case prosecuted well, only to have the evidence thrown out of court because some element of it was tainted after having been obtained improperly. Perhaps the best way to prevent that from happening, proponents of the separation posited, was to maintain a wall between these two government departments; let each group do its own work, but keep communication between the two to a minimum. Thus the wall grew spontaneously, higher and higher, throughout the Reagan and Bush administrations, but reached its apex with the Clinton administration when Deputy Attorney General Jamie Gorelick issued a memo touting that the wall was even higher than the law required it to be.

It wasn't that agencies couldn't interact or share any information about a case. During his tenure as director of the FBI, Louis Freeh purposefully tried to implement ways the FBI and CIA could better share information. But it became increasingly more difficult to do so without jeopardizing the perceived chance of a conviction. As more and more regulations were stacked on top of the wall, the lines of demarcation became less clear concerning what information could be shared and what could not—even if that information had to do with potential terrorist activity.

U.S. Attorney Patrick Fitzgerald experienced the wall firsthand. He testified in a congressional hearing, "I was on a prosecution team in New York that began a criminal investigation of Usama Bin Laden in early 1996. The team had access to a number of sources. We could talk to citizens, local police officers, other U.S. government agencies, foreign police officers—even foreign intelligence personnel, and foreign citizens. We did all those things. We could even talk to al Qaeda members—and we did. But there was one group of people we were not permitted to talk to. Who? The FBI agents across the street from us assigned to a parallel intelligence investigation of Usama Bin Laden and al Qaeda. We could not learn what information they had gathered. That was 'the wall.'"[3]

Not only did the wall prevent information sharing among the military, the CIA, and the FBI, it existed within the FBI itself. Agents pursuing cases involving surveillance authorized by FISA could not readily share information with agents or prosecutors working criminal investigations. The wall impeded the flow of information both ways: the information gathered by agents tracking a criminal case could not be passed along to an agent working on a counterintelligence investigation. While some communications were legal, the rules surrounding such interactions were extremely complex. After a while, most agents decided that the best way to stay out of hot water was to err on the side of caution and not share any information about intelligence cases at all. Why jeopardize your career if it was simply going to get you written up with a poor review?

Consider this hypothetical scenario: two agents—one working on the intelligence side of the wall and knowing that a potential terrorist was living in your town, and the other on the criminal side who had the capability of prosecuting that terrorist and putting him behind bars—could go out for lunch with both having information that could help the other, but by law they were not allowed to share that information. That's how ridiculously the regulations were perceived by 2001 when I became the attorney general.

In August 2001, my deputy attorney general, Larry Thompson, recognized the danger of these developments and issued his memo to Department of Justice personnel encouraging them to devalue the wall. Again, he reminded agents on both sides of the wall, "The 1995 procedures remain in effect today." But then Larry made the first sledgehammer blow to the wall by mandating that individuals involved in intelligence investigations who came across information relating to a felony federal offense should immediately provide notice of the offense to people on the criminal side of the house. It was a first step toward taking down the wall, but unfortunately it was not enough. Looking back, Larry said later, "In retrospect, I wish I'd have done a lot more to try to tear down that wall."[4]

Ironically, in August 2001, an FBI agent, frustrated at encountering the wall, courageously bucked the system, warning about the dangerous constraints the wall placed upon Americans who were doing their best to protect our people.

This agent had good reason to be concerned. Two and a half weeks before 9/11, he was tracking two known al Qaeda terrorists, Khalid al-Mihdhar and Nawaf al-Hazmi, who were already in the United States. The two terrorists were living openly, using their real names while attending flight school, obtaining California identification cards, and even earning frequent flyer points. But the agent couldn't track them by himself because he needed access to computer information available only from the FBI's criminal investigators. In response to legal advice about the wall, the FBI refused to allow its criminal agents to cross over the barrier to help the intelligence agent. The agent received a stern e-mail from the Bureau stating, "If al-Mihdhar is located, the interview must be conducted by an intel agent. A criminal agent CAN NOT be present at the interview. This case, in its entirety, is based on intel. If at such time as information is developed indicating the existence of a substantial federal crime, that information will be passed over the wall according to the proper procedures and turned over for follow-up criminal investigation."[5]

The agent returned a message that bristled at the ban against using criminal law enforcement information to help in such a potentially important investigation. Written days before 9/11, the agent's words seem eerily prophetic:

> Someday someone will die and, wall or not, the public will not understand why we were not more effective and throwing every resource we had at certain "problems." Let's hope the National Security Law Unit [the lawyers whose advice was followed] will stand behind their decisions then, especially since the biggest threat to us now, UBL [Usama Bin Laden], is getting the most protection.[6]

Sadly, the FBI agent's warning fell on deaf ears and blinded eyes. He was told that headquarters was also frustrated with the issues surrounding the wall, but rules were rules. Nobody found al-Mihdhar or al-Hazmi. As far as I know, nobody has ever found their remains either, since they flew American Airlines Flight 77 into the Pentagon. Maybe—and admittedly, it is a big maybe—had we not been so concerned about perceived legal problems of mixing intelligence and criminal investigations, somebody might have connected the dots well enough to have gotten to those men before they got to us. And maybe somebody would have noticed that they had shared addresses with Mohamed Atta, the terrorist who flew a commercial airliner into the North Tower of the World Trade Center, and his cohort Marwan al-Shehhi, who piloted the plane that slammed into the South Tower. Maybe.

We know this for a fact: for two and a half weeks in late August and early September, we knew the names of at least two al Qaeda terrorists who were here to kill us. And we missed them.

Similarly, we missed Zacarias Moussaoui. Mistakenly referred to as "the twentieth hijacker," Moussaoui was nonetheless an al Qaeda operative in the United States. He had trained in a terrorist camp in Afghanistan, and received large sums of money from Ramzi Binalshibh, one of the 9/11 financiers. He had been attending flight school in Eagan, Minnesota, when his instructor had misgivings about his motivations for wanting to learn to fly. The school shared its concerns with the FBI, and Moussaoui was detained on an immigration violation on August 16, 2001. When the Minnesota field office of the FBI sought to obtain a warrant to search Moussaoui's computer, the request was denied because FBI officials feared breaching the wall.

Homeland Security Secretary Michael Chertoff believes to this day that 9/11 might have been averted had a warrant been allowed. "Had we known a week before—had Moussaoui told us, or had we gotten into his files, that would have given us some information that may have made a difference in preventing 9/11. It seemed obvious to me—his flight training, the martial arts, and then when we put the money piece together, we discovered that there was a common funding stream to Moussaoui and some of the hijackers."[7] As prosecutors later argued in convicting Moussaoui, the information he had and withheld would have substantially sharpened the pre-9/11 picture for investigators.

Although it is impossible to know for sure, had a warrant been granted, FBI agents might have found the information in Moussaoui's possession that would have linked him to the financial flow of al Qaeda money that was used to pay expenses for the other hijackers as well as himself.

With the president's mandate in mind—"Don't ever let this happen again"—I knew that our intelligence and criminal prosecution people had to be able to work together to combat the terrorists among us, as well as those in the mountains of Afghanistan. Our investigators needed some expanded legal authority from our own government if we were ever going to pursue the terrorists on even terms.

So, with smoke still rising from the Twin Towers and other crash sites, alongside a team of people at the Justice Department I worked night and day to put a piece of legislation together that would give us the clout we needed to track down and arrest suspected terrorists. We were continually reminded of the importance of our work, as we grappled with the emotions evoked by the 9/11 memorial services. Graphic images filled television screens again and again, the planes hitting the buildings; how many times did we see those horrific moments replayed? Equally moving were the reports of rescue workers attempting to extricate people from the rubble, and listening for any signs of life. Each image I saw of the still-smoldering Ground Zero, or view of the devastation at the Pentagon, or report of another poignant story of the lives lost on United Flight 93, spurred me on and motivated me to keep working.

The 9/11 attacks occurred on a Tuesday. By Saturday, we had a full-blown legislative proposal. Part of the reason we were able to move so quickly was that a number of the provisions had been proposed to Congress in 1996, and Congress had rejected them. They hadn't wanted to give law enforcement that much power. But after the bloodshed of 9/11, few congressmen did not want to be aggressive in pursuing terrorists.

The bill was introduced by Wisconsin congressman James Sensenbrenner. It took six weeks of concentrated work with Congress to refine the bill and shape it into something that everyone could live with, and on October 26, 2001, President Bush signed into law the "Uniting and Strengthening America by Providing Appropriate Tools Required to Intercept and Obstruct Terrorism Act," otherwise known as the USA PATRIOT Act. Only one person voted against the act in the Senate—my principled friend Russ Feingold, who consistently voted against what he considered unacceptable government intrusions. It passed with strong bipartisan support in the House (357 to 66). The law provided our nation's law enforcement, national defense, and intelligence agencies with new or enhanced tools to disrupt, detain, and bring terrorists and other dangerous criminals to justice.

First, the Patriot Act facilitated information sharing and cooperation among government agencies. To put it bluntly, the act tore down the "wall," the legal barrier that prevented law enforcement, intelligence, and national defense communities from talking and coordinating their work to protect the American people and our national security.

Never again should our nation's efforts to protect its citizens from attacks such as those on 9/11 be restricted by boxes on an organizational chart. Because the wall has been torn down today, police officers, FBI agents, federal prosecutors, and intelligence officials can team together to uncover terrorist plots before they come to fruition.

Does the Patriot Act work? You bet! Prosecutors and investigators shared information in investigating the defendants in the "Virginia Jihad" case. This prosecution involved members of the Dar al-Arqam Islamic Center, who trained for jihad ("struggle" in Arabic, though usually interpreted to mean "holy war") in northern Virginia. Eight of these individuals traveled to terrorist training camps in Pakistan or Afghanistan between 1999 and 2001. These individuals are associates of a violent Islamic extremist group known as Lashkar-e-Taiba, which operates in Pakistan and Kashmir, and has ties to al Qaeda. As a result of using information obtained through electronic surveillance, prosecutors were able to bring charges against these individuals. Six of the defendants pleaded guilty, and three were convicted in March 2004 of charges including conspiracy to levy war against the United States and conspiracy to provide material support to the Taliban. The nine defendants received sentences ranging from a prison term of four years to life imprisonment. In this particular case, it would have been much more difficult to arrest, charge, and convict these terrorists had agents and prosecutors not been able to share information.

In clear terms the Patriot Act allowed the sharing of information that might help "connect the dots." For the first time in twenty-three years, law enforcement and intelligence agents were authorized to co-ordinate terrorism investigations without fear of running afoul of the law. Almost immediately this new ability to communicate informa-tion led directly to the disruption of terrorist plots, leading to numer-ous arrests, and eventually to prosecutions and convictions.

Ironically, the Patriot Act was largely made up of legal tools that were already in place and available to other areas of law enforcement but weren't available in the fight against terror. For example, in the 1980s, drug dealers developed a habit of throwing away their phones regularly. They had discovered that it often took law officers more than a week to get a new court order to monitor their phone calls on a particular telephone. If the drug dealers changed to a new phone every so often, that could give them at least a week to operate without surveillance. In response, the U.S. Congress authorized wiretapping of *individuals* rather than a physical *instrument* or phone. Conse-quently, if a drug dealer switched phones, the surveillance could switch as well, without officers having to go back to court for a new court order. The slang name for the newly mobile wiretap that fol-lowed the *person* not the *phone* was the "roving wire tap."

The Patriot Act did something similar for agencies fighting against terrorism. While allowing for robust surveillance, it also al-lowed for *roving* surveillance. This has been a much maligned por-tion of the act, causing some people to worry that the government is roaming around their neighborhoods with cameras and tape record-ers, tapping wires or looking in windows. After all, "roving wiretaps" sound so sinister.

In fact, this aspect of the act simply gives intelligence agents and law enforcement officers the court-ordered ability to change with a suspected terrorist when he or she switches phones, without having to go back to court to get a new warrant. Roving wiretaps still require a court order and still require the supervision of a member of the fed-eral judiciary. But the roving wiretaps allow agents to track continuously terrorism suspects who have become much more adept at camouflaging their telephone communications.

Also included in the Patriot Act was authority that allowed us to go after the purse strings of potential terrorists. The saying "Follow the money" is applicable with terrorists, too. Somebody finances international terrorism, and some of that money flows through U.S. banks. Prior to 9/11, we could do relatively little to impede or impound funds that were moving through the terrorist financial network. The Patriot Act gave us the ability to investigate and prosecute anyone who financially supports terrorism or funnels money to terrorists. This is a critical tool in choking off the supply lines of blood money and dismantling the financial network that makes terrorism possible.

In many similar ways, the Patriot Act has played a key part in protecting Americans from the deadly plots of terrorists dedicated to destroying our way of life. As I mentioned, the act allows investigators and law enforcement officials to use tools to fight terrorism that have been used for decades to fight organized crime and drug dealers. These tools have been reviewed repeatedly and approved by the courts. Many Americans were surprised to learn that they had not previously been available in the fight against terror. During the Senate floor debate about the USA PATRIOT Act, Senator Joseph Biden expressed his surprise at learning how the hands of the FBI had been tied. "The FBI could get a wiretap to investigate the Mafia, but they could not get one to investigate terrorists. To put it bluntly, that was crazy! What's good for the mob should be good for terrorists."[8]

Even before the Patriot Act, courts could permit law enforcement officials to conduct electronic surveillance to investigate many non-terrorism crimes, such as drug crimes, mail fraud, and passport fraud. But the Patriot Act enabled investigators to gather information looking into the broader, full range of terrorism-related crimes, including chemical weapons offenses, the use of weapons of mass destruction, and the killing of Americans abroad, as well as the various means of financing terrorism.

Imagine this scenario: Terrorists sneak a nuclear bomb into a major U.S. city and threaten to detonate it. The FBI learns that an individual has the plans in his house that describe the location and the detonation procedures for the device. The FBI searches the house without notifying the individual who lives there, and the agents discover the plan revealing the location of the nuclear device. Yet the FBI would not want the person living at the house to know that he had been searched until agents had found and disarmed the nuclear bomb. Otherwise, with one phone call, a simple signal, perhaps, the person at the house could notify his coconspirators to detonate the bomb before the agents would have a chance to interrupt the plan.

Permission and procedures for such investigations that can be conducted without tipping off the terrorists are now provided through the Patriot Act. Obviously, if suspected criminals are tipped off too early to an investigation, they might flee, destroy evidence, intimidate or kill witnesses, cut off contact with associates, or take other action to evade arrest. Consequently, federal courts have long allowed law enforcement to delay for a limited time when the subject will be told that a judicially approved search warrant has been executed. Notice is always provided, but the court-sanctioned, reasonable delay gives law enforcement time to identify the suspect's associates, eliminate immediate threats, and sometimes coordinate the arrests of multiple individuals without tipping them off beforehand.

This feature of the Patriot Act proved invaluable in the spring of 2003, when a court-authorized delayed-notification search warrant allowed investigators to gain evidence of a plan to ship unmanned aerial vehicle components to Pakistan. The UAVs would have been capable of carrying up to two-hundred pounds of cargo, potentially explosives, while being guided by a laptop computer. Two hundred pounds of explosives is more than enough to destroy a large building. Delaying notice to the suspects that investigators had obtained a warrant to search e-mail communications allowed the investigators to defer making an arrest until all the shipments of UAV components had been located. The suspect was then apprehended and pleaded guilty.

One of the more controversial elements of the Patriot Act allows federal agents to ask the FISA Court for an order to obtain business records including bank records, library records, or other items such as credit card receipts that might be relevant to national security terrorism cases. Examining business records often provides key information and can help solve a wide range of crimes. For instance, investigators might seek records from a hardware store or a chemical plant to find out whether a suspected terrorist bought materials that might be used in making a bomb. Agents may seek bank records in an effort to ascertain whether a suspected financier is sending money to terrorists.

While it is true that terrorists sometimes use public libraries and Internet sources to gather information about bomb-making, as well as to communicate with other cell members, the U.S. Justice Department has rarely used this portion of the Patriot Act to garner information—although it could.

Yes, in theory, under the Patriot Act an order can be issued to discover which books a suspect checked out of your local library, or what Internet sites such a person visited at the library. But if you are not searching out information on how to build a bomb, or poison a water supply, or some other act that might look suspiciously like a terrorist plot, there's little chance of your records being reviewed. The court can issue such orders only after the Justice Department demonstrates that the records are sought for an authorized investigation to obtain foreign intelligence information that has to do with a threat of international terrorism or clandestine intelligence activities. And such surveillance cannot be done solely regarding a U.S. citizen's activities protected by the First Amendment. (So feel free to encourage your friends and family members to check this book out of your library.)

The Patriot Act updated the law to counter new technologies and new threats. We no longer have to fight a digital-age battle with antique analog weapons, not to mention legal authorities left over from the era of rotary telephones. This is especially helpful when it is necessary under court orders to monitor e-mail. It has also been valuable where existing technologies can reveal the source, whereabouts, or destination of communications, such as those dialed by or received by telephones. The terrorist community is taking aggressive advantage of new technologies. The defense of life and liberty requires that law enforcement does the same:

"I am a Jew, my mother is a Jew," said the *Wall Street Journal* reporter Daniel Pearl moments before Islamic terrorists savagely sliced his throat, recording their barbarism on videotape.[9] When investigating the murder, law enforcement drew from one of the act's new authorities to use high-tech means to identify and locate some of the killers. Four Islamic militants were captured, charged, and convicted of the brutal slaying. In Pakistani court, British-born Ahmed Omar Saeed Sheikh was sentenced to death, and his three cohorts were sentenced to life prison terms.[10]

Other features of the act increased the penalties for those convicted of committing acts of terrorism, whether the convicted person actually plants a bomb or simply pays for the ingredients and parts with which it was built. Both are considered terrorists by our law now.

Harboring terrorists, a new offense, prohibits knowingly harboring or helping someone who has committed terrorist acts, such as the destruction of aircraft; the use of nuclear, chemical, or biological weapons or any weapons of mass destruction; the bombing of government property; the sabotaging of nuclear facilities; and air piracy.

Thanks to the Patriot Act we now have more severe penalties for those who commit terrorist crimes. Previously, many terrorism statutes did not specifically prohibit engaging in conspiracies to commit terror offenses.[11] They do now.

Altogether, the act President Bush signed into law provided

"more than one thousand antiterrorism measures, including the re-vamped intelligence sharing, to a raft of anti–money laundering powers."[12] The authorities substantially enhanced our ability to pre-vent, investigate, and prosecute acts of terror.

During the first week following 9/11, we also began doing press briefings from the FBI building. I was determined to keep the public informed for two main reasons: one, to assure people about what we were doing; second, to enlist the public in providing the information we needed to stop terror. "Report anything suspicious," I advised.

As part of that effort, one of the early debates we had with the FBI concerned whether or not we should release photos of the hijackers. We had photos of all nineteen of them by now, so undoubtedly some-body would have seen them prior to 9/11. If we could find out where they were operating, that might point us to the people behind the at-tacks. To the contrary, the Bureau felt that by putting the terrorists' pictures on television, we might color people's perceptions. More people would think that they had seen the hijackers than actually had.

When we finally convinced the FBI to air the photos, we were in-undated with leads. Hundreds of thousands of people responded with information, some of it quite valuable. Of course, we were also swamped with false leads, as well as all sorts of wacky information. But that was okay. If we received only one solid lead for every hun-dred or so that came in, it might be that one lead that could prevent the next attack. So calling on the public to help us made good sense. "If something looks suspicious, let us know about it," we told people.

Certainly, bringing the public into the fracas also put more "noise into the system." Potential terrorists could not operate with impunity because they knew that no matter where they worked, somebody was watching. This was a conscious part of the Justice Department's strat-egy to prevent more attacks. And everybody, to a person, worried that more attacks could be on the way.

And they were.

ENDNOTES

1. Interview with Michael Chertoff, June 1, 2006.
2. Information based on the U.S. Justice Department inspector general's June 2002 audit and report. The IG's audit for the Bureau of Prisons, the Drug Enforcement Administration, and the Marshal Service covered weapons and laptops reported lost or stolen between October 1999 and August 2001, while the FBI audit reflected property reported missing between October 1999 and January 2002. For the complete report, see http://www.govexec.com/dailyfed/0802/080502m1.htm.
3. *Preserving Life and Liberty: The Record of the U.S. Department of Justice 2001–2005* (Dept. of Justice Publication, U.S. Department of Justice), p. 9.
4. Interview with former U.S. Deputy Attorney General Larry Thompson, June 9, 2006.
5. Stewart Baker, "Wall Nuts: The Wall Between Intelligence and Law Enforcement Is Killing Us," *Slate*, December 31, 2003; www.slate.com/id/2093344.
6. The Malaysia Hijacking and September 11th: Joint Hearing Before the Senate and House Select Intelligence Committees (Sept. 20, 2002), written statement of New York special agent of the FBI. This information was included in U.S. FISA Court of Review Opinion, Sealed Case Number 02-001, decided November 18, 2002, p. 27.
7. Interview with Michael Chertoff, June 1, 2006.
8. Senator Joseph Biden's comments on the floor of the U.S. Senate; recorded in the U.S. *Congressional Record*, October 25, 2001.
9. Leon Wieseltier, "The Death of Daniel Pearl," *New Republic* (online version), February 25, 2002; www.tnr.com/doc.mhtml?i=express&s=weiseltier022502.
10. "Daniel Pearl Killers Appeal," *CBS News*, July 17, 2002; www.cbsnews.com/stories/2002/05/31/attack.
11. Portions of this material regarding the USA PATRIOT Act have been adapted from U.S. Department of Justice press releases and the book *Preserving Life and Liberty: The Record of the U.S. Department of Justice 2001–2005*, p. 5–11.
12. Liz Halloran, "One More Act for the Patriot Act," *U.S. News & World Report*, January 23, 2006, p. 30.

CHAPTER ELEVEN

TERRORISTS AMONG US

The Hunt for American al Qaeda

❦

The thought that al Qaeda terrorists could be living right next door to us never crossed the minds of most Americans prior to 9/11. Terrorists were over *there*, someplace far away, in countries with unusual names we could hardly pronounce, certainly not in Orlando, Buffalo, San Diego, or *Peoria*, of all places!

"How will it play in Peoria?" was the query often attributed to comedian Groucho Marx when road-testing his vaudeville shows. Over the years, the question became a common phrase to Americans when asking how an idea or product would be accepted by the American public. The midsize central Illinois city has come to represent quintessential American mainstream culture. How ironic that a man with direct ties to al Qaeda would set up operations in Peoria, in the heart of our nation.

Ali Saleh Kahlah al-Marri arrived in the United States from his native Qatar on September 10, 2001, less than twenty-four hours before the first plane struck the World Trade Center. Like many other suspected terrorists, al-Marri found easy access to our homeland through academic pursuits. He originally entered the United States in 1983, enrolling at Bradley University in Peoria, Illinois, in the summer of 1987, and earning a bachelor of science degree, with a major in management and administration in 1991. Following his graduation, al-Marri returned to his homeland of Qatar. He came back to the United States in

May 2000, and then traveled to Saudi Arabia. When he returned to Illinois, he brought along a wife from Saudi Arabia and five children.

Al-Marri came to the attention of federal agents when, according to the *New York Daily News*, "shortly after the 9/11 attacks, the Peoria FBI office received a lead from its Indianapolis office regarding a steamer chest that al-Marri had shipped to the United States. The Peoria office also had gotten a call from a salesman at U.S. Cellular who expressed concerns regarding al-Marri's cell phone account."[1]

When FBI agents interviewed al-Marri at his home in Peoria on October 2, 2001, they did not know about his involvement with al Qaeda, his training at an al Qaeda camp in Afghanistan, or his swearing of an oath of loyalty and a pledge of service to Osama bin Laden. Nor did the agents know that al-Marri had taken his commitment a step further, offering to lay down his life as a martyr for bin Laden.

The agents did, however, discover that al-Marri's Social Security number was being used by two other people, and he had written two completely different dates on his college enrollment forms under his date of birth. Al-Marri said that he was unaware of any problems with his Social Security number and explained the two birthdates by claiming that in Qatar birthdates were listed by year only.

During the initial FBI interview with al-Marri, one of the FBI agents asked al-Marri when he had previously traveled to the United States.

Prior to his arrival on September 10, he had last been in the United States during the 1983 to 1991 time frame, al-Marri told the agent. In fact, al-Marri had returned to the U.S. in May 2000.

Already suspicious, the FBI agents' interest piqued even more when they discovered that al-Marri had an alias, "Abdullakareem A. Al-muslam," under which he operated a phony company, "AAA Carpet." The company's "business office" was located at room 209, in the Time Out Motel in Macomb, Illinois, a motel at which al-Marri had stayed.

The agents left al-Marri after their initial interview, but returned on December 11, 2001. In the meantime, they had further investigated al-Marri's activities and discovered that he had indeed traveled from Peoria to Saudi Arabia and back in 2000. He had lied to the FBI, and on that basis alone they could detain and charge him. But the agents didn't move too quickly. They suggested that they had some questions for him, and asked him to accompany them to the FBI office in Peoria. Al-Marri consented.

While the agents waited for al-Marri, they asked if they could look around his apartment. Again, al-Marri agreed. The agents noticed a laptop computer and asked al-Marri if he'd bring his computer along as well.

Agents looking into al-Marri's telephone usage discovered that he attempted to make international telephone calls using pay phones and Quest calling cards to a man in the United Arab Emirates as well as other calls to Pakistan and Saudi Arabia. Al-Marri's cellular phone was activated in cells near the sites of the calling card calls, made from Illinois locations including Peoria, Springfield, and Chicago.

The calls in the UAE were to the telephone of Mustafa Ahmed al-Hawsawi, one of the 9/11 financiers—the same man who had funneled thousands of dollars to and from the nineteen 9/11 hijackers. Al-Marri's ties to al Qaeda were becoming alarming. According to court documents, al-Hawsawi's phone number in the United Arab Emirates had also been called by Mohamed Atta, the ringleader of the 9/11 hijackers. When the agents asked al-Marri if he knew al-Hawsawi or had made the telephone calls, al-Marri denied knowing al-Hawsawi and denied making the calls.

Originally arrested as a material witness to the 9/11 attacks, he also had an immigration detainer on him for violating his student visa. In addition, al-Marri was soon criminally charged with making "materially false, fictitious, and fraudulent statements and representations . . . to an agent of the Federal Bureau of Investigation," specifically noting the false claim that he had not entered the United States between 1991 and September 2001.[2] A second count charged al-Marri with lying to the FBI regarding telephone calls to Mustafa Ahmed al-Hawsawi. Al-Marri was held at the Peoria County Jail for several weeks, before he was taken to New York and incarcerated at the Metropolitan Correctional Center, a short walk from Ground Zero.

Although the FBI was not yet aware of the extent of al-Marri's involvement with al Qaeda, they held him as part of our concerted strategy to use any violation of the law to detain terrorists and suspected terrorists before they could harm Americans.

One of the virtues of the "spit on the sidewalk" policy was that we sometimes detained a person who was an important player in the overall war on terror, yet we didn't realize it at the time. All we knew was that he had spit on the sidewalk. Such was the case with Ali Saleh Kahlah al-Marri.

The FBI soon discovered more information about the young-looking, thirty-seven-year-old Bradley University graduate student. When the investigators opened al-Marri's computer carrying case, they found two pieces of paper on which were written thirty-six credit card numbers, along with the names of the account holders. While the expiration dates for some of the cards had passed, seventeen accounts were valid; none of the cards were issued in al-Marri's name. He was formally charged with credit card fraud on January 28, 2002.

Al-Marri certainly had an avid interest in numbers. Besides the unauthorized credit cards, in searching his home agents found falsified identification documents and several phony Social Security numbers. He also had computer software programs frequently used by hackers in their efforts to gather illegally personal information from unsuspecting victims' computers. This raised speculation among some officials that perhaps al-Marri planned to hack his way into the U.S. banking system to wipe out balances and otherwise wreak havoc with banking records and damage the U.S. economy.

The *New York Daily News* reported that "FBI computer expert Connie Lawler analyzed everything on al-Marri's 80-gigabyte hard drive. In addition to the anti-American, pro-Taliban rhetoric, she found files containing more than 1,750 credit card numbers. None of the numbers belonged to al-Marri."[3] Also found on his computer were lectures in Arabic by Osama bin Laden and photos of the 9/11 attacks. An almanac was discovered in al-Marri's home with marked pages depicting major U.S. dams, reservoirs, waterways, and railroads.

A computer file designated "chem" contained al-Marri's bookmarked Internet Web sites, including fact sheets for hazardous substances. Other sites provided information regarding the necessary amounts of certain chemicals that might be dangerous to life. Still other Web sites on al-Marri's computer related to weaponry and satellite equipment.

Although the FBI didn't know of al-Marri's significance when they first interviewed him, slowly but surely they became convinced that al-Marri was in fact part of an al Qaeda advance team, sent to the United States to facilitate the next round of terrorist attacks. Two separate detainees testified about al-Marri's loyalty to bin Laden and his training with al Qaeda at bin Laden's al-Farouq paramilitary camp in Afghanistan. After his al Qaeda training in the use of poisons and highly toxic chemicals, al-Marri returned to the United States, along with his wife and children, ostensibly to pursue a graduate degree in computers while living in Peoria. Several months later, a detained senior al Qaeda leader, whose credibility had been well established, identified al-Marri as an al Qaeda "sleeper operative," someone inside the country, lying low but working all the while for the enemy. The senior operative informed interrogators that al-Marri was tasked with providing support to newly arriving terrorists for the *next wave* of attacks inside the United States. With what we know now, preparations for that second wave may have been initiated before 9/11.

Al Qaeda's original attack plan for 9/11 was conceived as a two-part plot—to hit the East Coast of the United States *and* the West Coast. The initial plan included strikes at New York, Washington, and Los Angeles. Osama bin Laden himself decided that the plot should focus on the East Coast only, and that the plot for the attack on the West Coast should be held in abeyance as a follow-on attack.

This second wave was planned meticulously by Khalid Shaikh Mohammed (KSM), the same top al Qaeda strategist who planned the 9/11 attacks. In October 2001, KSM, working with the Southeast Asian terrorist "Hambali" (whose real name is Nurjaman Riduan Isamuddin), recruited and began training four Southeast Asian terrorist cell members. This time the terrorists planned to fly an airliner into the tallest building on the West Coast, the U.S. Bank building, formerly known as Library Tower, a seventy-three-story office building in the heart of downtown Los Angeles.

After the terrorist operatives were recruited by KSM and Hambali, they met with Osama bin Laden and swore oaths of loyalty to him. When they returned from Afghanistan to work further with Hambali in Southeast Asia, they began making preparations for the West Coast attack.

I believe KSM had planned to use al-Marri to help facilitate this next wave of attacks focused on Los Angeles. Al Qaeda sent al-Marri to the United States on September 10, 2001. He was back in place in Peoria, prior to the initial attacks, and then KSM began planning the second wave. After al-Marri was detained in 2001, I believe it frustrated al Qaeda's plan for new attacks.

The Los Angeles plot unraveled due to international cooperation among America's allies. When the cell leader was arrested in February 2002, the other three members of the team believed the plot had been canceled. They, too, were arrested and taken into custody shortly thereafter. Hambali, the terrorists' trainer, turned his attention to planning a 2002 attack on a nightclub in Bali. That strike, unfortunately, was not intercepted, and two hundred people died on the anniversary of the attack on the USS *Cole*. Hambali was captured in August 2003.

Al-Marri's case illustrates the value of the "spit on the sidewalk" strategy. At first, al-Marri was held in civilian custody, to be tried for criminal offenses. Al-Marri rejected numerous offers to improve his lot by cooperating with the FBI investigators and providing information. He insisted on becoming a "hard case."

Consequently, on June 23, 2003, President Bush, based on substantial, verifiable evidence of al-Marri's al Qaeda involvement, designated al-Marri an "enemy combatant," and he was transferred to military custody. Such designation removed al-Marri from the criminal justice system and meant that he could be kept on that basis at least until the war against al Qaeda was over.

In a written designation of al-Marri as an enemy combatant, parts of President Bush's statement included that:

> Al-Marri is, and at the time that he entered the United States in September 2001 was, an enemy combatant;
>
> Mr. al-Marri is closely associated with al Qaeda, an international terrorist organization with which the United States is at war;
>
> Mr. al-Marri engaged in conduct that constituted hostile and war-like acts, including conduct in preparation for acts of international terrorism that had the aim to cause injury to or adverse effect on the United States;
>
> Mr. al-Marri possesses intelligence, including intelligence about personnel and activities of al Qaeda that, if communicated to the U.S., would aid U.S. efforts to prevent attacks by al Qaeda on the United States or its armed forces, other governmental personnel, or citizens;
>
> Mr. al-Marri represents a continuing, present, and grave danger to the national security of the United States, and detention of Mr. al-Marri is necessary to prevent him from aiding al Qaeda in its efforts to attack the United States or its armed forces, other governmental personnel, or citizens. . . .[4]

Another enemy combatant was José Padilla, who presented a threat similar to that of al-Marri, except for a major difference between the two men: Padilla was a U.S. citizen. Born in Brooklyn, Padilla and his family had moved to Chicago early in his life. A former street gang member, Padilla was in and out of detention several times during his youth, serving time on aggravated battery and armed robbery charges in Illinois and then arrested over illegal use of a gun in Florida, later being convicted of aggravated assault. Although as a boy he had attended a Catholic church along with his mother and siblings, after his stint in prison he espoused Islam.

Published reports tell us much about Padilla, as does information declassified in June 2004 and made public by Deputy Attorney General James Comey. We know that in 1998 Padilla traveled from Miami to Cairo, Egypt, where he spent eighteen months. In March 2000, he joined a religious pilgrimage to Saudia Arabia, where he met an al Qaeda recruiter from Yemen who offered to sponsor him for al Qaeda training in Afghanistan.

In June 2000, Padilla made the trip, going by way of Pakistan, and then on to Afghanistan. He later told investigators that his travels were sponsored by friends interested in his education. Quite an education it was. The FBI found Padilla's July 24, 2000, application form to the al Qaeda training camp, along with one hundred other applicants. The form includes the information that Padilla is an American citizen who speaks Spanish and Arabic as well as English.

In a jihad camp, Padilla was trained in the use of weapons such as an AK-47, G-3, Uzi, and other machine guns as well as explosives. He met with known al Qaeda leaders such as Mohammed Atef, who although initially skeptical, became convinced and intrigued by the young American's willingness to betray his homeland. According to reports, Padilla also discussed with his al Qaeda mentors blowing up hotels, apartment buildings, and gas stations in the United States.

In early 2001, Padilla walked into the American consulate in Karachi, Pakistan, to request help. He had lost his passport in the Karachi marketplace, he claimed, and he needed to secure a new one.

It was a classic act of al Qaeda tradecraft designed to eliminate suspicious travel and cover the nature of the traveler's past visits to foreign countries. The consulate granted Padilla the passport.

Upon completion of his training, Padilla went to Egypt for two months before returning to Afghanistan in June 2001. During this trip, according to Padilla, Mohammed Atef again discussed with him the possibility of blowing up apartment buildings in the United States by trapping natural gas to produce a maximum yield explosion. Padilla trained for this mission with a man he had met in Florida known as Jafar the Pilot.

Jafar and Padilla couldn't get along for some reason, and Jafar eventually was moved to another mission. Padilla remained with Mohammed Atef, who had taken special interest in the young American's training. He stayed with Atef through September 11, 2001, and following, although his training for future attacks was interrupted by the arrival of "the Americans" in Afghanistan. When Atef was killed in a bombing, Padilla, armed with an assault rifle, joined numerous al Qaeda fighters and moved to the Pakistan border.

It was there that he met Abu Zubaydah, one of al Qaeda's key strategists. Zubaydah was in charge of sorting the fighters into two groups, those who should be relocated through Pakistan and those who should return to fight in Afghanistan.

Padilla met several times with Zubaydah. Whether it was al Qaeda's plan or Padilla's pipe dream, Padilla explained that he plotted to attack the United States with a "dirty bomb," a conventional weapon packed with radioactive waste, designed to disperse into the air when the bomb detonated. Besides those injured by the immediate explosion, a dirty bomb's radioactive spray could cause long-term contamination, possibly disease or death to greater numbers in the population at large.

Apparently Zubaydah was skeptical that Padilla could pull off such a dirty bomb attack but nonetheless sent Padilla and his new partner on to meet with Khalid Shaikh Mohammed (KSM), al Qaeda's top operational manager, now basking in the adulation of his peers as the readily acknowledged mastermind behind the 9/11 attacks. Zubaydah went so far as to write a recommendation letter regarding Padilla, sending it to KSM, informing him of the American's plan to detonate a radioactive bomb, and asking KSM to evaluate the possibilities.

KSM met with Padilla and encouraged him to pursue the plan to blow up high-rise apartment complexes using the natural gas method outlined by Atef, Padilla's former mentor. KSM instructed Padilla and his accomplice to rent two apartments in each building, seal off the apartments, turn on the gas, and then detonate using remote timers to explode the buildings simultaneously in the various locations. The al Qaeda leader suggested that Padilla enter the United States from Puerto Rico or through Mexico.

KSM gave Padilla authority to conduct the operation if he and his partner succeeded in entering the U.S. It was later learned that KSM remained hopeful that the explosives-trained Padilla could execute the dirty bomb, as he had presented the idea to Abu Zubaydah, but also gave Padilla permission to attempt the destruction of apartment buildings in New York, Florida, or Washington, D.C.

After receiving KSM's assignment, Padilla was trained by Ramzi Binalshibh, the coordinator of the nineteen 9/11 hijackers, in the secure usage of telephones for communication with al Qaeda. Padilla received $15,000 in cash, travel documents, a cell phone, and an e-mail address through which he could contact Ammar al-Baluchi, KSM's right-hand man, once Padilla had successfully entered the United States.

On April 5, 2002, Padilla departed for America, traveling through Pakistan and then on to Zurich. He arrived at Chicago's O'Hare International Airport on May 8, 2002. He was carrying more than $10,000 in U.S. currency, given to him by his al Qaeda mentors. He also carried with him the cell phone provided to him by Ammar al-Baluchi, as well as names and telephone numbers of his recruiter and sponsor, and al-Baluchi's e-mail address.

Meanwhile, according to *TIME* magazine, when Zubaydah was captured in Pakistan, he spilled the beans about Padilla's plan.[5] Federal agents tracked Padilla as he traveled. They picked up Padilla as a material witness on May 8, 2002, shortly after he stepped off the plane at Chicago's O'Hare Airport. Allegedly, Padilla had returned to his homeland to begin the process of scouting out American targets for a dirty bomb.

He was transferred to Manhattan and appointed a lawyer, and the Justice Department hoped that Padilla would tell us everything he knew about al Qaeda. On June 9, 2002, President Bush designated Padilla as an enemy combatant.

I was in Moscow meeting with leaders there, seeking to build our coalition against terrorism, when I reviewed Padilla's case. We arranged a video hookup, and in emphatic terms I announced the news that the FBI and the CIA had successfully prevented a potential terrorist from carrying out his plot to harm people in the United States. After consulting with Secretary of Defense Donald Rumsfeld and other senior officials, I recommended to President Bush that he designate Padilla (who had changed his name to Abdullah al-Muhajir) as an enemy combatant, which the president did.

Although Padilla's plot had not fully developed beyond the discussion stages, as far as I know, I felt then, and still do today that it merited serious attention. As Deputy Defense Secretary Paul Wolfowitz said of Padilla's plan, "We stopped this man in the initial planning stages."[6]

It was important to inform the public about Padilla as quickly as possible. Our primary reason for announcing any captures was to help Americans understand that Padilla-type terrorists were out there, and we wanted the public to be aware. We needed the public's help and involvement in our continuous efforts to detect and disrupt terrorist activity *before* the enemy could strike.

Beyond that, Padilla was the first American citizen to be captured on U.S. soil and designated as an enemy combatant, even prior to al-Marri. Consequently, we chose not to delay making his capture known. Imagine the uproar and potential panic if we had kept Padilla's capture quiet, and somehow word leaked—as it usually does—that the Justice Department was secretly snatching American citizens out of public airports and putting them in military custody! Better to tell the world as much as we could about the Padilla capture, recognizing that we were limited by the classified nature of much of his story.

As often happens, because the press is not privy to the behind-the-scenes details of the FBI's and CIA's work, many members of the media did not understand the significance of Padilla's capture. Some saw it as a great injustice, the American government trying to bully a disgruntled young man. Others mocked and poked fun at the Justice Department for making a big deal about picking up a "punk kid" in an airport. But José Padilla was much more than a disenchanted street kid.

José Padilla had transformed himself into an enemy of our nation, a trained, well-funded, and equipped terrorist. Much more than a mere thug stepped off that plane in Chicago. An al Qaeda terrorist who had accepted an assignment from the same man who had assigned nineteen other terrorists to attack America on 9/11 boldly reentered our country. This man intended to kill hundreds of men, women, and children by blowing up apartment buildings; he was an al Qaeda terrorist who hoped to wreak even more havoc among his former countrymen by detonating a dirty bomb that would release destructive radioactive materials. Padilla had spent time personally with at least three top al Qaeda leaders, and he possessed vital information about their whereabouts and resources and their evil intentions. Perhaps most frightening of all, as an American citizen, José Padilla would have been free to move around the United States without restriction, plotting, planning, and looking for opportunities to kill innocent people.

It was not only vital that we capture him, but it was equally important that we keep him off our streets and out of our communities. Although President Bush faced an unpopular and difficult decision, I believe he made the correct one, an extraordinary decision to declare José Padilla—an American citizen—as an enemy combatant, a terrorist determined to do immeasurable harm to other Americans.[7]

The al-Marri and Padilla cases were strong reminders that we could be safe in America only by maintaining constant vigilance and applying perpetual pressure on potential terrorists right here in our own nation.

Obviously, after 9/11 we realized that our defenses against terrorism were inadequate. The fact that nineteen terrorists could enter the country, and wreak the horror that they did without leaving significant footprints, astounded and alarmed us. One or two people slipping through the system would have been bad enough, but *nineteen* was a large number of terrorists to miss, and indicated a substantial vulnerability. One had to wonder, *How many other al Qaeda types are already in the United States, lurking below the surface, awaiting orders or preparing plans for future attacks?*

To better understand why the al-Marri and Padilla cases were so important, I need to take you back to 9/11 again. Because commercial flights were curtailed so quickly on September 11, 2001, few planes took off after the Pentagon was struck, and flights that were already airborne landed as soon as possible all around the country. That was the good news. The pattern of Middle Eastern passengers sitting near the cockpits on the hijacked flights was the bad news. We launched an exhaustive scrub of all manifests for flights of similar aircraft scheduled to take off that day at approximately the same times as the hijacked flights had taken off. In a number of instances, flights had been canceled or in some cases were forced to land because of the no-fly rule imposed. On their passenger manifests, the FBI found patterns similar to those on the hijacked aircraft. We could not ignore the obvious conclusion that several additional planes may have been "scheduled" to take part in the attacks of 9/11. We were forced to operate from the dangerous worst-case scenario that al Qaeda had additional active terrorist cells ready to strike again.

Once we had secured the names of the individuals who were seated in those locations, we pursued them vigorously. Several of them were picked up and detained that same day, or in the days immediately after 9/11. In several cases, men who were detained had on their persons or in their possession box cutters similar to those used on the hijacked flights. Unfortunately, it was not illegal to carry box cutters on a plane at that time, so we could not hold them on that basis. If we could not detain them on immigration or criminal violations, we deported them if they had violated the terms of their visas.

It was frustrating to let some of those people out of our custody to leave the country, but we could do only what the law allowed, and we refused to overstep our bounds. We had to turn them loose one way or the other, either in the country or out of the country, so we decided that turning them loose out of the country was better. In many cases, information may have been shared with other countries, letting them know that a suspected terrorist was returning to their land, having been deported from the U.S., but it was nonetheless wrenching to know that potential terrorists were walking away when we had them in our hands. But our justice system is not like that of many European countries that allow for prolonged detentions without charging a suspect. If we had no legal grounds for holding them, we removed them from the United States so they could do us no immediate harm.

The Justice Department received severe criticism for detaining so many people following the 9/11 attacks. Our critics chided, "You arrested all those people, yet not a single person has been convicted of anything associated with the 9/11 terrorists."

The truth is, we don't know how many people we caught who may have been involved in terrorist activities. But if they were involved in any criminal or immigration violations, we prosecuted them aggressively, incarcerated them, or sometimes expelled them from the country, if we had that option. Al-Marri was such a person who was picked up during that process. He was detained initially as a material witness, then later on charges of lying to the FBI and other immigration violations, and then later charged with other criminal acts including credit card fraud and other crimes.

Was it worth it to detain and charge hundreds of other violators in order to find one or more of the key men sent to America to facilitate a second wave of attacks on the United States? I thought so then, and I think so more today. Those we detained we either charged or released; and those we punished had been convicted after trial.

Significant controversy has attended the various methods we used against terrorists. But contrast our tactics with those used during World War II. President Franklin Delano Roosevelt initiated a military commission specifically to adjudicate eight German-born saboteurs who had been living in the U.S. prior to the war, one of whom claimed to be an American citizen (the Supreme Court declared otherwise).

In Germany, they devised a plot to blow up valuable infrastructure in the United States. Then in mid-June 1942, they infiltrated the United States from two separate Nazi submarines. Four men traveled aboard a U-boat that landed them under the cover of night in Long Island, New York, and four aboard a sub that put them ashore near Ponte Vedra Beach, Florida. The saboteurs carried with them a supply of explosives, fuses, incendiary devices, and timing mechanisms, which they buried on the shore where they landed. All eight were apprehended.

President Roosevelt hastily convened a military commission. The men were tried in a matter of weeks. They were sentenced to death;

the death sentence was appealed; the Supreme Court affirmed the process, adding that it would issue a full opinion sometime in the future. Six of the eight were executed in Washington, D.C., less than ninety days after their arrival. Months later, the Supreme Court issued its full opinion, validating the process. Two of the men's sentences were commuted to life in prison because they had assisted in the capture of their coconspirators.

Clearly a vast difference exists between what the United States did in 2001 in apprehending and detaining potential terrorists and what our country did during World War II. Ironically, the attack on New York and the Pentagon and the plane that went down in Pennsylvania on September 11, 2001, resulted in more deaths than the attack on Pearl Harbor on December 7, 1941. And in 1941, during the Pearl Harbor attack, Hawaii remained a decade away from becoming the fiftieth state in the union. Needless to say, the attacks of September 11, 2001, were all on states within the American homeland.

Yet our government's response was much more respectful of due process and citizens' rights. We detained only people who were in violation of the law. In contrast, during World War II, the United States interned thousands of American citizens of Japanese and German extraction—people who were not in violation of any laws at all. Many of those people had been born in the United States. Secretary of Transportation Norman Mineta, for example, was born in San Jose, California. He and his entire family were interned near Cody, Wyoming, and they had done nothing wrong. Their only reason for being swept out of their home and confined to a camp was their Japanese heritage. Certainly, the case can be made that these extreme measures were unnecessary during World War II.

I have to chuckle sometimes when I am painted as "hard-nosed." In truth, our Justice Department wasn't nearly as aggressive as Roosevelt's. And our respect for civil liberties was far more extensive than the response following Pearl Harbor. Yes, we were tough, but we always operated within the law; it was never our policy or practice to detain any noncombatant without charges. In our conduct, we never approached the limits of the law as closely as Roosevelt did.

Beyond that, we aggressively prosecuted people who acted violently or with discrimination against Arabs in general or Muslims in particular. I announced publicly that we would decisively curtail any violence or illegal activity against law-abiding people of Middle Eastern descent. My message to non-Arabs in the United States was simple: "Do not allow your sorrow or your rage to become hostility toward people on the basis of their ethnicity or their religious views. That is unacceptable; it is out of bounds, and if you break the law, we will prosecute you for it."

As soon as it was feasible, I invited Americans of Arabic ethnic backgrounds to meet with us in Washington, and we visited with Arab groups in Detroit and other cities in America. I also visited several mosques. With each group, I emphasized that we were focused on punishing wrongdoers; I stressed our adamant refusal to assume criminality on the basis of ethnicity or religious preference.

The al-Marri and Padilla cases further illustrated our need for a coordinated, centralized system of gathering and disseminating information about terrorist cases. If al Qaeda was staging operations in places such as Peoria, it is vital that FBI field offices around the country—not simply in cities such as New York, Washington, or Los Angeles—know what each other is doing. We did not have a centralized "clearinghouse" to assemble all the facts, seek to make sense of them, and then distribute that information rapidly to agents in the field. An agent pursing an investigation in New Jersey may have a piece of the puzzle, and an agent pursuing another case in Arizona may have another, and an agent in Florida may have yet another. But if they never see each other's information, it is unlikely that the pieces will ever fit together properly, or that the image will be readily discernable.

The terrorists we faced in the months following 9/11 and still battle today disperse and diffuse their operations as much as possible.

Regarding 9/11, they received their financing from the Middle East; they trained in Afghanistan; they did their planning in Germany; they did flight training in the United States, and they fine-tuned their operation at a meeting in Kuala Lumpur, Malaysia. Interestingly, for the final phase of their planning, they went somewhere totally different. Why? They didn't travel to Malaysia merely to enjoy the balmy weather. They went there because they wanted to keep the pieces of the 9/11 attack puzzle as dispersed as possible. They chose a face-to-face setting, rather than talking on the telephone or communicating on the Internet. They went to a place they could quietly get into and out of with relatively little notice, leaving minimal footprints for intelligence agencies to track.

Fragmentation on the part of the terrorist activities mandates integration on the part of law enforcement so we can work together to see the entire picture of how and where they are trying to attack us.

Our military forces can detain members of the opposing force indefinitely, pending the outcome of the conflict. Military forces detain enemy combatants; those that have violated the rules of conflict are eligible, once so detained, to be processed, charged, and adjudicated by a military commission. The others are detained pending the outcome. The al-Marri and Padilla cases represent examples of this defense capacity.

This means of dealing with detainees during a time of war was relied on extensively during World War II. Allied forces apprehended numerous German, Japanese, and Italian soldiers who had fought for their nations. Most detainees had observed the accepted rules of conflict. When we captured them, we detained them in camps to remove them from the conflict until the war was over. Then we sent them home.

There were some, however, who had flagrantly violated the rules of war. Their trials and adjudications became known as the the Nuremburg Trials. Because terror is a technique that intentionally violates the rules of war, many terrorist detainees today could be eligible for similar trials by military tribunals.

We faced a dilemma following 9/11. How do we adjudicate the villains who had part in the attacks on America, or were planning future attacks on our country?

Ali Saleh Kahlah al-Marri was determined to be a "sleeper" agent who would help others launch attacks. As such, he was considered "at war" with the United States. That's why President Bush, invoking war rules, declared him to be an "enemy combatant," authorizing the U.S. government to hold him if necessary without charge or trial until the end of the war. Padilla remained in military detention until November 2005, when he was formally indicted on new criminal charges flowing out of his alleged activities that became known after his initial detention. The charges label him as a codefendant along with members of a terrorist cell that operated in the United States and Canada. As a result, José Padilla will now stand trial in the criminal justice system on charges of conspiracy to commit murder of U.S. nationals, conspiracy to provide material support to terrorists, and conspiracy to murder, kidnap, and maim persons in a foreign country.

Soldiers defending a country at war are not subject to the rules of procedure designed for court trials. For example, if a soldier encounters an enemy, under internationally agreed upon rules of war, that soldier can take whatever action is necessary to protect himself and neutralize his enemy, whether it involves capturing and detaining the enemy or killing him on the spot.

Under the rules of law enforcement, police can use lethal force to contend with an imminent threat of death or serious bodily injury. Once a suspect is detained, he or she is normally charged and tried, or else released.

For those involved in national defense during armed conflict, a different set of rules governs. Under "war rules," unlike during peacetime, an enemy combatant can be shot without warning unless he is incapacitated, in custody, or trying to surrender. If any combatant is captured, he can be held in custody until the end of the conflict, without a trial.

War rules define combatants as anyone taking an active part in hostilities. Under this rule, even civilians who pick up arms and start fighting can be considered combatants and treated accordingly. Following 9/11, our government applied this definition to terrorists who were a part of attacking the United States.

We vigorously pursued breaking up terrorist cells within the United States. The "Lackawanna Six," for example, were charged with providing material support to al Qaeda. Originally a group of seven men, all of whom are U.S. citizens of Yemeni family backgrounds, were living in a tight-knit community in Lackawanna, New York, near Buffalo. The group traveled to Afghanistan during the summer of 2001 to train at Osama bin Laden's al-Farouq jihad camp. At the camp, they studied how to use explosives, rocket-propelled grenade launchers, land mines, and other military equipment. Six of the members returned to Lackawanna, but the seventh member remained in the Middle East.

Perhaps most disturbing, the members of the cell seemed to be good members of their community. Yasein Taher had been voted the friendliest person in his class in 1996. A former captain of the school soccer team, he married his childhood sweetheart, a former cheerleader. Five years later, Taher was in Afghanistan training to be a terrorist.

Sahim Alwan, another member of the group, was a college-educated, married man with three children. He worked as a counselor with the Iroquois Job Corp Center in Medina, New York. Alwan is reported to have met with Osama bin Laden personally.[8]

The Lackawanna Six came to the attention of the FBI through an anonymous letter suggesting that the group may be involved in criminal activity and associating with foreign terrorists. Thanks to the "noise in the system" and the active help of alert citizens, six potential terrorists were convicted and incarcerated.

As much as I was pleased about our progress in taking suspected terrorists off the streets of America, I recognized that we must remain constantly on guard. My convictions were reconfirmed on December 22, 2001, when an American Airlines flight departed Charles de Gaulle Airport in Paris, bound for Miami. About ninety minutes into the trip, a flight attendant smelled what she thought was a burned match near the seat occupied by Richard Reid of Great Britain.

When the flight attendant confronted the man, Reid put the match into his mouth. The fight attendant alerted the captain, just as Reid lit another match in an attempt to light the inner part of his shoe, from which a wire extended. Passengers seated nearby saw what was going on and pounced on Reid, restraining him and then subduing him. When the plane landed, FBI investigators discovered that Reid had loaded both of his shoes with high-tech explosives. Had he succeeded in detonating the explosives, 183 passengers and fourteen crew members could have been killed. Reid was sentenced to life in prison, plus 110 years.

While Reid was portrayed as a naïve, deluded dolt by television talk show hosts, the method of terrorism he had attempted was a favorite of none other than al Qaeda strategist Khalid Shaikh Mohammed, the mastermind behind the 9/11 attacks. KSM, as he is known to U.S. terrorist fighters, recommended the shoe bomb as an effective method of breeching the cockpit door and disrupting flight.

Some people don't like to think of the war on terrorism as a literal war; they prefer to think that President Bush was speaking metaphorically when he said on September 29, 2001, "Our war on terror will be much broader than the battlefields and beachheads of the past. The war will be fought wherever terrorists hide, or run, or plan."

Doubters bandy about philosophical concepts such as, "How do we know we are really 'at war,' with al Qaeda?" or, "How will we ever know if or when the war is over?" These are genuine questions by honest scholars with sincere intentions. Frankly, because of the nebulous nature of the war on terrorism, we may *not* be able to pin-point a certain date and say, "That was the day the war on terror ended." But while attacks persist around the world, and plots are disrupted here in America and Canada, we are well served to know that the war is still on.

ENDNOTES

1. Richard T. Pienciak, "Mystery Man in 9/11 Terro Case: Who Is Ali Al-Marri?" *New York Daily News*, January 12, 2003.
2. Charging documents: The U.S. District Court, Central District of Illinois, case number 03-1220. Other information in this chapter adapted from the charging documents of the *United States of America v. Ali Saleh Kahlah al-Marri* in the Southern District of New York.
3. Ibid.
4. White House Office–controlled Document, filed June 23, 2003, by John M. Waters, clerk, U.S. District Court, Central District of Illinois.
5. Amanda Ripley, "The Case of the Dirty Bomber," *TIME*, June 16, 2002; www.time.com/time/nation//printout/0,8816,262917,00.html.
6. Cable News Network, June 11, 2002; http://archives.cnn.com/2002/US/06/11/dirty.bomb.suspect.
7. Much of this information regarding José Padilla was made public by Deputy Attorney General James Comey on June 1, 2004, in response to the Senate Judiciary Committee's request that American citizens be informed about enemy combatants.
8. Public Broadcasting Service, *Frontline*, reported by Roya Aziz and Monica Lam, October 16, 2003.

CHAPTER TWELVE

PHANTOMS OF LOST LIBERTY

The Battle to Defend Justice

❧❧❧

How quickly they forget. The thought crossed my mind as I entered Room SD-106 in the Dirksen Senate Office Building. I was back on Capitol Hill, appearing before the Senate Judiciary Committee to answer their questions on the topic of "Preserving Our Freedoms While Defending Against Terrorism."

It was Thursday, December 6, 2001; slightly more than twelve weeks had passed since the atrocious 9/11 attacks on our nation. It was also the day before the sixtieth anniversary of the Japanese attack on Pearl Harbor, on December 7, 1941. Heightening the irony still further was the fact that we were meeting in the Dirksen Building rather than the Hart.

The Hart Senate Office Building—where many televised hearings are held—was closed. On October 15, 2001, a potentially lethal anthrax-laced envelope had arrived in the Capitol Hill mail, and had been delivered to the offices of then Senate Majority Leader Tom Daschle. Authorities shut down the entire building until Daschle's suite of offices and those nearby could be fumigated. Hundreds of senate office workers who may have been exposed to the anthrax received emergency three-day dosages of the strong antibiotic ciprofloxacin (Cipro) as a near panic swept across the Hill. Exacerbating the tension, a second anthrax-laced letter, addressed to Senator Patrick Leahy, had been intercepted by investigators on November 16, 2001.

Before the Hart Senate Office Building could be reoccupied, everything in the affected rooms that might harbor the deadly anthrax spores—computers, files, cabinets, books, and personal items—had to be carefully packed and taken to a company in Richmond, Virginia, for treatment with ethylene oxide, a substance commonly used to sanitize medical instruments. In eleven senators' offices located in close proximity to Daschle's, liquid and foam versions of chlorine dioxide fumigants and particle filtering vacuums were still in use even as I faced the Senate Judiciary Committee in the Dirkson Building.

If anyone should be aware of the need for a strong response to terrorism, it should have been the senators before whom I was to answer questions that day. But as I said, it is astounding how quickly we forget, when the threat of terror-inflicted death subsides into the normal routine of everyday partisan politics and personal agendas.

Senator Patrick Leahy sparked interest by striking what George F. Will referred to in a *Washington Post* editorial as Leahy's "overheated phrase," that we were "shredding the Constitution" in our attempts to protect our nation from terrorism.[1] David Lazarus, writing in the *San Francisco Chronicle* fretted, "Ashcroft Misses the Point."[2] The *New York Times* editorialized about "Justice Deformed: War and the Constitution."[3] *Times* writer Robin Toner characterized the upcoming hearings as "Ashcroft and Leahy Battling over Greater Police Powers."[4]

Perhaps even more frustrating to those of us in the Justice Department who were becoming more aware of the potential terrorist presence in our country every day, the Patriot Act was working, as the stack of statistics I carried with me clearly showed. None of that seemed to matter to the media intent on painting the Bush administration as overstepping the boundaries between safety and security to encroach on civil liberties. I wondered if the senators before whom I sat truly believed the drivel spouted by the talking heads as well as the multitudinous articles castigating the Justice Department's treatment of terror suspects. Not to mention the constant drumbeat by the media purporting that in our prosecution of immigration violations, we were setting up "kangaroo courts" and we were "shredding the Constitution."

I had found at least one of the many political cartoons semi-amusing. During the first week of December, a satirical cartoon appeared showing a child sitting on Santa Claus's knee. Santa is saying to the kid, "I know when you have been sleeping. I know when you've been awake. I know when you have been bad or good," and the kid looks up at Santa and says, "Who are you—John Ashcroft?"

Sometimes you just have to laugh.

The cast of characters on the U.S. Senate Judiciary Committee was familiar to me. Not only because I had previously served as a member of the Judiciary Committee—and quite possibly still would have been a member of the committee had I not lost my seat in the Senate, allowing the Democrats to gain a majority on the committee—but because it was the same group before whom I had been grilled during my confirmation process, when President Bush nominated me as attorney general. The faces were much the same, including the political heavyweights of the Democratic party: Leahy, Kennedy, Schumer, Durbin, Feinstein, Herb Kohl, John Edwards, Maria Cantwell, and Feingold on one side. Representing the other side were Hatch, Sessions, Thurmond, Kyl, Mike DeWine, Specter, Charles Grassley, and Mitch McConnell.

I was to appear before the committee to defend the Justice Department's aggressive campaign against terrorism. In the days before the hearing, Washington was abuzz with the expectation that the committee members would rake me over the coals. It was to be my confirmation hearing revisited.

The media must have expected some combustible moments; National Public Radio was broadcasting the hearing live from the crowded room in the Dirksen Building. Television news personalities

Ted Koppel and Bob Schieffer stood in the back of the room. Al Sharpton sat near the front of the room.

Prior to my appearance at the hearing, Chairman Leahy had made some strong comments to the press, criticizing me and the way the Justice Department was pursuing our "spit on the street" policy in an effort to disrupt potential terrorist acts against our nation.

Because the Patriot Act was working so well, I was somewhat surprised, a bit disappointed, and in no small measure concerned when the negative publicity began to paint the news regarding who we were detaining, for how long, and why. Indeed, prior to my testimony, the committee had welcomed several witnesses whose experiences as detainees had been less than pleasant. Considering the circumstances under which the FBI and the INS were working in the days following 9/11, it was not completely surprising that errors or overreactions could occur, or that a person was not treated with kid gloves, although those instances were rare and, when discovered, punished. It intrigued me that of the many people who were detained, the aberrations were asked to testify before the committee.

I recognized that the hearing represented a pivotal moment in the war on terror. Criticism of our policies and the provisions of the USA PATRIOT Act had reached a shrill pitch, and most of it was based on little more than accusations of bad faith. Also under fire was President Bush's decision to allow the use of military tribunals to try non-U.S. citizens suspected of terrorism. I made the decision to defend—and defend vigorously—our policy of relentless prosecution of legal violations by suspects associated with terrorist groups. In short, I entered the room expecting and ready for a fight.

The majority members of the Judiciary Committee seemed to have a publicly expressed agenda that was well rehearsed in the media in advance of the hearing. Namely, that the Department of Justice would be chilled in its aggressive approach toward terror.

At the same time, we had an agenda of our own: We refused to allow the safety and security of the American people to be sabotaged by political intimidation and senatorial histrionics. We wanted the committee members to understand that if they chose to restrain the Justice Department in our war on terror, I would not be restrained in signaling the intensity of our commitment to the safety of Americans. This hearing wasn't merely about the committee members haggling with me over the fine points of our policy, it had direct implications to our prosecutors and agents in the field on the front lines fighting the war against terror. We wanted them to know that they had the authority to track down suspected terrorists, and the Justice Department, the entire United States government, and the people of America would be behind them all the way.

Senator Leahy opened the hearing with an admonition that seemed to come right out of the newspapers. "The need for congressional oversight is not—as some mistakenly describe it—to protect terrorists," said the committee chairman. "It is to protect Americans and protect our American freedoms . . ."

Utah senator Orrin Hatch offered his usual eloquent opening remarks, including a quote from the Democratic senator from Georgia, Zell Miller, who said, "'They need to get off his back and let Attorney General Ashcroft do his job . . . These nitpickers need to find another nit to pick. They need to stop protecting the rights of terrorists. This is about national security. This is about life and death.'"[5]

I went straight to the heart of the matter in my testimony. "Thanks to the vigilance of law enforcement and the patience of the American people, we have not suffered another major terrorist attack. Still, we cannot—we must not—allow ourselves to grow complacent. The reasons are apparent to me each morning. My day begins with a review of the threats to Americans and to American interests that were received in the previous twenty-four hours. If ever there were proof of the existence of evil in the world, it is in the pages of these reports. They are a chilling daily chronicle of hatred of America by fanatics who seek to extinguish freedom, enslave women, corrupt education, and to kill Americans wherever and whenever they can."

I went on to describe the vicious enemy we face in our fight against terrorism. Some of the senators were old enough to recall their parents' descriptions of the horrors inflicted on the world by Hitler, Stalin, Mussolini, and Mao. Several of them had witnessed firsthand man's inhumanity to man in Vietnam. Strom Thurmond, at ninety-nine, had lived through it all. I wanted the senators to realize that the enemy we now must defeat is equally as formidable, far more insidious, and potentially more devastating than the worst tyrants the world has suffered.

"The terrorist enemy that threatens civilization today is unlike any we have ever known. It slaughters thousands of innocents—a crime of war and a crime against humanity. It seeks weapons of mass destruction and threatens their use against America. No one should doubt the intent, nor the depth, of its consuming, destructive hatred."

As I spoke, I reached for a large, homemade-looking book and held it up for the Senate Judiciary Committee to see. "This is a seized al Qaeda training manual—a 'how-to' guide for terrorists—that instructs enemy operatives in the art of killing in a free society." I paused long enough for the senators to look up from their notes and focus on the terror manual.

"Prosecutors first made this manual public in the trial of the al Qaeda terrorists who bombed U.S. embassies in Africa . . . In this manual, al Qaeda terrorists are told how to use America's freedom as a weapon against us. They are instructed to use the benefits of a free press—newspapers, magazines, and broadcasts—to stalk and kill their victims. They are instructed to exploit our judicial process for the success of their operations. Captured terrorists are taught to anticipate a series of questions from authorities and, in each response, to lie—to lie about who they are, to lie about what they are doing, and to lie about who they know in order for the operation to achieve its objective. Imprisoned terrorists are instructed to concoct stories of torture and mistreatment at the hands of our officials. They are directed to take advantage of any contact with the outside world."

I continued by describing the Justice Department's response to the incursion of the enemy, including some of the progress we had made thanks to the tools provided in the Patriot Act, legislation that most of the senators had voted for, though several of them had acknowledged earlier in the week, during the hearings prior to my appearance, that they had voted for the act reluctantly.

I informed the committee that to date we had detained 563 individuals on immigration violations, and had brought criminal charges against 110 suspected terrorists so far, with sixty of them in custody.[6] (These numbers would rise, of course, in the months ahead as we progressed.) I also told the senators that we had investigated more than 250 incidents of retaliatory violence and other threats against Arab Americans, Muslim Americans, Sikh Americans, and South Asian Americans. I wanted the committee to know that the Justice Department was equally committed to protecting our Arab citizens as we were in tracking down suspected terrorists.

Several of the members seemed intrigued by this information, perhaps because so much of the media coverage regarding our activities since 9/11 had given the impression that the INS and the FBI were badgering people of Middle Eastern lineage. Worse yet, civil liberties advocates grossly mischaracterized the Justice Department as though we were trying to spy on or manipulate nearly every aspect of American life. "Ashcroft and his secret police are trying to take away your liberties," the alarmists repeatedly spouted.

I had been easing into the confrontation that I knew could not be avoided. The time had come.

"The Department of Justice has sought to prevent terror with reason, careful balance, and excruciating attention to detail," I said. "Some of our critics, I regret to say, have shown less affection for detail. Their bold declarations of so-called facts have quickly dissolved, upon inspection, into vague conjecture. Charges of 'kangaroo courts' and 'shredding the Constitution' give new meaning to the term 'fog of war.'

"Since lives and liberties depend upon clarity, not obfuscation, and reason, not hyperbole, let me take this opportunity today to be clear: Each action taken by the Department of Justice, as well as the war crimes commissions considered by the president and the Department of Defense, is carefully drawn to target a narrow class of individuals—terrorists. Our legal powers are targeted at terrorists. Our investigation is focused on terrorists. Our prevention strategy targets the terrorist threat.

"Since 1983, the United States government has defined terrorists as those who perpetrate premeditated, politically motivated violence against noncombatant targets. My message to America this morning, then, is this: If you fit this definition of a terrorist, fear the United States, for you will lose your liberty."

I was dealing with fire and I knew it, but the words I was about to utter would become some of the most misunderstood words I had occasion to utter as attorney general. Although only a relatively small paragraph in my 2,400-word statement, it elicited an enormous response.

I told the committee:

We need honest, reasoned debate; not fearmongering. To those who pit Americans against immigrants, and citizens against non-citizens; to those who scare peace-loving people with phantoms of lost liberty; my message to you is this: Your tactics only aid terrorists—for they erode our national unity and diminish our resolve. They give ammunition to America's enemies, and pause to America's friends. They encourage people of good will to remain silent in the face of evil.

I stood by that statement then, and I stand by it yet today. I chose the phrase "phantoms of lost liberty" on purpose, because I was convinced that certain members of Congress, as well as various civil liberties groups, misconstrued the facts. They talked incessantly about things that didn't exist, people whose rights were supposedly being infringed upon or were supposedly losing their liberties on a whim, or for no reasons at all. They pandered to their constituencies using fearmongering tactics, and the concerns they needlessly engendered worked against the best interests of our nation, and especially our nation's fight against terrorism.

Almost immediately, the backlash of liberal voices in Congress and in the media filled the airwaves. I was roundly condemned for attempting to stifle "reasoned and appropriate debate" on the Bush administration's policies. Newspapers and magazines around the country ran editorials with titles such as "General Ashcroft's Detention Camps," "Ashcroft's Hypocrisy," "John Ashcroft: Minister of Fear," and a host of others. The *Oregonian* titled its December 7 editorial "The American Way of Name-calling"; The *Boston Globe* lamented, "Justice Decried." The *Houston Chronicle* interpreted my comments as anti-intellectual if not downright naïve or worse: "Raising questions and asking for answers does not equate to treason or aid and abettance for the nation's enemies."[7] David Cole, professor at Georgetown University Law Center, wrote a scholarly piece in the *Harvard Civil Rights–Civil Liberties Law Review* that included me as a prime example of "the New McCarthyism."

Talk shows abounded with critics discounting the numbers of arrests we had made or the "caliber" of suspected terrorists we had locked up. Pundits poked fun, mocking and sneering, implying that no "real" terrorists such as bin Laden or his closest cohorts were yet in custody.

Of course, they conveniently ignored the fact that numerous leaders of al Qaeda had been killed by our military. Hundreds of people had been interviewed by the FBI, and that number rose every day as potential suspects were identified and prosecuted. Also conspicuously absent from the critics' messages was that if even one Ali al-Marri or José Padilla type had succeeded, if any one of the many plots foiled by the FBI would have reached fruition, thousands of lives may have been lost. Nor did they acknowledge that al Qaeda's sharklike appetite for American blood had grown stronger, not weaker, after the attacks of 9/11.

Few of the critics mentioned the new threats we encountered every day, perhaps the most serious being the numerous "independent terrorists," thousands of minor players not necessarily directed by bin Laden or his organization but inspired and emboldened by the 9/11 attacks and looking for major opportunities to wreak havoc on our country.

Despite the avalanche of criticism from liberal sources, we had succeeded in emphatically declaring our position, and the American public rallied to our support. We also won ourselves a great deal of running room with Congress; even the Senate Judiciary Committee backed off and gave the Justice Department less grief about the steps we were taking to protect our country from terrorism. The additional operational support from the Judiciary Committee enhanced the protection of American lives and liberties in the years ahead.

That's all we really asked. We determined that the debate would be conducted on the basis of truth and facts rather than on rumor and innuendo, frightful suggestions that had no basis in fact—phantoms, if you will. The more liberal elements of Congress, no doubt, were disappointed that we were so successful in our attempts to secure our government's favor, that we could focus on fighting terrorism rather than feuding about emotional attempts to wedge one faction or group of Americans against another. At a time when our nation was still recovering from the devastating 9/11 attacks, any reckless falsehood designed for power-grabbing, attempting to pit one race, class, or ethnic group against another, was counterproductive and was helping the terrorists. We needed to unify our country around the principles of freedom rather than divide it.

Whether the liberal-leaning members of the Senate Judiciary Committee truly understood the message I'll never know, but the public caught on and agreed.

Few of us at the Justice Department thought our hard-fought, new-found antiterrorism measures granted through the USA PATRIOT Act would pave the way to wiping al Qaeda off the face of the earth. We knew our enemies would never give up and would never relent. What we didn't anticipate was having to fight the FISA Court itself for the right to protect Americans from terrorism.

Parts of the FISA system had been in serious disarray well before I became attorney general. Its difficulties, you will recall, had become one of the most serious impediments to cooperation among federal officials in identifying and neutralizing terrorists. In the days and weeks following September 11, we made the case for changes in the FISA system that would strengthen our antiterrorism capability, and Congress enacted these changes in the USA PATRIOT Act.

But despite the Patriot Act's explicit changes in the law, and our success in taking terrorists off the streets, the FISA Court ruled *against* allowing greater cooperation between prosecutors and the intelligence agents.

I refused to sit back and watch the wall—the same wall that had so severely impeded our ability to stop terrorism against our nation—be totally reconstructed without objection. Despite the fact that we were in the midst of a round-the-clock, all-out war against terror, I decided to appeal the ruling of the FISA Court.

People on my staff could hardly believe it. Career Justice Department officials objected vehemently. "Just let it go," they advised. "We can work around it. Don't mess with the FISA Court."

Their concern was legitimate. After all, the FISA Court had not been challenged, never since its inception—not once. Not only was it a secret court whose existence was unknown to most Americans, the decisions of the court were uniformly accepted edicts. Nobody ever contested them; no legal challenge had ever been brought concerning any of their rulings.

But with national security on the line, I informed the court that I disagreed with the outcome they had expressed and indicated to them my belief that such a disagreement should be resolved by submitting the issues to the FISA Court of Review. "We're going to appeal to the Court of Review."

"I think you should," one of the judges said.

On November 18, 2002, the United States Foreign Intelligence Surveillance Court of Review ruled for the first time in history. The review overturned the lower FISA Court's ruling that had limited the sharing of information between the criminal law enforcement and the intelligence agencies. The expanded authorities in the USA PATRIOT Act had survived their most serious challenge yet. It would not be the last.

ENDNOTES

1. George F. Will, guest editorial, *Washington Post*, November 22, 2001.
2. David Lazarus, "Ashcroft Misses the Point," *San Francisco Chronicle*, December 2, 2001.
3. Editorial, *New York Times*, December 2, 2001.
4. Robin Toner, "A Nation Challenged: Ashcroft and Leahy Battling over Greater Police Powers," *New York Times*, December 2, 2001, p. 1B
5. Senator Orrin Hatch, Department of Justice Oversight: Preserving our Freedoms While Defending Against Terrorism, December 6, 2001, p. 307.
6. Testimony given before the United States Senate Committee on the Judiciary, Washington, D.C., December 6, 2001. These numbers reflect where we were twelve weeks after 9/11. The numbers of detainees as well as suspects charged swelled greatly during the next twelve months.
7. "Ad Hominem; Attorney General need not stoop to such argument," *The Houston Chronicle*, December 8, 2001.

CHAPTER THIRTEEN

INTELLIGENCE-BASED IMMIGRATION

The Need to Secure Our Borders

❦

The red 2001 Mitsubishi Galant speeding northward on Interstate 95, about twelve miles south of the Delaware state line, caught the attention of Maryland State Trooper Joseph M. Cadalano. And well it should have: the trooper clocked the vehicle racing up the highway shortly after midnight at ninety miles per hour in a sixty-five mile per hour zone.[1]

Speeders on this section of I-95 were not unusual. The straight stretch of highway cutting through the largely rural edge of Maryland, Delaware, and Pennsylvania owned a well-deserved reputation as a speed trap, and more than a few residents as well motorists just passing through on their way to New York had paid their dues to belong to the "Need for Speed Club."

Trooper Cadalano noted the time/date function on his radar mechanism—September 9, 2001; 12:09 a.m. The officer reached over and switched on the patrol car's flashing emergency lights as he pulled onto the highway to give chase. He also turned on the car's dashboard-mounted video camera.

The chase was relatively short. As soon as the driver of the Galant realized the Maryland State Police car was signaling him to pull over, he slowed down and eased his vehicle to a stop along the right edge of I-95.

Cadalano called in the stop, giving the license number of the car to the dispatcher on the radio. The dispatcher immediately began running the usual checks on the license number. Meanwhile, the officer approached the car cautiously, being careful to stay behind the left shoulder of the driver. He noted that the new-looking Galant was occupied by only one person. A quick visual scan of the car's interior showed it to be clean—no obvious signs of alcohol, drug paraphernalia, or other suspicious items; nor were there any books, maps, luggage, or personal items in the passenger areas of the vehicle. In fact, the car looked brand new.

Trooper Cadalano spoke cordially to the dark-haired, dark-complexioned male driver, whom he guessed to be in his mid to late twenties.

"I stopped you because you were going ninety in a sixty-five zone. May I see your driver's license and registration, please?"

The man in the car didn't say anything as he handed the license and registration through the window to the officer.

The car's registration revealed that the vehicle was owned by the Garden State car rental company at the Newark, New Jersey, International Airport. The driver possessed a Virginia driver's license, including a valid photo identification. "Do you still live in Springfield, on Quicksilver Drive?" Cadalano wanted to know.

The man in the car answered affirmatively, but offered no other information. He seemed calm and cooperative, not agitated at all about being pulled over.

"Okay," Cadalano said. "I'll be right with you."

The trooper returned to his patrol car and radioed in the information, waiting to see if there were any outstanding arrests on the license bearer, or if the car itself might be stolen. Neither check turned up anything to worry about.

Trooper Cadalano wrote a citation for exceeding the posted speed limit, traveling ninety in a sixty-five zone, a high rate of speed to be sure, but he'd written tickets for worse on this stretch of highway.

Completing the citation, Trooper Cadalano walked back to the red Galant and handed the registration and license back to the driver, along with the speeding ticket. "Okay, sir. Ninety miles an hour in a sixty-five zone is a $270 fine. I need your signature down here at the bottom."

The officer passed his clipboard and pen to the driver as he explained, "The blue copy is a self-addressed envelope. Use a check or money order to mail it in. If you choose to do so, you have to do it within fifteen days. All your payment options are on the back of the white copy here. There is your information."

The driver quietly scribbled his name at the bottom of the citation, accepted his two copies, and passed the clipboard back out the window. Officer Cadalano looked at the signature on the citation to make sure it matched the name on the driver's license. The name was rather unusual, but then the wide variety of names Cadalano encountered on Interstate 95 never ceased to amaze him. Where do all these people come from? This name appeared to be Middle Eastern. Nothing unusual about that.

"You are free to go," Trooper Cadalano said.

The man eased out onto the night . . . and into history.

Cadalano read the name, "Ziad Samir Jarrah." The state trooper watched the car's taillights disappear into the traffic flow headed toward Newark, to the rendezvous location where he was to join his friends, to the parking lot at the airport where he would leave the Galant. Early Tuesday morning, Jarrah would hurry to Gate A-17 at Newark International Airport to board a United Airlines flight to San Francisco. A few minutes after breakfast had been served, he and his friends hijacked the plane, slit the throats of the pilots, and then Jarrah sat down at the controls of Flight 93. Two days later, investigators would find the signed speeding ticket in the glove compartment of the Galant, left in the parking lot at Newark International Airport.

The Maryland state trooper did not know what evil Jarrah had in mind. Nor did the trooper have any reason to check. Other than speeding, Jarrah had done nothing suspicious. A case could be made that the law officer had no time-efficient means of performing an elaborate check, anyhow. But what if he had? The trooper may have discovered that Ziad Samir Jarrah had legally entered the United States on June 27, 2000, at the Atlanta Airport on a B-2 tourist visa. He enrolled in flight training at Florida Flight Training Center in Venice, Florida, a violation of his immigration status since he never applied to INS to change his status from a tourist to a student. He stayed in flight school until January 31, 2001, and remained in the country for a total of fourteen months—until September 11, 2001, the day Jarrah died. He had been living in the U.S. illegally for more than a year; the six-month period of stay on his visa had expired a full year earlier.

On either count—for violating his immigration status or over-staying the time limit of his visa—Jarrah could have been detained, charged, and removed from the United States. Trooper Cadalano had the authority to detain for the INS the man who would be at the controls of United Flight 93 when it slammed into the ground in rural Pennsylvania, but the Trooper didn't know about Jarrah's immigration violations . . . so he let him go. What might have happened if the pilot member of the terrorist team in Newark had not shown up that fateful day? What if there had been a national clearinghouse the officer could have tapped into where he could find out immediately whether the person he had stopped had ties to terrorism? Would United Flight 93 have been hijacked without a terrorist pilot to guide the plane into a target? It is hard to believe that al Qaeda would not have called off its hijacking team if they had no pilot and could not complete its mission.

Similar questions piqued the interest of Kris Kobach, a sharp new White House Fellow who later became a counsel to the attorney general. Kris came to the Justice Department on September 1, 2001, and a few weeks later, when he heard me encourage the Justice Department to share ideas that might prevent another 9/11 from ever happening again, Kris brought me some possibilities. Some of these ideas formed the basis of a new program we called the National Security Entry-Exit Registration System (NSEERS), to help the Immigration and Naturalization Service (INS) get a better handle on who was coming to America and what they were doing in the country.

The need for a new immigration program was glaringly obvious. The events of September 11, 2001, showed that we had to improve control of our borders and do a better job of tracking foreign visitors who are in the United States on temporary visas as guest workers, tourists, students, or for business reasons. As we looked at our nation's immigration policies, one of the most threatening problems we faced was not the flood of Mexican workers illegally pouring across our southern borders—although that was and remains a significant security issue. The most serious concern, however, was that we didn't know much about those who were legally coming into the country, what they were really doing here, or how long they stayed.

The number of U.S. visa applications in 2001 grew to more than 10.6 million. But before 9/11 the Immigration and Naturalization Services operated in a "virtual intelligence vacuum," according to the Staff Report of the National Commission on Terrorist Attacks on the United States.

Occasionally, through some good detective work by a border patrol agent, or an extra inspection by an alert immigrations officer, we were able to thwart a terrorist's attempts to enter our country. The turning away of Mohamed al-Kahtani is a case in point.

A Saudi national, al-Kahtani was sent to the United States by Khalid Shaikh Mohammed to be the "twentieth hijacker" in the 9/11 plot. Because al-Khatani was intended to be what the hijackers referred to as "muscle," someone to subdue passengers or crew who interfered with their plan, al-Khatani did not know a great deal about the overall al Qaeda plan. Traveling from Dubai to Florida, al-Kahtani arrived at Orlando International Airport on August 4, 2001. As he attempted to go through immigration, inspector Jose Melendez-Perez grew suspicious. Al-Kahtani had no return ticket, limited funds, no hotel reservations, and he refused to identify the "friend" he said was waiting for him.

That friend, videotape from airport surveillance cameras showed, was Mohamed Atta, driving a rental car into an airport parking area which he entered shortly before al-Kahtani landed.

The immigration inspector thought something seemed odd about al-Kahtani, so he refused to allow him to enter the country. Melendez-Perez's supervisor backed him up on his decision, and before long, al-Kahtani was on a plane headed back toward Dubai. Military forces later captured him near the Pakistan-Afghanistan border and sent him to Guantanamo Bay, Cuba, under military guard. In Cuba, al-Kahtani refused to reveal his identity at first. It was seven months before his fingerprints were matched with those of the person attempting entry in Orlando. Thanks to an alert immigration inspector, the system worked, and KSM's twentieth hijacker was turned away. One has to wonder what might have happened had other hijackers encountered an officer like Melendez-Perez.

The 9/11 terrorists had entered the country legally, moved about our nation with impunity, and operated on our soil, some of them for more than a year, undetected and unhindered. Once inside the United States, they had no obligation to make further contact with federal law enforcement for any reason. Their only contact with any law enforcement was accidental, and most frequently that contact was at the local level, or as in the case of Ziad Jarrah, with a state trooper. We had no system to know where they were once they entered the country, or what they were doing. For the most part, we had no idea if they were still in the United States or if they had left the country. If they exited the country, in most cases we were unaware of it.

Prior to 9/11, the INS's system for handling legal, short-term foreign visitors was easily compromised. It was based on the honor system, and terrorists have no honor. When people entered the country, they completed the I-94 form; they were to retain a portion of the form, which they were asked to turn in to immigration authorities upon departure from the country. But the overwhelming majority of people leaving the country were not even reminded to turn in the form. Nor did they turn it in. Consequently, we knew that people had entered the country, but we were not certain whether or not they had departed. Most had left; some had stayed here illegally, but the INS did not know the difference because procedures for monitoring departures were not in place.

Even the processing of the I-94s, supposedly intended to help the INS know who was in the country, was done in North Dakota and later in Vermont—all done by paper transactions. By the time the INS got the list of people who were in the country, oftentimes their visas had expired and they would have already departed.

Consequently, it has been far too easy to overstay a visa in the United States. Indeed, five of the nineteen hijackers had overstayed their visas, but the INS was unaware of it, had no system in place to alert state and local officials that the overstays had occurred, and frequently did not respond to local officials who detained visitors with expired visas. If we'd had a stronger immigration system prior to 9/11, the five terrorists who had over stayed their visas might have been detected, deported, and al Qaeda's plan disrupted.

Interestingly, when they entered the United States, all of the hijackers filled out immigration forms as required by the INS. Not one of the hijackers filled out the form completely; all left blank data fields and questions not fully answered.[2] On the form is a request for information regarding the purpose of the visit—whether tourism, education, business, or other reasons. All of the hijackers informed the INS that they were going to be doing something other than the activities they actually did while they were here in the United States.

Because they were all doing something other than their stated purpose, all nineteen of the hijackers would have been deportable, had the INS known. But the INS did not know.

Part of the reason for that was the appalling lack of information we demanded from people coming into our country for short-term visits. For the vast majority of foreign visitors, the INS requires only an I-94 form, a simple questionnaire to be completed on the plane or ship just prior to arrival in the United States. If you've traveled outside the country and then returned to the United States, you have probably seen foreign visitors completing their INS form I-94. It's about the size of a traffic ticket and requires nothing more than basic information. It asks foreign visitors to state the reason for their visit and to provide an address, supposedly where they will be staying while in the United States. The answers accepted on such forms are often dangerously vague.

One of the hijackers wrote "Ramada Hotel, New York" on his I-94 form. Not even New York City, no address, no specific location, nothing—and that person was permitted to enter the country!

Prior to 9/11, Congress had mandated that the Justice Department and the INS develop a comprehensive immigration entry-exit system, with the original target date for implementation at the end of 2005. It became clear after 9/11 that we couldn't wait that long. We needed to take immediate steps to get control of our borders.

When we looked at the National Security Entry-Exit Registration System, NSEERS as it came to be known, that gave us a place to start. The program consisted of four simple, commonsense elements.

First, it required that all foreign visitors provide more information about themselves, their plans, and their whereabouts while in our country. Especially those visitors identified as presenting any sort of elevated national security concern must have a brief digital fingerprint taken and a background check run on them before entering the country. Beyond that, they were required to provide more thorough information than is otherwise required on an I-94.

While the I-94 form merely asks for an address in the United States, individuals from certain countries—especially those persons who match intelligence-driven criteria, such as males under forty years of age seeking to enter the country from nations known to be terrorist havens—would not simply pass through immigration desks with a quick passport check but would be asked to submit to a secondary inspection. This type of individual would be registered in NSEERS and required to provide specific information about where he or she is staying, with whom, or in the case of a student, where and what he or she will be studying. The individual must provide specific background information such as parents' names and addresses, past educational history, as well as contact information such as telephone numbers, cell phone numbers, e-mail accounts, or other addresses where he or she may be reached while in the United States.

The NSEERS program also required basic personal information such as height, weight, and eye and hair color—all innocuous matters for most people (many Americans who apply for a job provide far more background), yet information that was not being asked of potential terrorists entering our country prior to 9/11.

As an additional means of identification, NSEERS required that each person, especially those from countries known for terrorist activities, submit to a simple fingerprint check. The fingerprinting is done with a digital pad using the two index fingers. It takes ten seconds to obtain the prints, and it takes only a few minutes to run those prints against a database of tens of thousands of wanted criminals, people with criminal records, and known terrorists.

The military and other agencies have obtained numerous fingerprints from abroad, prints that have been obtained from captured terrorists, prints that allied governments have given to the United States, and so-called latent fingerprints, prints that don't have a name associated with them. Some of these latent prints were obtained from al Qaeda safe houses and from al Qaeda training camps inspected after coalition forces over-ran the Taliban forces in Afghanistan in 2001–2002.

A good fingerprint can last sometimes for more than thirty years, so even though al Qaeda had fled the training camps long before allied forces showed up, the camps themselves yielded a gold mine of fingerprints. The only problem with these prints, of course, was that we didn't have names to attach to them. We simply knew the owners of those prints had been in close proximity to al Qaeda.

By storing those prints in the NSEERS database, and obtaining prints from every person wanting to enter the U.S. from a foreign country that had been associated with terrorism in any way, it was possible to quickly compare the prints for matches. If they match, the person attempting to enter the United States is turned away. If no match comes up, the person is on his way with only minutes, if not seconds, of minor inconvenience and delay.

The second element of NSEERS turned out to be more controversial. Once in the country, if a person holding a nonimmigrant visa wishes to remain in the country, he is required to register at one of the seventy-six INS offices across the country after thirty days and every year thereafter, to verify that he is doing what he said he would do, and living where he said he would live.

Most European countries have required this sort of information for decades. If you establish an address while you are visiting in Europe and you change your location, you must report within a certain period of time, usually to the local police, and inform them of where you are living. Failure to do so is grounds for being detained, arrested, or even deported. Ironically, while most of our European friends have this system in place, the United States did not have such a system prior to 9/11. The NSEERS program was a step in that direction, requiring that those visiting in our country (especially from countries where known terrorism has been supported), should report their whereabouts and activities every thirty days. To me, it just made good common sense.

The third element of NSEERS was even more simple and practical. When a person who has entered the country on a short-term visa leaves the country, he must verify his departure at the airport or port from which he departs. This, too, is a regulation that has been required by many other countries for decades, but had not been well-enforced by the United States.

Finally, we had to determine which visitors were still in the country at the time NSEERS was started. Remember, the INS did not know who had stayed, and who had left. Therefore, the NSEERS program required the registration of anyone already present, visiting the United States on a temporary visa. This registration on the part of INS was intended to gather the same information from recent visitors who had not been required to provide the basic information when they entered the country.

These "call ins" involved individuals from specific countries known to be breeding grounds for terrorism, countries such as Afghanistan, Iran, Algeria, Yemen, and others. We did not ask for all nationals from all countries to report for registration at once, but required individuals from countries such as Iran, Iraq, Syria, Sudan, Qatar, and others to report early on in the program. We called in individuals from other countries shortly thereafter in a scheduled series of registrations.

The basis on which the calls went out was the country of origin, and more specifically, the calls were based on what passport a person was carrying. For example, a person of Norwegian heritage carrying a passport from Yemen would be questioned in the same manner as a person of Arabic heritage who grew up in Yemen.

We implemented the program nationwide in October 2002, including the expanded fingerprint checks, and saw almost instantaneous, positive results. The INS soon apprehended more than 330 aliens at the border who presented law enforcement threats, including wanted criminals, aliens who had committed serious felonies in the past that render them inadmissible now to enter the United States, aliens with fraudulent documents, and aliens who had previously violated U.S. immigration laws. More important, by May 2003 NSEERS had led to the identification of eleven suspected terrorists.

Any time a person was apprehended trying to sneak across the border or was in secondary inspection for some another reason, we would run their fingerprints to determine if they were in the database. The results were astounding. By the end of its first year, NSEERS resulted in the arrest of four thousand wanted criminals. We caught potential terrorists, too.

The NSEERS program allowed the INS to track the entry, exit, and whereabouts of the thousands of short-term foreign visitors enrolled. These registrants came from 148 different countries, quite literally people from almost every country on Earth.

Contrary to the criticism, the NSEERS program was not designed to screen people from one particular country. Granted, people coming to America from countries known to sponsor terrorism such as Iran, Iraq, Libya, Sudan, and Syria were asked to step aside at the point of entry for NSEERS screening. All visitors over the age of fourteen from those countries were registered, but thousands of visitors from countries around the world were picked for NSEERS because they met intelligence-based criteria used by the INS inspectors at the port of entry. Intelligence criteria, which has been classified, is the intelligence community's assessment of which foreign visitors represent the greatest security risks to the United States. These criteria should and did change as the terrorist threats to our country change. In sum, we should use reason, driven by the latest intelligence, to determine the highest risks to our security.

By this method, we avoided the random searches seen at most airports and ports of entry, searching Grandma going through the security checkpoint at the airport, or little babies. On the other hand, males under forty years of age, especially those in their mid-twenties to early thirties, hailing from certain countries on our list of terror potentials, were much more likely candidates to be checked.

They were fingerprinted and asked a series of questions about their activities; that information was added to our database and enabled us to follow up on them. If they lied or represented themselves falsely in any way, those actions could be grounds for them to be expelled from the country.

The aspect of NSEERS that turned out to be most controversial was the registration requirement for individuals who were already in the country, especially when we added countries such as Indonesia and Malaysia to the list. Individuals from selected countries had "call in" periods following a directive that went out requiring them to come in and register with the INS at sites around the country, where they would be asked the same series of questions asked of new arrivals. If they did not register, that was grounds on which they could be detained, arrested, and often removed from the country. This put the burden of responsibility on the people visiting America to honor their visa obligations, rather than on the government to catch them violating those obligations. We simply asked them to do what they said they were going to do when we welcomed them to our country.

One other impediment is worth noting that may have discouraged Trooper Cadalano from arresting Ziad Jarrah on September 9, 2001, even if he had known that Jarrah was in the country illegally. Under President Clinton, the Justice Department had issued a flawed interpretation of law in a 1996 Office of Legal Counsel opinion. That opinion indicated that state and local police were permitted to make immigration arrests for *criminal* violations of immigration law, but were *prohibited* from making arrests for *civil* immigration violations. The 9/11 hijackers had committed civil, not criminal, violations of the law by overstaying their visas and violating the terms of their admission to our country. If the 1996 opinion were correct, police officers on the front line would be powerless to arrest terrorists like Jarrah.

That 1996 opinion, however, was *not* correct; it was not based on any solid case law. Several appeals courts had come to the opposite conclusion—that local police possessed the inherent authority to make immigration arrests, both criminal and civil, of deportable illegal aliens. In addition, Congress indicated that this inherent authority was not displaced by the federal government. In 2002, the Office of

Legal Counsel withdrew the flawed portion of the 1996 opinion, and issued a corrected opinion—that local and state police officers can indeed make immigration arrests. We emphasized that point when we introduced the NSEERS program.

Civil liberties groups in the United States immediately complained that the INS was "racially profiling," targeting people from Middle Eastern and Southeast Asian backgrounds. Other countries complained about our program as well, as did academic institutions in the United States. It was a strange "I want to have my cake and eat it, too" situation. We were not to allow potential terrorists to strike the country, but we were attacked for tracking people who posed the greatest risk to our security.

The requirement to report after thirty days is especially valuable and yielded some strong investigative leads. We know immediately when a person doesn't show up. He has a ten-day window, if he is staying in the country for more than thirty days, after which he becomes "out of status." The majority of people on temporary visas stay in the country less than thirty days. But if a person doesn't show up to verify where he is living and what he is doing, then a signal will go up on day forty that the person is out of status. If a person violated this requirement, he may still exit the country—in fact, we would most likely "help" him to do so—but he would have difficulty ever legally reentering the United States. Importantly, we were able to notify police officers across America through the National Criminal Information Center to look for and arrest NSEERS violators. Had this system been in place on September 9, 2001, Trooper Cadalano could have arrested Ziad Jarrah, and he might have stopped the hijacking of United Flight 93.

From our perspective, the United States encourages people from foreign countries to visit our nation. We do an enormous amount of commerce with people from other countries, and it is conducive to business for these people to be able to visit the United States.

Similarly, many of our academic institutions are populated by students from foreign countries. But for the most part, prior to 9/11, the INS had no registry of where students were, what they were studying, whether or not they had dropped out of school, or when they had graduated. As such, in addition to NSEERS, we implemented a congressional mandate under which institutions were required to report any changes regarding the status of their students who were in the country on a short-term visa to attend school. For the first time, we maintained a central registry database in Washington to keep track of these student changes.

Some of the academic institutions in our country raised a ruckus about this "intrusion" into their business. They regarded it as an invasion of their academic freedom to provide information to the government that might just protect their school from violence, or from becoming the site of a bioterrorism attack or some other form of terrorism.

Unfortunately, when the Immigration and Naturalization Service moved from the umbrella of the Justice Department to the Department of Homeland Security, only parts of the NSEERS program survived. Registration call-ins stopped. In late 2003, the mandatory thirty-day reporting requirement, which had generated leads on suspected terrorists in the past, was eliminated. While it is still technically in place, it is not the comprehensive program it was when first implemented. In my opinion, to the extent that we do not make use of a program such as NSEERS, an intelligence-driven immigration system that spotlights potential terrorists as they come into the country, we are needlessly creating an area of vulnerability to potential incursions of the enemy.

While programs such as NSEERS are only part of the solution to preventing terrorist activities in our nation, we need some system designed on facts, not simply emotion. Everybody coming into the country does not need the same scrubbing as those who are coming from high-risk locations. Random searches based on computer selection or some other arbitrary mathematical formula rather than on intelligence data prove inefficient and ineffective.

Besides, the beauty of the NSEERS program was that it provided a way so that we did not need to register every mom and pop coming into the country. We didn't need to register Grandma or the toddler. We could focus on individuals who represented the highest risk to our country. A popular criticism of NSEERS was, "If you can't register everyone, then you shouldn't register anyone." The idea being, of course, that we should not separate people or particular nations for disparate treatment. Personally, every time I travel through the airport and see people of almost negligible terror threat being searched and screened, I shake my head, wondering how much time, effort, and money we are spending in vain while we hedge on making uncomfortable people who represent substantially greater terrorist risks to our security.

Our friends the Saudis loudly cried foul at NSEERS, yet anyone who has ever traveled to Saudi Arabia knows that their immigration controls are far more restrictive than ours, and are some of the most restrictive in the world. Beyond that, fifteen of the nineteen hijackers were citizens of Saudi Arabia. Should American immigrations officers not be more inclined to question carefully short-term visitors from that country, even though we deeply respect Saudi Arabia and its leadership?

How serious is this situation? Keep in mind that law officers encountered four of the 9/11 hijackers prior to that fateful day. Saudi Arabian Nawaf al-Hazmi entered the United States through Los Angeles International Airport on January 15, 2000. He rented an apartment with fellow hijacker Khalid al-Mihdhar in San Diego and lived there for more than a year. He was authorized to stay in the country for only six months. As such, from July 2000 on, al-Hazmi was in the country illegally. Had NSEERS been in place, the system could have been alerted and a search initiated for him. It wasn't.

In early 2001, al-Hazmi moved to Phoenix, Arizona, to join another 9/11 hijacker, Hani Hanjour. On April 1, 2001, al-Hazmi and Hanjour were stopped for speeding in Oklahoma. Had the officer known that al-Hazmi was in violation of his immigration status, the trooper could have detained him. But the officer did not know.

Similarly, Egyptian-born Mohamed Atta, the ringleader of the 9/11 terrorists and the man who was most likely at the controls of American Airlines Flight 11 when it slammed into the World Trade Center, had legally entered the United States several times on B-1 and B-2 visas, temporary visas granted to visitors for tourism, business, or pleasure. He first entered our country through Newark, New Jersey, on June 3, 2000. Like al-Hazmi, Atta too overstayed his visa's six-month legal time period. He spent thirteen months in America, planning, rehearsing, and preparing for the 9/11 attacks. At any point after the first six months, he could have been deported had authorities known that he was out of status.

Like his cohorts, Atta was also stopped by local law officers. On April 26, 2001, Atta was pulled over by a Broward County, Florida, police officer and ticketed for possessing an invalid driver's license. The officer did not know that Atta had overstayed his visa on a prior visit to the United States.

Amazingly, despite his prior illegal presence in America, Atta obtained a valid Florida driver's license in May 2001. When he failed to appear in court on his April 26 offense, a bench warrant was issued for his arrest. On July 5, 2001, Atta was pulled over on yet another traffic violation in Palm Beach County, Florida. The police officer was unaware of the bench warrant issued by the neighboring Florida jurisdiction and allowed Atta to drive away with nothing more than a warning.

Hani Hanjour, from Saudi Arabia, entered the United States on an F-1 student visa on December 8, 2000, at the Cincinnati/Northern Kentucky International Airport. He stated that he intended to take classes at the ELS Language Center in Oakland, California, but

Hanjour never showed up for classes at the school. At that point, he became illegal.

Hanjour, too, was pulled over on a speeding charge in Arlington County, Virginia, on August 1, 2001. The police officer apparently did not know that Hanjour was out of status. The officer issued Hanjour a citation and allowed him to drive away. Hanjour paid his $100 fine by mail.

As astounding as it may seem, of the five 9/11 hijackers who we later discovered were "out of status," four of them were stopped by local or state police within six months of the attack.[3] Had the officers known that those four men were in violation of their visas, the terrorists could have been detained and deported.

But the officers didn't know because the information was not available to them through the National Crime Information Center, the database through which most routine traffic stops are run.

The missed opportunities represented by the four traffic stops— the most common of law enforcement encounters—are even more poignant when you consider that of the four men stopped, three are believed to have piloted hijacked planes on 9/11. Beyond that, Atta and Hazmi were the al Qaeda operation leader and his second in command. Is it possible that the 9/11 attacks might not have been able to proceed had these men been taken out of circulation? Had the federal government acquired and disseminated information about basic immigration violations to local and state law enforcement agencies, several key terrorists may have been arrested, and the 9/11 plot may have been disrupted or discovered. Sadder yet, if they *had* been caught, they probably would have been released by the INS in the months before they were scheduled to be deported, thanks to the "catch and release" policies that were in place. Some may say that al Qaeda would have simply replaced them had they been detained. Perhaps so, but the time and training it might have taken may have given us a chance . . .

And in the battle against terror, the deadly combination of inefficient effort and ignored opportunities can cost lives and must be avoided. I hope we have learned the costly lesson that we need to capitalize on every opportunity we have to disrupt the terrorist network.

ENDNOTES

1. Marsha Kranes, "Hijacker Had Been Stopped for Speeding," *Milwaukee Journal Sentinel*, January 9, 2002, p. 8A. Also, Marsha Kranes, "MD Cops Let 9/11 Hijacker Go," *New York Post*, January 9, 2002, p. 7.
2. K. Lloyd Billingsley, "A 9/11 Anniversary Primer," *National Review*, September 10, 2004.
3. This material regarding the 9/11 terrorists' immigration violations and the NSEERS program has been adapted from information provided in an interview with Kris Kobach on June 7, 2006. Portions of this material were also adapted from "The Quintessential Force Multiplier: The Inherent Authority of Local Police to Make Immigration Arrests," by Kris W. Kobach, *Albany Law Review* 69 (2005), p. 185–87.

CHAPTER FOURTEEN

JUDGMENT IN MANHATTAN

The Prosecution of Lynne Stewart

❧ ❧

When President Bush declared war on terrorism, he made it clear that anyone who aides and abets terrorists in any way is an enemy of the United States. Against the backdrop of 9/11, it was unconscionable to me that anyone in our country would have the gall to assist terrorists or compromise the security of our nation because of a personal ideology or political agenda. Yet attorney Lynne Stewart chose to do precisely that.

In 2000, the liberal left had lauded Lynne Stewart as an icon and a hero at the defense bar. She was famous for defending controversial figures such as H. Rap Brown, the former 1960s radical turned Muslim cleric who was convicted and sentenced to life in prison for killing a sheriff's deputy. Stewart also defended Mafia boss Sammy "the Bull" Gravano and other clients who had fostered violence.

Stewart met one of her most dangerous clients in Sheik Omar Abdel Rahman, a blind Egyptian cleric who is the head of a terrorist organization known as Islamic Group. Osama bin Laden and his top lieutenants also regarded Rahman as a spiritual leader.

Sheik Omar Abdel Rahman's own involvement with terrorism precedes the plot to assassinate Egyptian president Anwar Sadat. Rahman was the spiritual mentor for a group of young people who had formed a new cell of the radical group called Jama'at al-Islamiyya

(Islamic Group). When they asked him what the fate should be of a ruler who has ignored the law of God, Rahman's reply was, "Death."

The next year, 1981, members of the group assassinated Sadat for pursuing peace with Israel. Rahman was indicted along with the assassins, accused of issuing a fatwa that pronounced a death sentence on Sadat. Rahman was acquitted, and continued to encourage Muslim extremists to engage in violent actions against their own governments. While traditional Islam requires believers to be obedient to the ruling powers, Rahman labeled non-Muslim political leaders as "illegitimate" rulers to be removed by force.

Upon relocating to the United States, Rahman continued preaching his brand of violent Islamic extremism, becoming a controversial figure within the Muslim community of New York City. Followers of the sheik included the terrorists who bombed the World Trade Center in 1993, causing six deaths and more than one thousand injuries. Rahman and nine of his congregants were indicted for seditious behavior, conspiring in 1995 to bomb bridges, the Lincoln and Holland tunnels, and other landmarks in New York City, including the United Nations and FBI buildings.

Lynne Stewart was urged to take the Rahman case by former Lyndon B. Johnson administration attorney general Ramsey Clark, also famous for defending leftist, anti-American clients (more recently known for his role in defending Saddam Hussein). Despite Stewart and Clark's best efforts, Rahman was convicted in 1995 and sentenced to life in prison for conspiring to wage a war of terrorism against the United States, including the plot that resulted in the 1993 bombing of the World Trade Center. Rahman's incarceration became a rallying point for Islamic militants around the world, including al Qaeda and Osama bin Laden.

With the blind sheik in prison, Rahman's devotees attacked a group of tourists in November 1997, at the Valley of the Kings, in

Luxor, Egypt, the country's most popular tourist area. Six terrorists disguised as policemen shot and slashed to death fifty-eight Japanese and Swiss tourists, including women and children, just as they exited their bus, looking forward to viewing the pyramids, King Tut's and Queen Nefertari's tombs, and other Egyptian archeological sights and antiquities. Four Egyptian law officials died in the slaughter as well. Initially, supporters of Rahman blamed Israel for the attack, but later, Rahman's group, I.G., claimed responsibility for the massacre.

It was no secret that if given the opportunity, Rahman might incite further incidents. No wonder the U.S. Department of Justice did not want Rahman communicating with the outside world. With captured terrorists like Omar Rahman in mind, I announced in the weeks following September 11 an expanded procedure for monitoring detained suspected terrorists' conversations with outsiders, including conversations with their attorneys. With the authorization of Justice Department officials, law enforcement had already been monitoring the communications of certain inmates since the 1993 World Trade Center bombing. But the new procedures gave law enforcement officials greater discretion to "listen in" on incarcerated terrorists.

It was a way to prevent convicted terrorists from running their networks from inside the prison as well as to protect our sources and methods from being secretly communicated from prisoners to the outside world. It is a known fact that incarcerated organized crime figures, drug dealers, and gang leaders often attempt to run their operations from inside prison. We didn't want terrorist organizations doing the same thing. Furthermore, we wanted to have a capacity to know what information incarcerated terrorists might be passing from the prison concerning what they knew about our intelligence operations. That way we could better protect our intelligence people, hopefully preventing them from being hurt or alerting them before an agent's cover was blown.

These types of surveillances, placed on Rahman in 1997 by Attorney General Janet Reno, are known as Special Administrative Measures (SAMs). Pursuant to regulations enacted in 1996, these restrictions could be placed on a federal prisoner's communications or contacts with the outside world—including visitors and the media—when the government believes "that there is a substantial risk that a prisoner's communications or contacts with persons could result in death or serious bodily injury to persons, or substantial damage to property that would entail the risk of death or serious bodily injury to persons."

When the Department of Justice announced expanded authority to listen in on convicted terrorists and their attorneys in October 2001, we knew—but could not publicly share for fear of exposing Americans to greater risk—that inmates such as Sheikh Abdel Rahman were attempting to subvert our system of justice for terrorist ends. In fact, the al Qaeda terrorist training manual offers detailed instructions to recruits on how to continue their terrorist operations in the event that they get caught. Imprisoned terrorists are instructed to take advantage of any contact with the outside world, to "communicate with brothers outside prison and exchange information that may *be helpful to them in their work* [emphasis added]. The importance of mastering the art of hiding messages is self-evident here."[1]

That's why the Justice Department promulgated the new rule creating the authority to monitor the attorney-client communications of federal inmates whom we suspected of facilitating acts of terrorism. At the time, we attempted to make clear that of the 158,000 inmates in the federal prison system, this authority would apply only to the sixteen inmates who, like Sheikh Abdel Rahman, were already under Special Administrative Measures (SAMs). The authority was carefully circumscribed to preserve inmates' rights and civil liberties.

For example, it was the policy of the Justice Department to notify both the inmate and his attorney in advance that all visits and conversations could be monitored, either by video camera, audio recording, or both. At the same time, both the inmate and attorney were informed that no information protected by attorney-client privilege that might be learned from the monitoring could be used against the prisoner in court. As I said, these measures were not instituted with "everyday" inmates, but only with terrorist subjects, and especially with those, like Rahman, who had a radical, loyal following outside prison walls. The primary purpose for monitoring any inmate's conversations with visitors was to stop impending terrorist acts and save lives.

Despite our best efforts to explain the program, a predictable outcry arose from the usual sources. The American Civil Liberties Union called the program adjustments "a terrifying precedent" and the president of the National Association of Criminal Defense Lawyers denounced it as "an abomination."

"How dare you listen in to conversations between lawyers and their clients?" the outraged civil libertarians lamented. "This will destroy America's legal system. How can an attorney ever again hope to defend a client in this country if their private conversations can be monitored?"

But Lynne Stewart was not representing her client for the purposes of defending him; Rahman was already tried and convicted. Nor was Stewart preparing an appeal. Instead, she was purposely participating in, assisting, and facilitating the client's involvement in terrorist activity.

As Sheik Rahman's attorney, Lynne Stewart had agreed in writing to the restrictions on his contact with the outside world, including a prohibition on passing or receiving any written communication to or from Rahman with outsiders. Neither was Rahman permitted to communicate with any member of the news media, and Stewart had agreed to restrictions in that regard as well. On June 14, 2000, Lynne Stewart flagrantly disregarded her agreement with the Justice Department, issuing a statement by Rahman to Reuters news service, in which the convicted terrorist rescinded his support for the cease-fire on the part of terrorist groups in Egypt.

A logical question regarding Stewart's crime was: Did the Bush Justice Department know at the time we put in place Revised Special Administrative Measures for captured terrorist subjects that Lynne Stewart was passing along communications from Sheik Rahman? The answer is yes, we knew it. We had clear-cut evidence.

Despite that fact, the Justice Department kept silent for months as the case wound its way through the courts, even though we were severely criticized by the news media, liberal activists, legal professional organizations, and others accusing the Justice Department (and me in particular) of destroying the long-established lawyer-client privileges. But we knew these protections were necessary, based on what we had seen of Stewart's actions.

I knew at the time when I announced the new procedures that during several visits with Rahman in 2000 and 2001, Stewart acted knowingly and deliberately in violation of these restrictions in support of the terrorist activities of Islamic Group.

During a May 2000 visit with the blind sheik in prison at Rochester, Minnesota, Stewart attempted to disguise a conversation as her translator read letters to the blind sheik. The translator spoke quietly in Arabic with Rahman regarding his instructions about whether the Islamic Group should continue the cease-fire with the Egyptian authorities that had been in place since members of the Islamic Group had brutally killed fifty-eight tourists and four law officers in Luxor.

When Stewart announced to the news media that Rahman had withdrawn his support for the cease-fire, her message from the blind sheik was tantamount to waving a red flag in front of terrorists in Egypt who had been lying low, awaiting further word from their incarcerated leader.

On April 9, 2002, the FBI raided Stewart's Manhattan office and home. That same day, after a moving visit to Ground Zero in New York City, I stepped in front of news cameras and reporters to announce the indictment of Lynne Stewart, along with three men— Mohammed Yousry, Rahman's translator; Ahmed Abdel Sattar, a resident of Staten Island, New York, a paralegal, and an active Islamic Group leader; and Yasser al-Sirri, the former head of the London-based Islamic Observation Center, who was in the United Kingdom at that time. All four were charged with aiding Sheik Abdel Rahman in continuing to direct the terrorist activities of the Islamic Group from his jail cell, by facilitating communications among Islamic Group members, and providing financing for their activities. In so many words, Stewart and her codefendents violated the "Special Administrative Measures" that restricted Rahman's communications with the outside world by helping the convicted terrorist pass messages back and forth between Rahman and his terrorist organization.

Was Stewart merely performing her duties as a lawyer with her client? No; during her visit with Rahman in Minnesota, she had loudly spoken gibberish and nursery rhymes to distract anyone listening in on the meeting, and attempted to cover the conversation between Yousry and Rahman, who were speaking in Arabic and discussing potential acts of terrorism. Stewart's assistance with Rahman and Yousry amounted to "material support" to terrorists. And the Bureau of Prisons caught it all on tape.

Many people were critical of the Justice Department's surveillance of Stewart and her client, saying these actions were inappropriate, that such an indictment would ruin the attorney-client relationship. But besides obtaining the legal warrants for such surveillance, our objective of securing the safety of society went beyond Stewart's objective of serving her client. We had allowed her to do whatever she needed to do to help her client, but we forbade her from helping her client direct additional acts of terrorist violence against society. The fact that she was free to talk to her client did not mean that she was free to help him commit another crime.

In what would seem to some as an ironic twist, later that evening I appeared on the CBS program *Late Show with David Letterman,* where David and I briefly discussed the indictment of Lynne Stewart and other 9/11-oriented issues. While many observers wondered at the timing, the *Letterman* show had actually been in the works for some time prior to the Lynne Stewart arrest.

For several weeks during the spring of 2002, David Letterman had been doing a parody of a song I had written and performed, "Let the Eagle Soar." The song is a patriotic ballad filled with symbols of freedom and opportunity, deeply meaningful to many Americans and to me. Whenever I performed the song—and especially in the months after 9/11 when American patriotism was running high—audiences responded favorably.

The *Late Show* staff obtained a grainy, poor quality videotape shot from the back of a room with a simple home video camera at a private function where I had sung the song in Charlotte, North Carolina. The lighting and sound quality of the tape were horrible. But that made it all the better for Letterman to ridicule.

The *Letterman* show used the video clip, milking it for weeks as a comedy bit, running it at oddball times when the audience least expected it, never in any context that might hint at the patriotic or spiritual overtones the song carried. The bit went over so well somebody on Letterman's team got the wise idea of inviting me to appear on the program. Of course, the producer who contacted my office asked if I would be willing to come on the show to talk with Letterman about 9/11 and how the nation was faring, and, oh, yes, would you be willing to sing your song?

At first, I was reluctant to appear on the program. After all, Letterman's trademark irreverent humor did not lend itself to the serious subjects with which we were dealing at the Justice Department on a daily basis. While I was more than willing to offer encouragement to any audience regarding our effective war on terrorism, especially in New York, where Letterman's show is taped, I did not in any way wish to trivialize our efforts to track down terrorists and to prevent further attacks. On the other hand, if the public could better grasp what we were trying to do, using the authorities of the USA PATRIOT Act to arrest and detain potential terrorists, it would be worth the hassle. Finally, we agreed that I would appear on Letterman's program.

David Letterman wanted me to sing on the show, but I preferred not to do so. I love to sing—especially the old gospel songs I learned as a boy in Missouri and the great American patriotic songs like "The Battle Hymn of the Republic," "God Bless America," and "America the Beautiful." While serving in the U.S. Senate, I enjoyed singing in a quartet along with Senators Trent Lott, Larry Craig, and Jim Jeffords. We called ourselves "The Singing Senators" and performed patriotic music at numerous events. And yes, we even released an album called *Let Freedom Sing* in 1998. While audiences appreciated the spirit of my singing, I was reminded frequently not to quit my day job.

My reluctance to sing on David Letterman's program stemmed not from nervousness. I simply chose not to sing because I thought it might reinforce the wrong stereotype of the singing attorney general and would expose the office to ridicule.

Letterman insisted; he called down to the greenroom and urged me to sing; I politely refused. But Letterman was persistent. He called again, ebulliently encouraging me to sing "Let the Eagle Soar."

"Hey, you gotta do this," Letterman urged. "People want to hear you sing. This will be great!"

I had told the show's producers that if they wanted me to perform some music, I would be glad to play the piano. I played a Beatles song, "Can't Buy Me Love," along with band leader Paul Shaffer. In light of some of the scathing news reports regarding the USA PATRIOT Act, and the immediate outcry by liberal media regarding the Lynne Stewart indictment, the song seemed eminently appropriate. Paul and his band members accorded me great kindness as we sat down in the studio and played a variety of tunes together during rehearsal. When I expressed a twinge of insecurity, Shaffer simply said, "You keep moving your hands. We'll give you plenty of cover."

And they did! When we performed the song before the television cameras, it went off without a hitch.

Clearly, Letterman wanted to interview me as part of a series of conversations in which he engaged public leaders following 9/11. I believe he wanted to demonstrate his ability to confer intelligently about serious matters, and he did. He is an insightful entertainer who obviously engages in "duficism" as a shtick. From my vantage point, appearing on his program presented an opportunity to counter the myth of the nasty and mean attorney general, and give people a sense that, contrary to media images, the Justice Department is filled with real human beings, people with hearts filled with concern for our country as well as having a sense of humor. But I didn't want to play into a stereotype: "That Ashcroft is just a religious nut."

I wanted John Ashcroft to be humanized; David wanted me to be satirized. He kept saying things like, "You are a decent singer; that tape doesn't do you justice, why don't you just sing your song? Everybody will like it." He may have been sincere, but I didn't want to risk learning he wasn't at the expense of the Office of Attorney General and the Justice Department.

In a sense, both David Letterman and I got what we wanted. He identified himself in the interviews as someone conversant with serious issues. I didn't particularly distinguish myself in my responses to David's questions, but I had some fun playing the piano with Paul Shaffer and his band. And David was his affable self as we talked, one Midwesterner to another. Hopefully, people who saw the show went away with a better impression of what I was trying to accomplish at the Justice Department.

The Lynne Stewart trial commenced in June 2004, and was actually based on a second set of indictments brought against Stewart. The first indictments, brought in April 2002, were dismissed by U.S. Judge John Koeltl in July 2003 as too vague. In November 2003, the Justice Department filed fresh charges that Stewart and her codefendants— Ahmed Sattar and translator Mohammed Yousry—had conspired to provide material support to Islamic Group, which is designated a terrorist organization by the State Department.

The new indictments charged that Stewart helped disguise prison conversations in which Rahman passed messages to his translator and assistant. The indictment said Stewart "pretended to be participating in the conversation with Abdel Rahman by making extraneous comments such as 'chocolate' and 'heart attack'" as well as gibberish words.

In his opening statement at the trial, Assistant U.S. Attorney Christopher Morvillo described Stewart as complicit in a virtual "jailbreak." Morvillo reminded the jury concerning the Islamic Group's horrific 1997 attack on tourists at Luxor and the 2000 kidnapping of tourists in the Philippines by the terrorist group Abu Sayyaf, demanding the release of Ramzi Yousef—both apparently carried out on behalf of Sheik Rahman. Morvillo said of the blind sheik, "His words and speeches were as dangerous as weapons."

In court, prosecutors played a tape of Lynne Stewart on a visit with Rahman at Rochester Federal Prison during which she chanted gibberish to cover up his conversations with Yousry, the principal facilitator. The translator turned out to be one of Rahman's coconspirators, and Stewart was cloaking what Rahman and his translator were talking about. The tape showed Stewart clearly trying to help them have a conversation about their activities. She did so in direct violation of the court order and the antiterrorism laws.

Several attempts were made to get the case thrown out of court. Notwithstanding, on February 10, 2005, after deliberating for twelve days, a New York jury convicted Lynne Stewart and her cohorts of aiding terrorism. Stewart was convicted on all five charges she faced— including "providing material support" to terrorism, conspiracy to abet terrorism, and lying to the government about her actions.

The *New York Times* coverage of the Justice Department victory called it "one of the country's most important terror cases since the Sept. 11 attacks." Our concern was that terrorists whom we imprisoned could not continue to direct or otherwise encourage or perpetrate terrorist attacks from inside prison. Stewart facilitated Rahman's participation in terrorist activities from his place of incarceration. Lynn Stewart deserves to be in prison, not simply because she was trying to help a client, or because she read a press release to a news agency, but because she violated the law in a way that endangered the security of our nation. In convicting Lynne Stewart, the jury acknowledged that America is taking the president's definition of "terrorist" to heart. If someone aids a terrorist, that is the same as being a terrorist.

Some defense attorneys and other supporters of Stewart charged that her actions deserved nothing more than a sanction by the bar association, claiming that her prosecution would cast a "chill" on defense attorneys across the country. Why couldn't Lynne Stewart have been punished in some other way? Why not disbar her; why not fine her or find some other way of reprimanding the lawyer for her misdeeds?

But when a person willfully commits a crime, a serious crime that threatens the security and the safety of United States citizens, that deserves serious punishment. Perpetrators of such crimes don't receive less punishment because they are lawyers, or because they were operating according to their own code of ethics. Nobody is above the law; the penalties for these crimes are prescribed in the statutes, and Lynne Stewart received one of the penalties that is prescribed in the statutes.

What Lynne Stewart did was not merely a violation of ethics; it was a crime, and a crime against our country.

Whether the bar association took any action or not is irrelevant. The bar did act; it acted on the basis that Lynne Stewart had been proven guilty beyond a reasonable doubt. Disciplinary actions by the variety of agencies in the culture require various levels of proof for them to be successful. If you are in the civil court system, for example, generally all you have to prove is a more likely than not preponderance of the evidence. But on the criminal side of the American justice system, it takes an extremely high level of evidence to convict. In Stewart's case, it was proven beyond a reasonable doubt that she was guilty.

Lynne Stewart and Sheik Abdel Rahman were determined to exploit the rights guaranteed him in the United States system of justice to pervert and destroy that very system. But the United States cannot stand by and allow such perversions of justice to happen.

Following the attack on America on September 11, 2001, I sought to reassure the American people that the actions of the Department of Justice were carefully designed to target terrorists and to protect American rights and freedoms. Never again should we look away when our institutions of justice are subverted. We dare not ignore those who claim rights for themselves while they seek the destruction of others. We must, in the words of President George W. Bush, "defend freedom and justice, no matter what the cost."

Doing what is right in the face of adversity is not always easy or popular. Critics may assail you, but the critics don't always realize what they don't know or don't understand, because they don't have access to all the information. In the Lynne Stewart case, we knew that we had clear justification for our actions, that she was passing information, and that others would attempt to do something similar if we didn't act.

The Lynne Stewart case reminded us of the valuable lesson that sometimes when you are doing the right thing, you have to stay strong, steely, and silent, even though you are getting beaten up by others for doing what is right. Often, it takes a long time for the truth to emerge.

Concerning the attacks of 9/11, it took more than three years, but the truth eventually came out.

ENDNOTE

1. Quoted from an al Qaeda terrorism handbook seized overseas in the mid-1990s and declassified after September 11, 2001.

CHAPTER FIFTEEN

UNCOVERING THE TRUTH

The 9/11 Commision, Part 1

⊱══⊰

I've been relatively healthy throughout my life, having missed work only a handful of days in my entire career. But early in 2004, Dr. Dan Parks, the White House doctor shepherding my health, expressed concerned about my borderline blood pressure, so he suggested checking me more frequently. During one such appointment, I felt some discomfort in my stomach, as though I had overeaten at lunch, not a severe distress, but enough to make me uncomfortable. I didn't pay much attention; in my line of work, an upset stomach goes with the territory. It ought to be part of the job description. Without mentioning the pain in my stomach to the doctor, I hurried from the White House medical office to another meeting.

The FBI security detail, along with a delegation from the Justice Department picked me up at the White House, transporting me to a briefing and a news conference across the Potomac in eastern Virginia. We were expecting a verdict in the Northern Virginia terrorist cell case, so more people than usual accompanied us to handle the media arrangements. On the way, I slouched down on the seat, trying to position my body in a way that allowed some relief from the discomfort. It was impossible, especially once we started moving. The black armored FBI Suburban that my security guards insisted I use for transportation around Washington since 9/11 was extremely uncomfortable. The suspension in those armored vehicles is similar to riding in a dump truck, hard as a rock. Every bump sent searing pain through my body.

I sat quietly, feeling miserable, breathing with difficulty. I loosened my tie, and unbuttoned the top button of my shirt. David Ayres looked over at me quizzically. He'd rarely seen me "go casual" in the middle of the day, especially on the way to an event in which I'd be representing the Justice Department. After all, I was the AG who ordered two "casual days" each week—Saturday and Sunday!

We arrived at the office of U.S. Attorney Paul McNulty in Alexandria around two-thirty in the afternoon, and I walked inside with my tie still somewhat askew. That in itself tipped off several people traveling with me that something was wrong.

Upstairs in the reception area, numerous people awaited the verdict—prosecutors, police officers, and FBI agents as well as state and local officials who had helped on the case. With such a group, I'd usually greet everyone quite gregariously, but because I felt so awful, I simply said a hasty hello. Paul McNulty expected the verdict soon, so he invited me to wait in his personal office while the men and women who accompanied me went out to prepare for the press conference.

"You go ahead," I said to the others. "I don't feel well. I think I'm going to lie down on the couch here." A stomach flu had been going around in the Washington area, so I thought perhaps I had caught the bug. The pain in my stomach had intensified, and I thought, *If I can just stretch out for a few minutes, it will go away.*

It didn't. In fact, it grew worse. Lying on the couch exacerbated my discomfort, so when everyone left the room, I slid onto the floor. I was still lying there when the verdict came down.

"Sir, Attorney General Ashcroft," I heard somebody say. "It's time for you to attend the news conference."

"I don't think I can," I whispered.

FBI agent Craig McGroarty and David knelt down beside me. "We better get you home," said David. Craig helped me to sit up, and I slowly eased to my feet. "Come on, let's leave," David urged.

"I don't want to move, David." I grimaced as I spoke. "I don't think I can go anywhere right now."

"We need to get going before the traffic gets bad," Craig implored.

"Don't worry; we have the situation covered here," David said.

Subbing for me, Paul McNulty went out to speak to the media. I shuffled to the service elevator and, along with several members of the FBI detail, made my way out the back door of the building, every step causing me to wince.

Driving back from Alexandria, David convinced me to call Dr. Parks, the White House doctor whom I had seen earlier that day. Not accustomed to running to doctors for every little sniffle, bump, or kink, I played down my symptoms to Dr. Parks on the phone. "I'll be fine," I said. "Can't you just prescribe something for a stomach flu?" Thankfully, Dr. Parks saw through my bravado. In the course of the conversation, he said, "I'll meet you at your house." I resisted that as well, but the pain won out and I agreed to see the doctor.

By the time we arrived at my home, I could hardly stand or walk. Janet met us at the door and helped me to our bedroom, where I stretched out on the bed. When Dr. Parks arrived, he didn't even examine me. He took one look and said, "Get this guy to the emergency room."

The FBI detail helped me back to the Suburban, and we raced to George Washington University Hospital. I was rushed into the emergency room. The doctors examining me discovered that my pancreas was radically inflamed and leaking acid into my stomach, causing the searing pain. A person's normal amylase and lipase enzyme release count runs around 200 and mine was close to 27,000! The way the doctors explained it to me, if a person's pancreas continues to overreact like that, the stomach will literally start digesting the internal organs, just as the stomach normally digests a piece of meat.

The next day, the doctors informed me that they planned to operate, but they didn't dare touch the pancreas until it settled down and the burning subsided. In most cases, that is accomplished by a total fast of both food and water. They tubed me up with intravenous lines so they could shut down my pancreas and digestive system. For the next five days, I ate and drank absolutely nothing; I was allowed a few ice chips on my lips, but nothing could be swallowed as my stomach "cooled down." Meanwhile, the doctors discovered that my pancreas was being negatively affected by my gall bladder. Fortunately, gall bladders are optional. So, operating to delete it would relieve the offense to my pancreas. I felt weak and emaciated, but my doctors assured me that when they got me patched up, over time, I'd be close to good as new.

The doctors kept me in intensive care, lying on my back for almost ten full days, pumping me full of antibiotics and morphine. They then sent me home, where I needed another three weeks to recuperate. Following my bout with acute pancreatitus and the necessary surgery, I returned to work in the early spring of 2004. I had relinquished my official responsibilities as attorney general during my stay in the hospital and through the recuperation. I was in no position to exercise judgment or to make decisions on behalf of the United States government.

But almost immediately after my return, I was drawn into a raging conflict, called to testify before the National Commission on Terrorist Attacks Upon the United States, more popularly known as the 9/11 Commission.

The Commission had subpoena power similar to that in a judicial process. They could request information from the government, but because of the classified status and the sensitivity of so many topics concerning the terrorist attacks, they conducted some interviews in private prior to the actual hearings. They also used these private meetings to determine which witnesses they wanted to call before the entire Commission in a public hearing. Two members of the Commission questioned me in private, but I had little doubt that I'd be giving testimony at the public hearings as well.

Unlike members of Congress who conducted the televised Watergate hearings, the Iran-Contra hearings, and others, the 9/11 Commission members were not accountable to the American people, in the sense that they would not be voted in or out of office based on the quality of their work. They were simply a fact-finding commission, similar to the Warren Commission called together after the assassination of President John F. Kennedy.

The National Commission on Terrorist Attacks Upon the United States—charged with uncovering the truth behind 9/11 and making recommendations as to how we can better protect our nation against future attacks—seemed to many, from time to time, to be veering dangerously out of control. Ostensibly, the Commission's overriding purpose was to find the facts surrounding the terrorist attacks. Everyone in the nation wanted to know how the best intelligence organizations in the world could be blindsided by the terrorists who caused such death and devastation. Why couldn't we have stopped al Qaeda before they attacked us? And what about those rumors that said we had missed opportunities to find some of the 9/11 hijackers already inside our country in August 2001? What should we be doing differently in the future? And were we really secure in the present? These questions and many others deserved thoughtful, truthful responses.

Before the 9/11 Commission ever opened the first public hearing, information they had obtained in private prehearing testimony seeped into news coverage. When the Commission staged its televised hearings, juicy tidbits had been leaked stimulating media interest, and members of the Commission had been interviewed, previewing what they intended to discuss.

Unfortunately, from the early stages it became apparent that on occasion the hearings were not so much about discovering the truth as they were about assessing blame and grandstanding. Before long, the public hearings disintegrated into show trials. Even while deliberations continued, before the evidence had been completely examined, certain members of the Commission offered themselves ubiquitously on network and cable news programs, and anywhere else someone would put them on camera to discuss their findings and hype their hearings.

Certain members became "personalities" in demand in the media.

Unlike the way a court proceeds in its quest of the facts, limiting press access and avoiding any announcements of conclusions in advance, the Commission members chose to do the opposite. They didn't simply send out a press secretary or a spokesperson to make announcements; instead the members themselves took to the streets, almost with a "Tune in tomorrow to see who we grill" attitude.

But far more serious than the theatrics that had come to dominate the 9/11 Commission hearings was the Commission's neglect—inadvertent or otherwise—of what I believed to be several of our nation's most glaring vulnerabilities to terrorist attack. Beyond that, at least one member on the Commission had been a prime player in helping to create some of those vulnerabilities.

Compare that to a court of law: in a courtroom, a judge is not permitted to hear a matter if he has been part of the case. But a member of the 9/11 Commission who had been at the heart of developing a policy that inhibited the discovery and pursuit of terrorists could sit in judgment on others responsible for terrorist fighting policy.

Not only were the Commission members sitting in judgment, they shaped and tailored what information would be requested from potential witnesses. One member in particular had a definite conflict of interest. Jamie Gorelick served as deputy attorney general under Attorney General Janet Reno during the Clinton administration. A bright, articulate woman who left the Justice Department in 1997, Gorelick was working in the private sector prior to being tapped by Democrats to serve on the 9/11 Commission. According to media reports, her name had been on the short list of potential candidates for attorney general had Vice President Al Gore won the presidential election in 2000. Even most Republicans considered her a logical choice to be included on the Commission. But Jamie Gorelick knew something the other members of the Commission either didn't know or had chosen to ignore.

In 1995, Jamie Gorelick wrote a memo in which the Justice Department reinforced and heightened "the wall" inhibiting communication between the criminal investigators and intelligence officers investigating terrorists. The idea of "the wall" originally followed the enactment of the Foreign Intelligence Surveillance Act of 1978. The deputy attorney general's memo raised the wall higher than the law required. The wall impeded our law enforcement and intelligence agents from sharing vital information that might have led them to the hijackers before the terrorist attacks of 9/11. Knowing this, one might wonder how Jamie Gorelick could fairly serve on the Commission. The answer was simple: her memo was classified. Few people knew that Jamie Gorelick had actually caused information not to be shared between intelligence and law enforcement agents.

In the 1995 memo, classified as SECRET and addressed to U.S. Attorney Mary Jo White, FBI Director Louis Freeh, Richard Scruggs of the Council of Intelligence Policy and Review, and Assistant Attorney General for the Criminal Division Jo Ann Harris, regarding the investigation and prosecution of the terrorists involved in the 1993 World Trade Center bombing cases and others, Gorelick wrote:

> During the course of those investigations, significant counterintelligence information has been developed related to the activities and plans of agents of foreign powers operating in this country and overseas, including previously unknown connections between separate terrorist groups. Although information and evidence relevant to possible future criminal prosecutions is still being sought, it has become overwhelmingly apparent that there is a compelling need to further develop and expand that foreign counterintelligence information. Consequently, the FBI has initiated a separate full field counterintelligence investigation.

Clearly, the deputy attorney general understood that potential terrorists groups existed within the United States, maintaining connections with other terrorist groups abroad. Yet she felt compelled to raise the wall higher.

> Because the counterintelligence investigation will involve the use of surveillance techniques authorized under the Foreign Intelligence Surveillance Act (FISA) against targets that, in some instances, had been subject to surveillance under Title III, and because it will involve some of the same sources and targets as the criminal investigation, we believe that it is prudent to establish a set of instructions that will clearly separate the counterintelligence investigation from the more limited, but continued, criminal investigations. These procedures, which go beyond what is legally required, will prevent any risk of creating an unwarranted appearance that FISA is being used to avoid procedural safeguards which would apply in a criminal investigation.

In theory, the memo's enhancement of "the wall" was supposed to help avoid legal challenges to terror prosecutions. But with the simple phrase "which go beyond what is legally required," the memo acknowledged that this enhancement of the wall was not necessary. I do not believe that Deputy Attorney General Gorelick comprehended the danger of maintaining and elevating the wall.

On the other hand, Mary Jo White certainly did. Arguably the most prominent U.S. Attorney during the Clinton administration—a most formidable prosecutor wisely appointed by President Bill Clinton—Mary Jo White nonetheless challenged Jamie Gorelick's order regarding the raising of the wall. And with good reason. As U.S. Attorney for the Southern District of New York (sometimes referred to by Justice Department insiders as "the sovereign district" of New York because of its high-profile cases and independence), White had been the lead prosecutor on the case of Ramzi Yousef, the menace who planned the 1993 World Trade Center bombing. She and her talented team of prosecutors knew what the real risks were. They knew then more about the inner workings of global terror than many government intelligence agencies. They had fought and won a series of convictions against terrorists in the United States—including blind Sheikh Omar Abdel Rahman, who plotted to bomb the Statue of Liberty and New York's Holland Tunnel. In my view, for Mary Jo White, breaking down the wall was not a matter of appearances; it was a matter of survival.

Mary Jo White recognized that the wall made it more difficult to disrupt and stop such potential terrorist attacks. In a memo responding to Jamie Gorelicks's instructions, White pleaded with the deputy attorney general to tear down the wall between intelligence and prosecutors. "This is not an area where it is safe or prudent to build unnecessary walls," White cautioned, "or to compartmentalize our knowledge of any possible players, plans or activities."

In an almost prescient warning, Mary Jo White stated bluntly the reason for her concerns:

> The single biggest mistake we can make in attempting to combat terrorism is to insulate the criminal side of the house from the intelligence side of the house, unless such insulation is absolutely necessary. Excessive conservatism . . . can have deadly results.

She added: "We must face the reality that the way we are proceeding now is inherently and in actuality very dangerous."

White wrote the memo after her earlier uneasiness about the wall was ignored. In a June 13, 1995, memo to Attorney General Janet Reno, Mary Jo White responded to the heightened procedures. Reno had asked her if she was comfortable with the new instructions. White replied:

It is hard to be totally comfortable with instructions to the FBI prohibiting contact with the United States Attorney's Offices when such prohibitions are not legally required. These instructions leave entirely to OIPR [Office of Intelligence Policy and Review] and the Criminal Division when, if ever, to contact affected U.S. Attorneys on investigations including terrorism and espionage. While I understand the need for centralization and control, this mechanism cuts out the U.S. Attorneys until the Criminal Division decides with FBI Headquarters to open up a criminal investigation. Our experience has been that the FBI labels of an investigation as intelligence or law enforcement can be quite arbitrary, depending upon the personnel involved and that the most effective way to combat terrorism is with as few labels and walls as possible so that wherever permissible, the right and left hand are communicating.[1]

Enlisting the help of her team, U.S. Attorney White presented six pages of detailed reasons why it was a mistake to create too much of a wall between intelligence and prosecutions. White forwarded that analysis to Gorelick and added her own notes. "What troubles me even more than the known problems we have encountered," Mary Jo White revealed, "are the undoubtedly countless instances of unshared and unacted-upon information that reside in some file or other, or in some head or other, or in some unreviewed or not fully understood tape or other." She concluded, "These can be disasters waiting to happen."

Unfortunately, no one in the Clinton Justice Department acted on their premier prosecutor's warnings.

We had dismantled the wall through the USA PATRIOT Act in October 2001. Yet as I watched portions of the televised 9/11 Commission hearings while I struggled to recuperate from acute pancreatitis at

George Washington University Hospital, it struck me that most of the country still did not realize how we had ceded an advantage to terror by withholding information from our best agents. The wall had not gotten the attention it deserved in the Commission's deliberations up to that point. I knew something had to be done to bring the truth to light or, one day, the wall could be reinstated.

The 9/11 Commission had requested that I appear in a public hearing, and I had agreed. From what I had seen so far, I seriously questioned whether anything good would come of it. Still, this Commission represented the best chance for our country to hear the truth, and hopefully to set the historical record straight as to how our nation had become so vulnerable to terrorist attacks. If there were any possibility of making recommendations that would keep the American people safer and more secure, I wanted to testify.

I knew appearing before the Commission would not be a picnic. Several Commission members had already leaked information to the press about how they were going to draw and quarter me for not making counterterrorism a higher priority in our Justice Department. Major newspapers carried front-page stories with leaked private testimony before the Commission. Certain members, it seemed, were all too eager to interrogate me before the cameras.

When I entered the Hart Senate Office Building, I was ushered to a side anteroom before the hearings commenced. In the room were several members of the Commission. They looked surprised at my appearance. Thin and gaunt from my illness, I still felt rather weak. I had lost twenty pounds, and had only recently begun to eat solid food. A few of the Commission members came over to greet me. "My, you look great, John." It reminded me about the three stages of life: youth, middle age, and "you're looking great."

Tom Kean, chairman of the Commission, greeted me warmly. Tom and I have known each other for years and have enjoyed a strong friendship, even when we have disagreed on particular issues. Tom spoke quietly, "Don't worry," he said in an almost fatherly tone. "Things are going to come out all right. This Commission is going to write a valuable report."

I thanked Tom, and I truly appreciated his goodwill, but I felt the conduct of the Commission, the leaked hearings and processes were not harbingers of good things to come.

The hearing was held in the Hart Senate hearing room, the same room in which I had testified a few years earlier during the second day of my confirmation hearings. It was a hearing room constructed with television broadcasts in mind. As I took my seat, I noticed several members of the Commission fumbling through their notebooks. "I can't seem to find your testimony," one of them groused.

"Nor can I," another chimed in.

Ordinarily, when a witness appears before a commission in Washington, the initial testimony is already submitted in writing prior to the actual hearing. The members of the commission then have time to study the testimony and prepare further questions. Given the numerous leaks and "extra-hearings announcements" hyping the proceedings, I did not submit prior written testimony that the Commission members could "spin" in advance, or "cook" in the press.

I did, however, carry some important and unanticipated information with me.

Few experiences in my life have been couched in more daunting terms than my appearance before the 9/11 Commission. In theory, I was there to shed light on how we could prevent future attacks on America, but it was obvious to me that the Commission really wanted to know what the Justice Department was doing prior to 9/11, what we knew, and why our best efforts failed to prevent the 9/11 attacks. The Commission seemed obsessed with trying to lay the blame for the terrorist attacks at the feet of the Bush administration, while virtually absolving the previous administration of responsibility.

In the days just prior to my appearance before the Commission, I felt that the members had been disrespectful, patently rude, and offensive to National Security Advisor Condoleezza Rice. During Rice's testimony, Commission members interrupted her statements at times and seemed to be lecturing her almost contemptuously at others.

I certainly expected no better treatment. Looking up from my table and chair on the floor toward the Commission members seated at the raised tables in front and above me, it struck me how alone and isolated I was in this process. In such an environment, the attorney general sits alone, facing a dozen Commission interrogators and their staffs, who are busy passing notes, conferring with one another. The attorney general confers with no one during the hearing. He is alone, knowing that some of the people before whom he sits have already passed judgment and pronounced sentence: they are planning to nail me to the wall.

I also felt strongly that someone in the Bush administration should make it clear that the absence of responsible behavior on the part of the 9/11 Commission members had not gone unnoticed. It occurred to me that this might be one of my last public opportunities to present the truth about 9/11, so I decided to make my case as straightforwardly as possible.

Ironically, the Commission was about to swear me in to tell the truth—and there was a lot of truth that needed to be told—but I wasn't sure they wanted to hear it, nor would they be happy about the truth once I had told it.

Sitting right behind me in the hearing room were Larry Thompson, the deputy attorney general, and Ted Olson, the solicitor general whose wife, Barbara, had died aboard the plane that had smashed into the Pentagon on 9/11.

I raised my hand and stood as erect as my health would allow, and with as much intensity as my weakened constitution permitted I swore that the testimony I would give before the 9/11 Commission would be the truth. My first remarks expressed my profound sorrow for the victims who died on 9/11, and their families who still grieved.

I wasted no time in plowing into sensitive areas. Acknowledging the criticism the Justice Department incurred as a result of our aggressive efforts to arrest or detain potential terrorists, I targeted my first volley:

> We have been aggressive. We have been tough. And we have suffered no small amount of criticism for our tough tactics. We accept this criticism for what it is: the price we are privileged to pay for our liberty.
>
> Had I known a terrorist attack on the United States was imminent in 2001, I would have unloaded our full arsenal of weaponry against it—despite the inevitable criticism. The Justice Department's warriors, our agents and our prosecutors, would have been unleashed. Every tough tactic we have deployed since the attacks would have been deployed before the attacks.
>
> But the simple fact of September 11 is this: we did not know an attack was coming because for nearly a decade our government had blinded itself to its enemies. Our agents were isolated by government-imposed walls, handcuffed by government-imposed restrictions, and starved for basic information technology.

I remained focused on my remarks, but I could feel the tension in the room increasing exponentially as I spoke. My opening statement included four central issues that had not been developed fully during the hearings. First, I addressed the issue of covert actions—or the lack of them—directed at Osama bin Laden prior to 2001.

> Let me be clear: My thorough review revealed no covert-action program to kill bin Laden. There was a covert-action program to capture bin Laden for criminal prosecution. But

even this program was crippled by a snarled web of requirements, restrictions, and regulations that prevented decisive action by our men and women in the field.

When they most needed clear, understandable guidance, our agents and operatives were given the language of lawyers. Even if they could have penetrated bin Laden's training camps, they would have needed a battery of attorneys to approve the capture.

I informed the Commission of a conversation I'd had with National Security Advisor Condoleezza Rice prior to 9/11, during one of our first meetings on the subject of bin Laden's fomenting of terrorism. "We should find and kill bin Laden," I said. Rice concurred and gave CIA Director George Tenet responsibility for drafting new authorities that would allow for decisive, lethal action against bin Laden.

The atmosphere in the Hart hearing room was charged as I moved to my second point. No doubt, by now, some members of the Commission were wondering why they had invited me to their party. I pressed forward, knowing before I said the words that my next statement could be provocative, a turning point that might change the complexion of the hearings.

The single greatest structural cause for September 11 was the wall that segregated criminal investigators and intelligence agents. Government erected this wall. Government buttressed this wall. And before September 11, government was blinded by this wall.

Several members of the Commission appeared nervous as I spoke, but I persisted, describing how the wall worked in greater specificity:

In the days before September 11, the wall specifically impeded the investigation into Zacarias Moussaoui, Khalid al-Mihdhar, and Nawaf al-Hazmi. After the FBI arrested Moussaoui, agents became suspicious of his interest in commercial aircraft and sought approval for a criminal warrant to search his computer. The warrant was rejected because FBI officials feared breaching the wall.

When the CIA finally told the FBI that al-Mihdhar and al-Hazmi were in the country in late August, agents in New York searched for the suspects. But because of the wall, FBI headquarters refused to allow criminal investigators who knew the most about the most recent al Qaeda attack to join the hunt for suspected terrorists.

At that time, a frustrated FBI investigator wrote headquarters, "Whatever has happened to this—someday someone will die—and wall or not—the public will not understand why we were not more effective in throwing every resource we had at certain 'problems.' Let's hope the National Security Law Unit will stand behind their decision then, especially since the biggest threat to us, UBL, is getting the most protection."

FBI headquarters responded, "We're all frustrated with this issue . . . These are the rules. NSLU does not make them up."

But somebody did make these rules. Somebody built this wall.

The basic architecture for the wall in the 1995 Guidelines was contained in a classified memorandum entitled "Instructions on Separation of Certain Foreign Counterintelligence and Criminal Investigations." The memorandum ordered FBI Director Louis Freeh and others, "We believe that it is prudent to establish a set of instructions that will more clearly separate the counterintelligence investigation from the more limited, but continued, criminal investigations. These procedures, which go beyond what is legally required, will prevent any risk of creating an unwarranted appearance that FISA is being used to avoid procedural safeguards which would apply in a criminal investigation."

This memorandum established a wall separating the criminal and intelligence investigations following the 1993 World Trade Center attack, the largest international terrorism attack on American soil prior to September 11. Although you understand the debilitating impact of the wall, I cannot imagine that the Commission knew about this memorandum, so I have declassified it for you and the public to review. Full disclosure compels me to inform you that the author is a member of the Commission.

At no point during my testimony did I mention former Deputy Attorney General Jamie Gorelick by name in my opening remarks before the 9/11 Commission. I had purposely avoided naming her as the person who had heightened the wall, since I wanted to frame the discussion in the best possible light, focusing attention on the wall itself, not on those who had extended it beyond the requirements of the law. Still, as Commission members realized the implications of my statement, recognition dawned on their faces that we were in a whole new ball game.

The third issue I raised with the Commission was the limitation the U.S. government placed on our ability to connect the dots of the terrorist threat prior to September 11 because of the lack of support for information technology at the FBI.

After I became attorney general in February 2001, the Hanssen and McVeigh cases made it indelibly clear that the FBI's computer technology and information management was in terrible shape. The Bureau had at least forty-two separate information systems, none of which were connected or could readily communicate with each other. Agents lacked access to even the most basic Internet technology. These problems didn't merely hamper interagency communication; they hindered information sharing in the Justice Department, the intelligence community, and communication with state and local law enforcement. It's no wonder, given the state of this technology, that the Phoenix memo—a warning that Osama bin Laden may be sending students to the U.S. to attend civil aviation universities and colleges in Arizona, training in commercial aviation—was lost in the maze of antique computers across America and at the Washington headquarters.

Year after year, the FBI was denied funds requested to improve its information technology. Over eight years, the bureau was denied nearly $800 million of its information technology funding requests.

On September 11, 2001, the FBI's annual technology budget under the Clinton administration was actually $36 million less than the last Bush budget eight years earlier. The FBI's information infrastructure had been starved, and by September 11 it was collapsing from budgetary neglect. On September 11, 2001, and for a considerable time afterward, the FBI's ability to process, manage, and exchange information was seriously hindered by the fact that agents were working with 1980s-type equipment.

When the Hanssen and McVeigh failures fully exposed this neglect and its cost to national security, I ordered four independent external reviews of the FBI's information infrastructure under the coordination of Deputy Attorney General Larry Thompson. And my first two budgets, both proposed before 9/11, requested a 50 percent increase for FBI information technology. The budget under which we were operating on 9/11 was a budget established by the prior administration. No budget of the Bush administration was in place on September 11, and none had yet been enacted.

The 2002 budget proposed by President Bush had the largest counterterrorism increase in five years. Of course, after 9/11, Congress's cooperation on the FBI's budget requests was significantly improved, with a ready willingness to provide serious assistance not only in counterterrorism but in information technology as well.

As I shared these insights with the 9/11 Commission, several of the individuals who had touted their intentions to verbally dismember me now sat back in their chairs. Leaks from the Commission had advertised to the media that my head would roll, but I felt that certain necessary truths had been revealed. Several Commission members, appearing grateful, smiled openly.

If there had been any doubt previously, the Commission members knew now, even before the question and answer period, that I had come to tell the truth. And we weren't finished yet.

ENDNOTES

1. Memorandum from Mary Jo White, United States Attorney for the Southern District of New York, to the Honorable Janet Reno, Attorney General; Re: Instructions FI and FCI Investigations, June 13, 1995, made public by the U.S. Department of Justice, April 28, 2004, at the request of Senator Lindsey Graham and Senator John Cornyn.

CHAPTER SIXTEEN

THE MILLENNIUM PLOT

The 9/11 Commission, Part 2

≈≈≈≈≈

Victoria, British Columbia, looks like a scene from a painting, even on a chilly December afternoon. With picturesque mountains in the background and the blue-green sea in the foreground, the charming Canadian town evokes images of peace and tranquility. A ferry boat from Victoria's inner harbor shuttles passengers and their vehicles across the strait to Port Angeles, Washington, about a two-hour drive from downtown Seattle.

On Tuesday afternoon, December 14, 1999, a green Chrysler 300M pulled onto the boarding area in front of the Coho ferry, a scant ten minutes before the four o'clock departure for Port Angeles. U.S. Immigration inspector Gary Roberts asked the driver of the rented Chrysler for his passport and driver's license.

The driver complied, producing documentation showing his name as Benni Noris, from Montreal.

"Where are you going?" the immigration officer asked.

"Seattle," responded the driver with a marked accent. "Two-day business trip."

It struck the officer as odd that a businessperson would drive to Victoria to get to Seattle. A tourist enjoying the scenery might travel that route, but for a short business hop? Something didn't make sense.

"Pull aside here, please," the officer instructed. Officer Roberts checked Noris's name in his computer, looking for any outstanding arrest warrants, immigration violations, or other offenses. There were none. Just a mention that Noris had been checked at Los Angeles Airport in February.

The officer asked the driver to open his trunk. Inside, Roberts found a backpack, a satchel, and a suitcase, which he searched and found only the usual assortment of clothes a person might have for a short trip. The officer waved Benni Noris onto the ferry.

But it wasn't Benni Noris boarding that ferry traveling to America from Canada. The passenger's real name was Ahmed Ressam, a thirty-two-year old who had illegally immigrated to Canada from Algeria by using a fake passport. Ressam had spent much of 1998 in Afghanistan training at a terrorist camp closely connected to Osama bin Laden. He had returned to Montreal by way of Pakistan, traveled on to Seoul, Korea, and from there to Los Angeles. While waiting at LAX for his flight to Canada, Ressam observed and calculated how long it might take security guards to discover a bomb if hidden in a piece of abandoned luggage, plainly visible, out in the open, in a busy, congested passenger area. He boarded his flight, fully intending that the next time he saw LAX, he would bring it to ruin.

Now, comfortably aboard the Coho ferry, Noris/Ressam was on his way to fulfill his mission. Darkness enveloped the ferry as it eased in and tied off at the dock in Port Angeles shortly before six o'clock. U.S. Customs inspectors stopped each vehicle as it rolled off the ferry. There were so few passengers aboard the boat it wouldn't take long to finish up their duties, and they'd be on their way home. The Coho was the last vessel scheduled to arrive that evening, and the final car in the inspection line was a green Chrysler.

U.S. Customs inspector Diana Dean stopped the 300M bearing British Columbia license plates. As she had done to all of the previous passengers leaving the ferry, Inspector Dean rattled off a few basic questions, her normal routine before wishing the drivers a safe trip.

"Where are you going?" she asked.

"Seattle," Noris answered.

"Where do you live?"

"Montreal," came the reply.

"And who are you going to see in Seattle?"

"No. Hotel," Noris said in broken English.

With nineteen years of experience, Diana Dean noticed little things—things such as a man fidgeting while going through customs—and especially noticed when someone seemed unusually nervous. She noticed that Noris was perspiring on the chilly December evening. She decided to take a closer look, so she gave the driver a customs declaration to complete.

When he finished, Dean asked Noris to turn the car off, open the trunk, and get out of the car. The Algerian feigned as though he couldn't understand. Inspector Dean repeated the instructions several times before Noris reluctantly complied.

U.S. Customs inspectors Mark Johnson, Dan Clem, and Mike Chapman watched nearby. Finished with their inpections, and waiting to head home, they came over to help Inspector Dean check over the last vehicle of the day.

Mark Johnson addressed Noris while Chapman, Clem, and Dean searched the trunk. When Johnson asked Noris for his identification, the jittery Noris handed him a Costco card.

Johnson took Noris aside and told him to empty his pockets on a table. Meanwhile, Dan Clem reached inside the trunk and unscrewed the fastener on the spare tire compartment. When he looked inside, he found no spare tire, but he did find several green bags filled with white powder, two jars of brown liquid, two pill bottles, and four black boxes that looked similar to electronic devices.

Thinking they had found a stash of drugs, Johnson grabbed Noris by the shoulders. While patting him down, Johnson felt something odd in Noris's coat, and began taking off the Algerian's coat.

Noris bolted, literally leaving his car on the ferry and his coat in

Johnson's hands as he fled across a parking lot. Johnson and Chapman chased after him, spotting Noris hiding under a parked pickup truck.

Chapman drew his gun and ordered Noris to come out with his hands above his head. Noris complied, but then with Chapman aiming directly at him, less than twenty-five feet away, Noris turned and ran again, this time into a busy street. He was hit by one car, but he kept running with the Customs inspectors close behind. At the intersection, Noris attempted to commandeer a car that had stopped for the traffic light. He grabbed the driver's side door handle, startling the woman at the wheel. Instinctively, she stomped on the gas, sending Noris spinning, right into the grasp of Inspectors Johnson and Chapman.

The inspectors turned Noris over to the police, who placed him in the backseat of their cruiser, while the officers examined the stash in the trunk of Noris's rented car. The inspectors took samples of the white power and other contents. What was it? It wasn't cocaine; nor was it heroin. Could it be some sort of new chemical high? Johnson took out one of the jars of brown liquid and gently shook it. As he did, Noris, who was watching him from the back of the police cruiser, ducked.

No wonder. When the liquid was tested, it was found to be a highly explosive form of nitroglycerin, enough to make at least four large bombs. The mysterious chemicals proved to be ingredients for bombs as well, and the black boxes were found to be homemade timing devices.

When FBI agent Fred Humphries read Noris his Miranda rights in French and asked him if he wanted to talk, Noris responded that he did not want to discuss what had happened. Although he didn't say much, it was enough for Humphries. The agent recognized immediately that Noris was most likely not from Montreal. Instead, Noris's accent sounded a lot like that of a language instructor Humphries had once known in the military. That man was from Algeria.

Eventually, with the help of the Canadian Royal Mounted Police, the FBI discovered the man they had in custody was not Benni Noris, but instead was Ahmed Ressam, a suspected terrorist with ties to people close to bin Laden. A number of his coconspirators were found in Montreal and other locations—some within the United States—and arrested as well. Ressam's testimony represented another in a series of strong leads that indicated terrorist cells were thriving in Canada and the United States. With our northern borders so porous, it was only a matter of time before terrorists slipped into the U.S. through Canada, or launched some sort of attack originating in the north.

Investigators at first thought that Ressam had planned to use his explosives to blow up Seattle's Space Needle, because his cohorts had booked a hotel room near the popular tourist area. Beyond that, Ressam had mentioned twice to the Customs inspectors that he was headed to Seattle. Because of the threat, on December 27, 1999, Seattle's mayor, Paul Schell, reluctantly canceled the city's New Year's Eve Spectacular, scheduled at the Space Needle and expected to draw upward of one hundred thousand revelers.

It was later discovered, however, that Ressam had his sights trained on an entirely different target, the Los Angeles International Airport, which he hoped to blow to bits sometime on or near the New Year's celebration, as the world welcomed the new millennium.

The foiling of the "Millennium Plot"—as this incident along with the other thwarted al Qaeda–encouraged attacks near the end of 1999 collectively came to be known—received generous accolades as the pattern of how to prevent terrorist attacks. By 2004, when I testified at the 9/11 Commission hearings, certain Commission members pointed to the millennium case as an example of how an effective counterterrorism operation should be run. Senior officials, they said, from the president on down, should call everyone together and "shake the trees" (as the Clinton Administration had been shaking the trees) to prevent potential attacks.

While it is true that the FBI and CIA and other intelligence personnel did an outstanding job of disrupting terrorism around the millennium celebrations, even the people involved with the millennium counterterrorism efforts admitted that America and the world had gotten lucky.

In Jordan, for example, al Qaeda members had planned to attack a variety of tourist sites, including the four-hundred-room Amman Radisson hotel, which was sold out for the millennium celebration. Most of the guests staying at the hotel that night were Americans and Israelis. The terrorists also planned to bomb a site on the Jordan River where John the Baptist baptized Jesus; they intended to launch terrorist activity on Mount Nebo as well, another site revered by Christians and Jews as the mountain from which Moses was allowed to view the Promised Land, although he was not to enter. Moses is thought to be buried nearby, thus making the area all the more sacred to those of the Judeo-Christian faiths.

Fortunately, Jordanian intelligence intercepted a telephone call between Abu Zubaydah, al Qaeda's leader of the plot, and a Palestinian militant. Zubaydah is reported to have said, "The time for training is over."[1]

Jordanian police moved in and arrested sixteen conspirators in the plot, including Raed Hijazi, a taxi driver from Boston who, it was reported, helped assemble the bombs. Rather than pulling body parts from the rubble, the millennium celebration at Amman proceeded relatively uninterrupted.

In Yemen, similar favor surrounded personnel aboard the USS *The Sullivans*, a U.S. Navy destroyer in port at Aden harbor on call. Terrorists loaded a small boat with explosives and planned to either sidle up next to the huge American vessel or drive their boat directly into the ship. But by sheer luck, the al Qaeda boat, overloaded with explosives, got stuck in the mud and sank before the crew could detonate its powerful bombs.

Lest anyone regard these frustrated attempts at mass murder as the terrorists' version of the Bad News Bears, let me remind you that when al Qaeda launched a similar attack a second time, on October 12, 2000, they nearly sank the USS *Cole*, a U.S. Navy guided missile destroyer on call in Yemen, just as the USS *The Sullivans* had been. Seventeen U.S. sailors died in that attack. And the United States seemed powerless to retaliate.

The capture of Ahmed Ressam should also be considered a stroke of luck, not a national policy triumph. Granted, U.S. Customs inspector Diana Dean alertly followed up on her suspicions that something was awry. She and her fellow inspectors saved countless lives through their individual initiative. And that is a credit to Inspector Dean and her colleagues at Port Angeles, but it is hardly a testimony to aggressive national "get tough on terror" efforts.

In the aftermath of the millennium celebrations, the National Security Council and other agencies prepared "After Action Reviews" similar to those done when military operations are conducted. These reports specifically focused on what went well, what went wrong, and what could have been done better.

The Millennium After Action Review, assembled and written largely by Richard Clarke, President Clinton's counterterrorism czar, recommended twenty-nine strategies, mostly directed toward rooting out, disrupting, and destroying terrorist threats within the United States. While Richard Clarke and I might disagree on many issues, I concurred generally with his report, particularly the conclusion reached by the study that we had been lucky. Prior to 9/11, much of America's focus on terrorism had been on threats in foreign countries, at our embassies, or at military installations such as Khobar Towers in Saudi Arabia, where nineteen Americans died and more than three hundred were injured when a five-thousand-pound truck bomb was detonated by terrorists. Few people in the government or in the agencies tasked with keeping our nation secure gauged the threats within the U.S. borders as serious. Overseas? Certainly. In our homeland? Not hardly.

When I sat before the 9/11 Commission, I encouraged them to study carefully the classified Millennium After Action Review, which amounted to President Clinton's National Security Council plan to disrupt the al Qaeda network in the U.S. and abroad. Unfortunately, our government had failed to implement fully that plan, even though deterrents were spelled out clearly, a full seventeen months before the horrendous attacks of September 11, 2001.

Ironically, the NSC Millennium After Action Review itself declares that the United States barely missed major terrorist attacks in 1999, and cites luck as playing a major role. Among the many vulnerable areas of homeland defenses identified in the review as needing improvement, Justice Department surveillance and FISA operations were specifically criticized as "glaring weaknesses."

It was clear from the review that actions taken in the millennium period should not be the operating model for the U.S. government when it comes to preventing terrorist strikes against our homeland. The March 2000 review warned the Clinton administration of a substantial al Qaeda network and affiliated foreign terrorist presence within the U.S. capable of supporting additional terrorist attacks here.

Furthermore, fully seventeen months before the September 11 attacks, the review recommended disrupting the al Qaeda network and terrorist presence in the United States by using immigration violations, minor criminal infractions, tougher visa restrictions, and stronger border controls—destabilizing terrorist groups and taking them off the streets.

Interestingly, as I explained to the 9/11 Commission, "These are the same aggressive, often-criticized law enforcement tactics that we have unleashed for thirty-one months to stop another al Qaeda attack. These are the same tough tactics we deployed to catch Ali al-Marri, who was sent here by al Qaeda on September 10, 2001, to facilitate a second wave of terrorist attacks on Americans."

But despite the warnings and the clear vulnerabilities identified by the NSC in 2000, no new pre-9/11 disruption strategy to attack the al Qaeda network within the United States was deployed. It was ignored in the Justice Department's five-year counterterrorism strategy. From my perspective, it was buried.

I did not see this highly classified review before September 11, 2001. It was not among the thirty items on which I was briefed in the transition period when I took office. Nor was it advanced as a disruption strategy to me during the 2001 summer threat period by the NSC staff, the same agency that had written the review more than a year earlier.

Why the blueprint for security was not followed during the Clinton years, and particularly after the report raised warnings in the year 2000, we may never know. I do know from my personal experience that those who take the kind of tough measures called for in the plan will feel the heat in modern America.

Some people in our country seem more concerned about respecting the dignity and privacy of criminals and terrorists than they are about having an airport full of people obliterated, or a completely booked hotel blown to bits. Perhaps they think, Let's not get so upset about attacks on our embassies or military bases. Maybe, they surmise, the terrorists have good reason for attacking us. We have no right to be harassing innocent people in our country. For some people, not even the grotesque images that filled our television screens after al Qaeda's blatant attacks on 9/11 seem enough to wake them out of their utopia feel-good world.

I've been there, and I've heard the impassioned, amorphous rhetoric about infringing on the "civil liberties" of potential terrorists in our towns, cities, malls, and sporting arenas. Frankly, the sense of urgency in America may not have been enough to overcome concern about the outcry and criticism that most certainly would have followed such tough tactics. But the tactics themselves were right; the suggestions made by the Millennium After Action Report worked. I know they worked because, although we did not have access to that particular report until much later, the Justice Department put into practice those very tactics, what I called our "spit on the sidewalk" policy: detain or arrest suspected terrorists on any legal grounds possible. And the attacks stopped.

Certainly, we must never forget that terrorists take a long view of history—they waited for eight years between attacks on the World Trade Center—but after 9/11 there has not been a successful terrorist attack on our nation for more than fifty-eight months, since implementing the aggressive "spit on the sidewalk" strategy, or to date as I write these words. That fact alone causes one to wonder what might have happened—or not have happened—had the Millennium After Action recommendations been fully deployed rather than discarded, had they been fully implemented upon delivery rather than lost in the bureaucracy.

It is impossible to say that the Justice Department was not aware of the report in 2000. They knew the review warned of a substantial al Qaeda network and affiliated terrorist presence within the United States, and it was critical of the nation's security measures taken prior to 2000.

Yet something about that report must have seemed either profoundly valuable or extremely embarrassing. Former National Security Advisor Sandy Berger apparently felt the classified report was telling enough that he would risk smuggling draft copies of it out of the National Archives, ostensibly to prepare testimony for the 9/11 Commission. Berger went even further, taking copies of the classified after action report to his office and destroying them.[2]

As a former national security advisor for President Clinton, Berger occupied the same position that Condoleezza Rice filled for President Bush during the first four years of his administration. The national security advisor holds a position of great trust, advising the president on a multitude of issues and coordinates all items related to national security, bringing together the secretary of state, the secretary of defense, the attorney general, and dealing with the internal and external security of the country.

After the Clinton administration left office, Sandy Berger, even as a former national security advisor, would not normally have had access to classified materials in the National Archives. But he was designated by the former Clinton administration as their official person to review documents on the administration's behalf in preparation for the 9/11 Commission hearings. Berger was charged with the responsibility of going through the thousands of pages of material relating to the Clinton years in office, and managing the document flow from the Clinton administration to the 9/11 Commission. He was not a casual person with access; he had access to the documents because of his official responsibility to the 9/11 Commission.

Nor was Sandy Berger a buffoon, clumsily grabbing classified documents that would put him at such risk. Apparently, he knew what he was after and why. And when he was caught, he chose to plead guilty to his crimes. In court, Berger characterized his brazen theft as a lapse of judgment, stating, "I let considerations of personal convenience override clear rules of handling classified material." Berger continued, "I believe this lapse, serious as it is, does not reflect the character of myself."[3]

U.S. Magistrate Judge Deborah Robinson disagreed; she ordered Berger to pay a $50,000 fine, a substantial increase over the $10,000 recommended by government lawyers, but considered a slap on the wrists by many others. The question of why Sandy Berger took the documents about the Clinton administration's unimplemented plan to disrupt terrorism in the United States continues to rankle many who heard so much about how that administration was "shaking the trees" searching for potential terrorists in our country.

As I concluded my opening remarks to the 9/11 Commission, I offered them a rejoinder that I hoped would cause them to consider their real purpose for being commissioned in the first place:

This Commission's heavy burden—to probe the causes of September 11—demands that the record be complete. Our nation's heavy burden—to learn from the mistakes of the past—demands that this Commission seeks the whole truth.

May this Commission be successful in its mission. And may we learn well the lessons from history.

Not surprisingly, the first response to my testimony before the Commission regarded former Deputy Attorney General Jamie Gorelick and the wall. Former Illinois governor James Thompson asked, "General, does a member of your staff have the copy of this declassified memorandum about the walls? And if so, could we have it?"

With a slight hint of tongue in cheek, I replied, "I believe the memorandum is available, and we'd be glad to provide it to the Commission."

Technically, Jamie Gorelick recused herself from the hearing during testimony regarding the wall and her involvement at the Clinton Justice Department. Yet although she was recused, she remained on the panel of commissioners, scribbling notes and passing them to others, who then directed questions to me.

For more than an hour, the Commission members tossed questions my way, several of which seemed intended to discredit my four basic premises. I had hoped that the Commission would have wanted to pursue positive recommendations based on those four neglected areas of their deliberations. Instead, they seemed more intent on disproving them.

At least one pleasant by-product resulted from my testimony. After my appearance before the Commission, the members' television theatrics dropped off precipitously. After all, any time they showed up on a news program, or were interviewed in a "live" news segment, the show host could ask them how or why they had missed the Gorelick memo and its profound impact on the pre-9/11 conduct of our intelligence agencies, or why she remained on the Commission.

Not surprisingly, in its final report, the 9/11 Commission gave little credence or attention to my suggestions. Equally troubling was the fact that the 9/11 Commission ignored Mary Jo White's stunning memos and related documents. It makes no mention at all of White's passionate warnings. Such obvious omissions beg the question whether the Commission ignored White's pleas because they were potentially embarrassing to one of their own members, Jamie Gorelick.

Perhaps most outlandish of all, the Commission's report danced lightly around issues pertaining to "the wall," allowing only three pages (out of 567) to discussing the dangerous and dramatic role "the wall" played in the attack on our nation. Moreover, the 9/11 Commission avoided recommending that the USA PATRIOT Act be extended before many of its important provisions would expire. The Commission instead suggested that a "robust debate" should take place. "Because of concerns regarding the shifting balance of power to the government, we think that a full and informed debate on the Patriot Act would be healthy."[4] How the Commission could downplay the importance of such an important and effective tool in preventing terrorism surprised and disappointed me. In their refusal to support the reenactment of the Patriot Act, their position was basically, "Let's talk about it." The fact that the Commission chose to make no stronger recommendation after hundreds of hours of hearings, resulting in a massive report, at enormous costs to the American taxpayers, struck me more as gutless political dodgeball rather than noble national service.

Although the Commission may have served a good purpose, and many of its recommendations may prove helpful to preventing future terrorist attacks, its final report remains seriously flawed by these omissions. How sad, that the group with the most access to the truth chose in several strategic instances to look the other way.

ENDNOTES

1. *The 9/11 Commission Report*, "The Millennium Plots," 6.1, p. 174.
2. Hope Yen, "Judge Orders Berger to Pay $50,000 Fine for Taking Classified Material," Associated Press, September 8, 2005; reprinted online

in the *San Diego Union-Tribune,* SignOnSanDiego.com/new/nation/
20050908-1121-bergersentenced.html.

3. U.S. District Court for the District of Columbia, September 8, 2005;
www.dcd.uscourts.gov/.

4. *The 9/11 Commission Report,* p. 394.

CHAPTER SEVENTEEN

TRANSNATIONAL TERROR

*The Surprising Truth About International
Cooperation in the War on Terror*

The transnational nature of the terrorist threat that confronts the
United States was dramatically illustrated in the September 11
attacks. The terrorists underwent basic training in Afghanistan. They
planned their attack in Western Europe. Their finances were developed from the Middle East. That bin Laden's minions drew resources
from around the globe is well known. The perpetrators trained in flying skills across America, they fine-tuned their operation in Southeast Asia and launched their specific efforts from three different
American states.

If one were to have attempted prosecution of the offenders, the
trail of evidence would have circumnavigated the globe. Extensive
multi-jurisdictional cooperation would have been difficult, but necessary.

Just as prosecution would have required an integrated cooperation to coalesce the fragments of evidence, so prevention in the face
of purposefully fragmented and disintegrated conspiracies requires
the cooperating, integrating efforts of those seeking to disrupt the
plots.

Simply put, international terrorism made international cooperation mandatory rather than elective. Collective security has become

the only real security against the hydra-headed monster of international terror.

Consequently, international cooperation and activity became a specific object in the Justice Department's fight to prevail over terror.

Nothing would be allowed to displace the framework of interdependent cooperation of allies against the war on extremists. All of us in the cabinet remembered some rather unflattering, unjustified, gratuitous derogations of our president by one or two notable heads of European states. I personally resented the wrongful maligning of President Bush. Nevertheless, it became clear that our cooperative efforts with these countries would be of great value in the fight against international terrorism.

Knowing just how "frosty" it was "upstairs," I inquired about whether I should proceed with an important trip to Western Europe. Without a moment's hesitation, I was instructed to keep the schedule and to maintain the highest degree of integrated efforts for working together to secure our safety and freedom. It was gratifying to witness a White House totally unhesitant in placing our national security above multinational politics.

The 9/11 assault was not merely an assault on America but an assault on the entire civilized world. Great Britain was with us in our counterterrorism efforts right from the start. Even some of our allies who may have been reticent about helping to fight terrorism in the past recognized that we were in this battle together, whether we wanted to be or not.

The United States received unprecedented assistance and cooperation from numerous countries, including France and Germany. Germany, in particular, worked with us right from the beginning, almost immediately following the attacks. Part of their willingness to cooperate may have been because at least three of the 9/11 terrorists and three of their accomplices had spent a great deal of time in Germany, and like their American counterparts, the German intelligence agencies had not stopped them.

Three of the 9/11 hijackers had been students and roommates in Hamburg, Germany. Mohamed Atta, the ringleader and terrorist pilot on American Airline's Flight 11, first entered Germany in 1992 and attended the Technical University in Hamburg from 1992 to 1999. Atta continued to use his German bank accounts after entering the United States on June 3, 2000, traveling back and forth to Hamburg throughout the early part of 2001. Atta's name was on the lease of a four-bedroom apartment located at 54 Marienstrasse, in Hamburg. During the twenty-eight months that Atta leased the apartment, twenty-nine Middle Eastern or North African men called the apartment home at one time or another, including fellow hijacker Marwan al-Shehhi.[1]

Marwan al-Shehhi, a hijacker on United Airline's Flight 175, entered Germany in approximately 1996 and attended both the University of Bonn and the Technical University from 1997 to 1998. He left Germany and entered the United States in May 2000. Ziad Jarrah, one of the hijackers who commandeered United Airlines Flight 93, first entered Germany in 1996 and attended school in Greifswald in 1996 and Hamburg from 1997 to 2000, studying flight training and aeronautics. He left Germany for the United States in June 2000.

Soon after 9/11, the Germans issued arrest warrants for several other key individuals associated with the terrorist cell in Germany. Ramzi Binalshibh, Said Bahaji, and Zakariya Essabar were all part of the same al Qaeda cell that operated freely since 1999 in Germany.

Their connections to the hijackers were extensive. Ramzi Binalshibh is a Yemeni citizen who lived with Atta, Bahaji, and Essabar in Hamburg. He was one of the few al Qaeda members to attend two key planning sessions regarding the 9/11 attacks, one in Spain as well as the fine-tuning meeting in Malaysia. Hijacker Ziad Jarrah attempted to enroll Binalshibh in flight school in Venice, Florida, to no avail.

Apparently, Binalshibh wanted to be part of the 9/11 team, but he failed four times to obtain a U.S. visa. He remained involved to the end, however, becoming a key conduit for money and communications between the hijackers.

Binalshibh left Germany on September 5, 2001, and made his way to Pakistan, where he laid low for nearly a year. Then in early September 2002, Binalshibh appeared in a documentary that aired on Aljazeera, the Arabic television network, boasting about his involvement in the 9/11 attacks, and even claiming that his friend Mohamed Atta had called him on August 29, 2001, with a coded message setting the date for the attack.[2] I am personally deeply grateful to the Pakistani InterService Intelligence agents who captured Binalshibh and others on September 11, 2002, after a fierce 9:30 a.m. gun battle in a five-story Karachi apartment building.

Bahaji, a German citizen, also attended the Technical University in Hamburg, and together with Atta petitioned the university for a Muslim prayer room. He left Germany on September 3, 2001.

Essabar, a Moroccan citizen, made arrangements to travel to Florida in February 2001, when Atta and al-Shehhi were also in Florida. Essabar appears on Bahaji's wedding video with Jarrah, al-Shehhi, and Bahaji. Essabar was last known to be in Germany on September 6, 2001.

It was clear that Hamburg, Germany, had served as a central base of operations for these six individuals during their planning of the 9/11 attacks.

I had not really known German Interior Minister Otto Schily prior to 9/11, but I met with him within weeks after the attack and found a man who cared passionately about justice and rooting out terrorism. Minister Schily launched an intensive investigation regarding the Hamburg cell and the associates of the hijackers who perpetrated the terrorist acts on 9/11. The German government dedicated hundreds of investigators and executed dozens of searches to hunt down the terrorists.

We had a substantial force of investigators on the ground, working along with the German investigators, tracking past patterns of the Hamburg terrorist cell and others. We enjoyed a robust, unprecedented sharing of information with the Germans, as the agents worked night and day trying to thwart any follow-on attacks that might be in the works. Many of the terrorists had "gone to ground," a trade term for being in hiding, but we believed further attacks would be forthcoming.

The Germans took a personal interest in helping us investigate the 9/11 attack. As many as one hundred German citizens were among the nearly three thousand victims lost on September 11, 2001. The United States and Germany shared the goal of tracking down, arresting, prosecuting, and punishing those who were responsible for the heinous acts of terrorism that took those lives. More important, we shared a profound desire to see that no more lives were lost to terrorists. Having worked with Minister Schily "in the trenches," I consider him a wonderful friend of the United States and of mine personally. Schily was merely a lad when our troops controlled West Germany at the end of Word War II. He has long remembered the kindness of our soldiers and has repaid the United States in kind many times over.

Cooperative law enforcement and antiterrorist efforts flourished in France as well. For instance, one of the FBI's Ten Most Wanted Fugitives was James Charles Kopp, who had murdered Dr. Barnett Slepian in 1998. Through an extensive investigation Kopp was traced to France, where he was arrested on March 30, 2001, and extradited by the French back to the United States to stand trial.

The French also cooperated with us in the case of Richard Reid's attempted shoe bombing, which took place on an American Airlines flight. They were instrumental in helping on the Moussaoui case, and helped disrupt six men involved in a 2001 suicide bombing plot against the American Embassy in Paris. The six were given maximum sentences in French courts in 2005.

In the U.S. Justice Department's efforts to prevent terrorism, I was able to work closely with the French Minister of Justice, Dominique Perben, as well as Minister of the Interior Nicolas Sarkozy. Despite differences and public disagreements at the top levels of our governments, cooperation between law enforcement officials and antiterrorism efforts worked together smoothly and effectively.

Clearly, an international terrorist movement is a threat to the security of every country on earth. The challenges faced by the United States regarding border security, immigration, and tracking known terrorists affect other countries as well. Shortly after 9/11, I attended a conference comprised of interior leaders of more than twenty countries, and we attempted to lay out some plans for improving our security procedures. We needed to establish some standards by which we could uniformly help one another track terrorists. For instance, we recognized that we needed common information-sharing practices. Similarly, if we were to have secure uniform documents that could not be easily counterfeited, we needed technologies that were compatible. If we used biometrics such as fingerprints, the fingerprint readers in our country should be able to read fingerprints made from French, British, or Dutch technologies.

Some countries are considering more advanced technologies than others in these areas. For instance, some countries anticipate fingerprinting as a primary means of identification; others retinal scans; still others may embrace more advanced facial scans, which can read the unique subcutaneous patterns of blood vessels under a person's skin. All are valid means of identification, and to be most effective in helping one another, we need to use technologies that are compatible. Further, databases that house records of various threatening extremists should be readable and searchable on a basis of mutuality and interoperability.

September 11 made it clear that we had to tighten security in regard to passport distribution. Most countries want to receive "visa waiver status" with the United States. Individuals with passports from countries in this category are welcomed into the United States with relatively few interruptions or delays. But after 9/11, to maintain this status, we began to require that foreign countries be responsible in policing their passport issuance policies. If they did not have integrity in their passport program, it was impossible for the United States to allow special standing to individuals carrying travel documents of those countries.

The Belgians issued passports on a county level, rather than through a national clearinghouse. They reported as many as seventy thousand stolen passports in one year. Obviously, we could not allow just anyone with a Belgian passport to come waltzing through the U.S. Immigration checkpoints. We encouraged the Belgian government to tighten up its passport program. We said, "If you want us to grant special 'visa waiver status' to your nation, you can't simply allow passports to be exposed to theft in various local offices."

We intensified a program of assessing the travel document security policies of various countries that had visa waiver privileges. When we found shortcomings that were dangerous to the American people or could otherwise threaten our national and international security, we explained the necessity of foreign countries to either fix the problems—and fix them quickly—or run the risk of losing the visa waiver standing with the United States.

Of course, some counterparts squawked to high heaven, saying, "The United States Justice Department is trying to interfere with the way another country handles its internal affairs."

That simply wasn't true. In protecting our community we merely informed those countries, "You are not going to have special access to our country if you do not maintain the integrity of your passport program. We must be sure that the people coming through our ports of entry from your country are actually who they purport to be."

Most of the overtures in reaching out to our allies took place in a context of mutual respect, and through personal contact. I traveled to

Germany, France, Russia, Canada, Indonesia, Austria, Japan, China, Mexico and Central America as well as other foreign countries to meet with their ministers of the interior to compare notes on terrorism, but beyond that, to establish a friendship out of which a new spirit of cooperation could grow. In almost every country, I found open doors to communicate our concerns, and was well received in almost every instance. In China, for instance, for the first time in history we established an FBI legal attaché office in Beijing to enrich our cooperative efforts against terrorism. We brought to fruition and signed a treaty on extradition and mutual legal assistance with Japan that had been stalled in the negotiating process for well over a decade. We were the only nation to sign a similar treaty with the European Union. I probably signed more treaties than any attorney general in history. The effort to cooperate with a united Europe meant we needed to sign working agreements with well over a dozen nations. To encourage these treaty adoptions, I pledged to travel to each individual national capital for treaty signing ceremonies, which I gladly did. Never had the need for cooperation been greater. Never had the eagerness to cooperate been higher.

The cooperation that resulted was not seen so much on the evening news, as it was in the intelligence areas of the fight against terrorism. For instance, in Newark, New Jersey, Hemant Lakhani, a sixty-eight-year-old British weapons dealer who had been born in India, was charged with attempting to sell shoulder-fired missiles to terrorists for use against American targets. The indictment against Lakhani alleged that he brokered the initial purchase of one shoulder-fired antiaircraft missile and was arranging for a subsequent purchase and sale of fifty more missiles. Lakhani was captured after engaging in dozens of recorded and videotaped conversations indicating that he desired the missiles for the shooting down of American commercial airliners, and that Osama bin Laden "straightened them all out" and "did a good thing." Lakhani was convicted by a federal jury and sentenced to forty-seven years. Three other defendants involved in money transfers related to the transnational missile deal were brought to justice and pleaded guilty.

The Lakhani investigation would not have been possible had American, Russian, and other foreign intelligence and law enforcement agencies not been able to coordinate and share the intelligence they gained from their various investigative tools. The Russians actually infiltrated Lakhani's pipeline to the weapons supplier.

We went to great lengths to be responsive to our allies' needs as well. Often, I would get involved personally with leaders from various countries. If they needed someone extradited from the United States, for example, we tried to expedite that process as best we could without violating our own laws or standards. We wanted them to know that we were working together in every way possible.

Fortunately, as governor of Missouri and as a United States senator, and working with international trade organizations, I had developed a certain sense of comfort that allowed me to communicate comfortably and establish friendships with counterparts. Dealing with foreign leaders and treating them with the respect appropriate to their office was something that I enjoyed. These efforts allowed me to work from a position of friendship and mutual national interests. Such relationships were often a more effective means of securing cooperation than the more formal settings.

I wrote a multitude of notes and letters, many written by hand, to further personalize our relationships. Some may have considered my efforts as "hokey or corny," but I sent personal notes, sometimes even including personal pictures of Janet and me outside America. I meant this to demonstrate my valuation of other countries and my gratitude for the cultures of the nations with whom we cooperated.

Almost immediately following 9/11, certain countries called and expressed their willingness to help. A few countries, of course, implied that this was "an American problem," but most recognized that more than eighty countries had lost people in the attacks on the World Trade Center. They expressed a genuine consciousness that we are all in this together. Besides, almost every country in Europe had been dealing with some serious forms of terrorism long before America was so abruptly attacked in September 2001.

Great Britain had experiences with the Irish Republican Army, the Italians had the Red Brigade, the Germans had numerous indigenous terrorists, Spain had their own groups of terrorists they had been fighting as well. And of course, Israel had been living in a constant battle against terrorism for years. For most of our allies, international terrorism was not a new issue. Nevertheless, the sheer magnitude of the al Qaeda attacks, part of which were purposely centered on the World Trade Center, was a statement that elicited the support of our allies in a way we had not experienced since World War II.

Great Britain has a much more open immigration system than does the United States, and a more lenient asylum system that tends to attract people fomenting violent jihadist causes. Terrorists such as Zacarias Moussaoui and Richard Reid found havens there, as have numerous other suspected terrorists. Canada functions in much the same manner. Since these countries are such good friends of our nation, it was sometimes a delicate matter to encourage them to be stricter in their dealings with potential terrorists. Canada was of special concern to us, of course, because of our thousands of miles of mutually shared borders.

Causing no small matter of consternation to many of our foreign allies are the United States' policies on capital punishment. Many of our allies are reluctant to extradite even known terrorist suspects if they may possibly be executed in the United States. Some of our more lenient friends were even averse to life sentences.

Despite the popularity of multinational commissions now adjudicating war crime charges from Central Europe, many of our allies in the war on terror expressed serious reservations regarding our use of military commissions for war criminals apprehended in the war on terror.

This was one of the reasons why it was so important that the Zacarias Moussaoui case be adjudicated carefully. We needed to bring Moussaoui to justice, and we also needed to show the world that the judicial system in the United States could fairly try individuals charged with terrorist crimes.

In some foreign countries, authorities have the right to restrain a person prior to a crime being committed, called "preventive detention." In some cases a person can be detained without being charged for a significant period, much longer than in our country. In the United States, our justice system does not allow for such detentions. In the weeks and months following 9/11, some of our allies made extensive use of this preventive detention, to hold suspected terrorists until they could be investigated. Such detentions would not be allowable in the United States, but their use by others was helpful to us.

While we continued to pursue terrorists throughout Europe and the Middle East, at the same time I hoped to forge a better relationship with our neighbor to the south, Mexico. Clearly, the flood of illegal immigrants pouring across our southern border represented a major security concern. Although no al Qaeda–type terrorist attacks had been launched from Mexico, the porous border was an open opportunity, and we knew it.

I had been trying to emphasize this point to our Mexican counterparts when one night a group of twenty-eight illegal immigrants were known to be lost in the desert, trying to make their way into the United States. The Mexican immigration authorities with whom I had been working seemed shocked when, rather than expressing satisfaction that twenty-eight fewer illegal immigrants were going to enter the United States, I said, "We need to go find those people and rescue them. Otherwise they are going to die in the desert."

I worked throughout the night with Mexican Foreign Secretary Jorge Castañeda, National Security Adviser Aguilar Zinser, Attorney General Macedo de la Concha, Secretary of the Interior Santiago Creel, and their staffs attempting to find a way to reach the twenty-eight lost people. I was calling all over our countries trying to find a way to help.

At one point in the night, I called a Mexican official, and he offered, "We can get back to this search in the morning."

"We have people who are dying in the desert," I replied, "and if we wait until morning it will be too late. I'm going to keep working on this and I'll be calling you back."

That was a turning point in our relationship. The Mexican officials recognized that, to me, the people out in the desert were not merely illegal immigrants trying to break into the United States. These were fellow human beings in need, and I was willing to do whatever necessary to help save their lives.

We worked throughout the night, and were able to save fourteen of the lost immigrants. Sadly, the others died in the desert that night. Nevertheless, out of that heartrending incident came a stronger relationship between our two countries.

I sought to establish better communications between our nations by taking an interest in the Mexican culture, trying better to understand their rich history, and demonstrating a respect for their achievements. At the same time, I emphasized to them that we could not allow the unrestrained flow of illegal immigrants into our country. Admittedly, we had very few reports of al Qaeda's presence in Mexico, but we knew our enemy would attempt to exploit any area of vulnerability. Of greater concern was our neighbor to the north, Canada, where an open extremist Islamic presence could be found and terrorist activity was suspected, and later discovered.

The Canadian law enforcement and justice officials were tremendously cooperative and helpful in tightening security along our border. In a candid moment, a friendly high-level Canadian official told me, "John, you live in the greatest nation on earth, and it has been a privilege for me to live my life as your next-door neighbor. And if you don't defend freedom, we're all in trouble. We will do all that we can to help you."

One of the ways that I sought to improve our relationship with foreign officials was to bring them to Janet's and my home for informal times of conversation. We chose dinners in our home rather than formal "state" dinners, because we wanted to personalize our relationships with our international neighbors. On occasion, I made craft ideas reflecting our appreciation to give to our guests. Together, Janet and I assembled wreathes out of vines from our farm, replete with pine cones, acorns, nuts, stones from the streams, and other items that I had gathered. When possible I included natural items from the homeland of our foreign guests. I gave the handmade wreaths to our visitors as gestures of friendship and appreciation for our mutual working together. It was always amazing to see how small, personal gestures opened doors of communication, strengthening our national ties.

The friendship that grew between me and Otto Schily became a model for other efforts. Rather than meeting with him in a stately Washington office, I took him out to our farm, where we hiked the hills and along the river and talked informally. It was a delight to include Otto's family members at events when he visited. Otto expressed his appreciation on one occasion when I petitioned for God's blessing on him and his family prior to one of our meals together.

It became abundantly clear that the values that bind us together, human dignity and liberty, were profoundly more important than anything that might separate us. That is the foundation of the international cooperation necessary to the security of our lives and the value of our freedom.

ENDNOTES

1. *New York Times*, September 15, 2001.
2. CNN.com transcripts, "Arrested al Qaeda Operative May Tell Secrets," aired on CNN September 14, 2002.

CHAPTER EIGHTEEN

NEVER AGAIN

The Moral Imperative for Toughness

❧❧❧

The United States will suffer more terrorist attacks during this war with al Qaeda. They are fanatical, relentless, and patient. Their leadership is scattered, killed, or captured; their safe haven in Afghanistan is destroyed; their command and control structure has disintegrated. We are now at war with a diffuse, loosely organized network, united and motivated by a hatred for our nation and our core values. They are fed spiritually by bin Laden, and thrive in our society on the basic liberties they loath. The advance of civilization has dispersed technology, information, and destructive capacity so thoroughly that their network easily exploits these advances for their cause. This network will hit us again when they can.

I fear most the al Qaeda network's access to weapons of mass destruction, because if they have them, they will use them. But we must concede that if al Qaeda shifted its focus in the United States from spectacular attacks against national symbols to "soft targets" such as schools, subways, and shopping centers, they would be more difficult to stop. Their affiliated networks have launched successful attacks on "soft targets" in other countries such as Spain, Great Britain, and Russia since 9/11. They have planned such attacks in the United States, but so far, they have failed. We can expect them to try again.

One simple but difficult principle provides the opportunity for the United States to achieve "never again." That is: The will to win.

The will to do whatever is necessary within the Constitution to protect America separates us from more death and destruction within our shores. It is the will to sacrifice, to persevere in the face of adversity and criticism just as generations of Americans did before us. It is no guarantee, but if we falter, grow complacent, or fail to do what we can, we give the terrorist network opportunities that, with time and patience, they will exploit to kill more innocent Americans.

A moral imperative for toughness exists if we are asking America's young people to go out and stand in harm's way, to risk getting shot, or to lay their lives on the line. Then we are not eligible to be "nice guys" who will take a soft and easy approach to the enemy when we realize what is needed to preserve American lives. When we ask for the lifeblood of the next generation of Americans in Afghanistan, Iraq, or on other fields of battle, the moral imperative demands we defend our freedoms with an unyielding mental toughness. If we lose our resolve, our will to win, by mistaking the tranquillity of our daily lives for peace with terrorism, or caving in to propaganda campaigns built on a false sense of security, we will fail our moral obligation to young Americans who risk all to protect us.

These days my son Andy spends much of his time traveling in a rubber raft launched from a U.S. Navy destroyer. He crosses the divide between the huge ship and a suspected gun-running or contraband-carrying vessel and climbs aboard not knowing what threat to his life he is about to encounter in the theater of war. He does this not simply for the thrill of the experience but so we can live in safety and freedom thousands of miles away.

What sort of father would I be if I am unwilling to surveil suspected terrorists or ask probing questions of suspected terrorist detainees that might save the life of my son or thousands of other young men and women defending our liberty? Why should we send our young people into danger around the world in our fight against terrorism if we are going to coddle and succor terrorists in our own country? It would be a travesty if because of our lack of moral resolve and the will to win we turn our own country into a haven for terrorists that they no longer have in other lands.

This moral imperative demands toughness not simply on the next generation's part but on ours.

Another aspect of the moral imperative for toughness is the recognition that America at its best represents the values of freedom and goodness, and the terrorists represent imposition and evil. Osama bin Laden and his ilk intend to dictate the conditions of a person's existence; Americans believe that liberty and freedom are God-given rights. If we are truly endowed with life, liberty, and the pursuit of happiness by our Creator, how dare we acquiesce in the face of terrorists, implying that we don't care enough about those freedoms to defend them?

The legendary football coach Vince Lombardi used to say that the will to win is not the most important thing; the will to *prepare* to win is most important. Anyone who gets into a fight wants to win, but if he hasn't prepared ahead of time, he will be at a distinct disadvantage. Similarly, in our fight against terrorism, we must prepare to win. We must have the discipline to prepare for the next attack, and take the necessary steps to prevent it.

While sensational news stories about terrorism receive a lot of attention, Americans should understand that the hunt for terrorists in the United States is a "game of inches." Every incremental step matters; each tiny bit of information can make a difference; seemingly insignificant clues may provide the crucial piece that helps solve the puzzle.

We should debate the government's powers to protect the American people, for their exercise will shape our destiny. We should understand that the debate and our decisions are choices with consequences of life or death for innocent Americans. Which authority under the Constitution, one that is necessary to hunt terrorists inch by inch hiding in our country, will we surrender to suit our sensibilities? If you've heard the taped cries of the passengers about to die on United Flight 93 as I have, you believe minor steps such as helping local police to detain immigration violators can have profound consequences in the lives of individuals and in the nation.

I still see the doomed leaping from the World Trade Center, and smell the stench of the rubble. I remember the cost of weakness; misguided decisions have consequences. In this war, fought within our shores, a moral imperative for toughness exists. What will separate us from the mistakes of the past is the will to win; the will to do whatever is necessary under the Constitution to win this war will allow Americans to maintain an attitude of "never again."

Following my surgery in the spring of 2004, I tried to ease my work pace, but the constant swirl of events at the Justice Department, the never-ending flow of new challenges, and my sense of obligation kept me from slowing down. More and more, however, as we headed toward the presidential election of 2004, I felt that I should offer my resignation to President Bush. Neither he nor anyone in the administration ever gave me any indication that my resignation was expected. Every workday I met with the president, and at any point had he wanted me gone, it would have been a simple matter to drop a hint.

Certainly, I had no intention of resigning before the election, perhaps signaling a nonexistent rift, or creating a media frenzy as to who President Bush would nominate to replace me. When the time was right for me to leave, I knew I would know it.

That time came, and I knew it—on the day of the 2004 election. In resigning as attorney general, I sent President Bush a handwritten letter. I expressed my personal thanks for the privilege of serving our country:

November 2, 2004
Dear Mr. President:
    Nothing in my life compares to the high honor of serving America as Attorney General in your administration.

The cause of justice is indeed a serious calling. Americans have been spared the violence and savagery of terrorist attack on our soil since September 11, 2001.

During the last four years our violent crime rate has plunged to a thirty-year low. Under your "Project Safe Neighborhoods" the number of gun crimes has fallen to its lowest level in modern history. Drug use among America's young people has fallen and continues to fall significantly.

Corporate integrity has been restored with the work of your Corporate Fraud Task Force. As a result United States markets have reinforced their position as the trusted allocaters of the world's capital resources.

Thank you for your leadership which has made these and many other Justice-related achievements possible.

The demands of justice are both rewarding and depleting. I take great personal satisfaction in the record which has been developed. The objective of securing the safety of Americans from crime and terror has been achieved. The rule of law has been strengthened and upheld in the courts. Yet, I believe that the Department of Justice would be well served by new leadership and fresh inspiration. I believe that my energies and talents should be directed toward other challenging horizons.

Therefore, I humbly state my desire to resign from the office of United States Attorney General.

It would be my pleasure to structure the announcement of this resignation and the ensuing transition in conjunction with you so that your administration and the cause of justice are served optimally.

I have handwritten this letter so its confidentiality can be maintained until the appropriate arrangements mentioned above can be made.

I am grateful to you for the profound honor of serving clear, principled leadership.

May God continue to bless, guide, and direct you and your family as you lead America forward in freedom.

Most Sincerely,
John Ashcroft

We'd had a record-setting run at the Justice Department during the four years I had served as attorney general. As I thought back through some of our accomplishments, I felt a deep sense of satisfaction. Most of all, I was grateful to God that during our tenure, no further terrorist attacks had succeeded after 9/11.

America's defense—the defense of life and liberty—requires a new culture of prevention, nurtured by cooperation, built on coordination, and rooted in our constitutional liberties. We had carefully dismantled many of the excessive constraints imposed in the late 1970s that erected barriers to cooperation among government agencies, segregated law enforcement and intelligence gathering, and prohibited information sharing. That process needs to continue, including congressional oversight, certainly, but continue, nonetheless. Our survival and success in this long war on terrorism demands that we continuously adapt and improve our capabilities to protect Americans from fanatical, ruthless enemies. We must build a culture of prevention and ensure the resources of our government can be dedicated to defending Americans.

I'm often asked, "How will we know when the war on terror is over?" Perhaps that is a cover for the more troubling question: "Will it be over?"

One of Missouri's most famous native sons, Yogi Berra, is renowned for garbled anomalies such as, "That place is so crowded nobody ever goes there anymore" and "It ain't over til it's over."

Terror as a technique of war presents confounding questions: when will it be over and how will we know when it is over?

We must never allow the idea that it may be difficult to know someday whether the war is over to keep us from understanding that it can be crystal clear that the war is going on now. This conclusion is easy, considering continuing plots in Canada and the United States as well as attacks around the world. It is also painfully apparent that the war is not over when terrorist leaders offer aggressively threatening statements in the media or on the Internet.

To assume that, because we may have difficulty knowing someday that the war is over makes it impossible to know now that the war is still on, is nothing short of stupidity.

One more observation regarding the termination of the war on terror: this has been cited as a problem relating to the disposition of battlefield detainees. And it is more difficult knowing how or when to release detainees if there is no controlling, receiving authority to restrain these captured terrorists from restarting the battle. Nevertheless, in answering the question of which party should bear the risks of indeterminate detention pending the definitive cessation of the war, the answer is clear. The attacked, innocent culture should not bear the risk of additional injury. The risk should be borne by the terrorist aggressor who assaulted the innocent.

Much discussion has centered on the absence in the enemy of a clear, controlling governing authority capable of ending the fight with the United States. We have witnessed terror morph and evolve in the past five years. It has included airplanes, subways, schools, theaters, churches, and police stations—in short, civilian targets. It is the ultimate goal of terrorists to displace by force and fear the freedom and the will of the people. The goal of terror is not traditional territorial enlargement; rather the war target of the terrorist is the dismemberment of the will of the community it terrorizes.

One thing is certain, the risk of concluding that the war is over if and when it is not over is a very substantial risk indeed. Time and time again the patience of terror has been misinterpreted as the end of terror. When such misinterpretation has occurred, this mistake has invited disaster on a grand scale and an invigorated reemergence of terror.

When average Americans no longer believe there is a risk of terrorist activity, it becomes easier for terrorists to operate and succeed. I am thoroughly convinced that alerting and sensitizing the public to the risks of terrorism in our early effort to forestall further attacks decreased the risks of those attacks. When the public is alert, attacks are disrupted. If we cannot conclude this after the thwarting of Richard Reid's shoe bomb effort on the American Airlines flight we are without vision or hope.

The anomaly is that sensitizing the public probably stops the attack and then the absence of attacks undermines the idea that threat of attack existed. Ironically, the success of the elevated public alert thus undermines its credibility over time. Warning and alertness provides safety and defense, which lead to the misperception that there never was a real threat in the first place.

Nowadays, technology endows state, nonstate, and individual players with extensive destructive capabilities that were previously available only to substantial nation-state-scaled war participants. When the founders of our country and the writers of the Constitution put all the safeguards in place, at the time of the American Revolution, a single individual might have been able to carry explosives that could damage a room or a small structure. Today, a single terrorist could do more damage than a frigate sailing through Boston Harbor might have threatened during the Revolution. Today, one man might transport catastrophic explosive capacity or evil biology or radiology and, in worse cases, combine them to threaten metropolitan areas and hundreds of thousands of lives.

Is it possible that some of the concerns that led us to beware of nation-states—formerly the exclusive agents of widespread calamity—might now be necessary to safeguard against even greater modern threats, deployable by individuals and small groups? The enormity of the potential destruction and the speed at which it can be accomplished have drastically changed our world. That destructive capacity was unthinkable when the Constitution was carefully crafted.

The Constitution gives general power for defense to the chief executive of our nation. This makes good sense when one witnesses how long it takes a congressional committee to decide whether or not to send a matter to a vote. No wonder the writers of our Constitution said that defending our nation should be an "executive power"; there is a need for adroit decisions and to have the agility to change course for purposes of national defense based on the activities that are threatening.

At my retirement, I sensed and still feel today that the United States is winning the war on terrorism. First, the Central Intelligence Agency and the Federal Bureau of Investigation have set new standards for cooperation and coordination. The FBI's domestic intelligence operations were substantially strengthened by the CIA's information sharing, intelligence analysis, and operational coordination.

Second, in the new FBI as restructured under Director Bob Mueller, America's domestic counterterrorism force integrates intelligence and law enforcement capabilities to protect American lives.

A good example of how the FBI now functions to dismantle terrorism would be their clandestine operation against two Yemeni citizens, Mohammed Ali Hassan al-Moayad and Mohammed Mohsen Yahya Zayed. Both men were charged with conspiring to provide material support to al Qaeda and Hamas terrorists through al-Moayad's worldwide fund-raising operations. In the FBI undercover operation, al-Moayad boasted that he had personally handed Osama bin Laden $20 million from his terrorist fund-raising network.

In November 2001, the FBI's International Terrorism squad began working with a confidential informant who had known al-Moayad for more than six years. During several meetings with an FBI informant, al-Moayad boasted "jihad" was his field, and trumpeted his involvement in providing money, recruits, and supplies to al Qaeda, Hamas, and

other terrorist groups, and said he received money for jihad from col-
lections at the al-Farouq mosque in Brooklyn. Al-Moayad also
claimed to be Osama bin Laden's spiritual adviser.

On January 7, 2003, al-Moayad and Zayed flew from Yemen to
Frankfurt, Germany, to meet with the FBI informant. Al-Moayad allegedly went to the meetings intending to obtain $2 million from a
terrorist sympathizer who wanted to fund al Qaeda and Hamas. At
these meetings with FBI informants in Frankfurt, al-Moayad confirmed that the $2 million contribution would be used to support the
mujahideen fighters of al Qaeda and Hamas. Zayed even "swore to
Allah" that he would get the money to al Qaeda and Hamas if anything
happened to al-Moayad. Al-Moayad and Zayed were subsequently
arrested and charged.[1] In March 2005 a federal jury convicted al-
Moayad. He was sentenced to seventy-five years in prison. Zayed was
sentenced to forty-five years in prison.

This one FBI counterterrorism operation blended human intelligence sources, advanced electronic surveillance, deep undercover
operations, terrorist financing savvy, and criminal subpoenas and
search warrants, along with seamless law enforcement and intelligence cooperation. The breadth and talent of the team fielded in this
case literally spanned the globe—from the New York City police to
prosecutors in Frankfurt, Germany.

This is a good example of the new FBI—focused on preventing
terrorism, integrating intelligence and law enforcement, and deliver-
ing results. During the time I served as attorney general, I observed
Director Mueller and FBI agents around the world as they transformed their intelligence and counterterrorism operations to achieve
these kinds of prevention missions. Their efforts make Americans
safer, often in many ways the public does not see and cannot be
disclosed.

Third, the Justice Department continues prosecuting the war on
terror by integrating our law enforcement and intelligence capabilities as authorized under the Patriot Act. Between late 2001 and May

2004, we had a 100 percent increase in FISA orders, doubling in less than three years. We increased by 63 percent our intelligence sources—people who were informing our intelligence agents about potential terrorist activities.

During our time in the Justice Department, hundreds of suspected terrorists were identified and tracked throughout the United States. We disrupted numerous potential terrorist threats including terrorist cells in Buffalo, Detroit, Seattle, and Portland. More than 375 individuals were charged in terrorism-related investigations; 195 people were convicted or pleaded guilty on terrorism-related charges, including shoe bomber Richard Reid, who was sentenced to life in prison in 2003. Another 113 individuals in twenty-five separate judicial districts were charged with material support to terrorism, and 57 were convicted or pleaded guilty; "American Taliban" John Walker Lindh also pleaded guilty to one count of providing services to the Taliban and a charge that he carried weapons while fighting on the Taliban's front lines in Afghanistan against the United States–backed Northern Alliance. Lindh was sentenced to twenty years in prison.

More than 150 terrorist threats and cells were also disrupted. Members of a Portland cell, including Patrice Lumumba Ford and Jeffrey Battle, pleaded guilty to criminal charges. Ford and Battle were each sentenced to eighteen years in prison.

The Lackawanna Six, a terrorist cell operating near Buffalo, New York, also pleaded guilty to charges of providing material support to al Qaeda. They were sentenced to terms ranging from seven to ten years in prison.

Hamant Lakhani, the British national convicted of attempting to sell shoulder-fired missiles to what he thought was a terrorist group, was sentenced to forty-seven years in prison. Numerous other convictions have been obtained by the Justice Department in cases against terrorism. As I looked back over my time as attorney general it was clear that we had helped prevent terrorists from harming Americans.

During my tenure we also charged and deported nearly five hundred immigration violators linked to the 9/11 investigation. We made major strides toward dismantling the terrorist financial network and we disrupted terrorist movements around the world. We launched seventy investigations into terrorist financing, designated forty entities as terrorist organizations, and froze $136 million from terrorist organizations around the globe. Thousands of terrorists and criminals were stopped through the National Security Entry-Exit Registration System (NSEERS) including some suspected terrorists with ties to al Qaeda.

We added more than one thousand FBI agents to counterterrorism and counterintelligence; we also added 250 new assistant U.S. Attorneys. Fifty-six Joint Terrorism Task Forces were created to facilitate the fight against terror from the Capitol to the states and localities.

Throughout this process, the Department of Justice acted thoughtfully, carefully, and within the framework of American freedom, the Constitution of the United States. Time and again, the actions in the war on terrorism were subjected to thorough judicial review, and time and again, our department consistently defended the legal challenges. Just as the president's powers to protect the American people are rooted in the Constitution, our actions against terrorist threats were rooted in the Constitution, while adapting to the changing methods of our terrorist enemies.

Ironically, the attack of 9/11 led to the creation of a climate in America that actually helped reduce crime and drug usage. The attacks on our nation galvanized the morale, the will, and the determination of law enforcement, and unified Americans within the law enforcement community like nothing in recent memory. Who wore ball caps bearing the initials NYPD or NYFD before 9/11? After 9/11, the positive identification of the public with law enforcement and responders skyrocketed. How sad that it took bin Laden to wake us up to appreciate the people who work so diligently at protecting us every day, but we should be grateful for the American people's embrace of the law enforcement community in response to the most horrendous attack in our history.

The intense focus of law enforcement, the stronger coordination among local, state, and federal authorities, and the enhanced vigilance of the American people all worked against criminals and drug lords as well as terrorists. Violent crime dropped every year that I was attorney general to its lowest recorded level in American history in 2004. Rape and sexual assaults, aggravated assaults, and violent crime overall were cut by a quarter. The murder rate dropped to record levels with federal gun crime prosecutions climbing 76 percent to a record high, while gun crimes plummeted 24 percent to a record low. We did this, by the way, without any new gun-control laws.

If the crime rates in 2003 had remained at 1993 levels, 34.6 million more Americans would have been victimized by violent crimes. Additionally, 2.5 million more Americans would have been raped or sexually assaulted, and 6 million more gun crimes would have occurred. These numbers may not mean much to you merely reading them, but consider that they may represent your family, friends, or neighbors who did not suffer the pain or loss of a rape or murder.

With a restructured and refocused drug strategy, we experienced a 108 percent increase in drug seizures, dismantled a quarter of the major drug organizations, and arrested a quarter of the drug kingpins. Teenage drug use dropped for the first time in a decade—by 17 percent. Again, you may not appreciate that drop, unless you have a teenage son, daughter, or grandchild.

We recovered 150 missing children through the use of Amber Alerts, and we expanded the Amber Alert capability from four states to forty-nine states. Moreover, we were the first Justice Department in many years to come away with a clean financial audit.

Most of all, we were able to enlist the support of the American people in protecting our country from terrorism. As I write these words, America has not suffered another major terrorist attack. I pray that record continues to grow daily. But our safety has been the result of an alert, vigilant, and supportive public as well as thousands of unsung, dedicated public servants, many of whom I was privileged to work with on a daily basis.

At the same time, we must never forget that the war against terror can only be won one day at a time. When I wrote in my resignation letter to President Bush that "the objective of securing the safety of Americans from crime and terror has been achieved," the news media objected vociferously. "How can you say it is achieved? The war is not over."

Yes, we did; we won the war yesterday, and the day before, but the president well knew and so did I that victory is achieved one day at a time. We must remain constantly vigilant. We dare not underestimate our enemy. Al Qaeda is committed to the destruction of America, and they are in it for the long haul. They are much smarter than many give them credit for being, and they are definitely much more patient than the pace of our fast-food society conditions us to be. Their commitment does not depend on bin Laden or any other single leader. In June 2006, American forces in Iraq killed insurgency leader Abu Musab al-Zarqawi. A truly evil man is dead, but others will rise to take his place. Defeating them will take prayerful creativity, imagination, energy, persistence, and determination.

It may indeed be true that the terrorists thought that America was weak, that we would implode in the face of their attacks. After all, we had not responded effectively to their strikes in Nairobi, Khobar Towers, the USS *Cole*.

They may have dreamed they would sink the American economy by their strikes, and while we must admit the economic impact of 9/11 was enormous, the resilience of Americans and the ability of Americans to pull the economy back together after the attack was nothing short of inspiring.

America refused to be defeated. The United States responded with greater unity, resolve, and intensity than the terrorists expected.

In the hearts of each one of us rang the unspoken words "Never again."

Thankfully, the one question I'll never have to answer is, "Why did you allow us to be attacked again?" But my great satisfaction is, we were able to disrupt numerous terrorist attacks during my stay in office, and of all the accomplishments about which I am most pleased, I am happiest about what did *not* happen.

Certainly, people may have tried to pull things off that didn't work or of which we were unaware. But whenever we found any potential terrorists, we acted swiftly and effectively to get them off the street or out of the country.

An old saying purports, "An ounce of prevention is worth a pound of cure," and that is so true. But we needed a pound of prevention to deal with the terrorists America faced, and to prevent a war from being fought against them on our soil, in our own backyards . . . and we still do.

On the home front, our constant efforts in defense of liberty took heat at every step, but we considered the fight worth making. And that unseen war must continue as well.

My prayer is not merely that God will bless America—He has done so abundantly—but that we would be granted wisdom in protecting this grand experiment that many of us believe was His idea in the first place.

One senior administration official described my role in President George W. Bush's administration as one of "spear-catcher." Every spear caught is injury avoided; the ones you don't catch—the ones that catch you—are the ones that really hurt.

After I left my position in the cabinet, I met many people who said, "My, you certainly had to work through some difficult times," and perhaps we did. But I'm grateful that God allowed me to be there during those times, as challenging as they were.

At my Justice Department retirement ceremony on January 25, 2005, Daniel Bryant, director of the Office of Legal Policy, quipped that the caricatures of me in the press "served as a full-employment program for cartoonists and pundits." He then cited David Letterman's jab whenever he heard that I was retiring: "They say Attorney General John Ashcroft may be stepping down. Apparently he wants to spend more time spying on his family."

Actually, Letterman was probably more right than he knew. I was indeed looking forward to seeing my family members far more frequently.

These days, I enjoy working with my own company, the Ashcroft Group, which counsels corporations on enhancing corporate integrity, developing homeland security technologies, navigating strategic crises, and managing risks. I also enjoy keeping relatively normal hours, and eating dinner with Janet most evenings.

I relish the outdoors and the farm Janet and I have away from Washington, where there is nothing but a couple of toolsheds. I enjoy fighting back the brush, picking blackberries, and harvesting tomatoes in the garden.

Every once in a while, I'll be working up a good sweat when I notice a jumbo jet high above in the crystal sky, on its way toward Washington, D.C. Occasionally, a thought may dart through my consciousness that, similar to what happened on 9/11, there could be some evil-intentioned person at the controls.

Then I'll stop and mop my brow, watch the airliner continue on its way, and gratefully pray, "Never again."

ENDNOTE

1. Attorney General John Ashcroft; www.usdoj.gov/archive/ag/testimony/2003/030403senatejudiciaryhearing.htm.